THE MYTH OF DEMOCRATIC FAILURE

AMERICAN POLITICS AND POLITICAL ECONOMY
A SERIES EDITED BY BENJAMIN I. PAGE

DONALD A. WITTMAN

THE MYTH OF DEMOCRATIC FAILURE

Why Political Institutions Are Efficient

THE UNIVERSITY OF CHICAGO PRESS
CHICAGO & LONDON

DONALD A. WITTMAN is professor of economics at the
University of California, Santa Cruz.

The University of Chicago Press, Chicago 60637
The University of Chicago Press, Ltd., London
© 1995 by The University of Chicago
All rights reserved. Published 1995
Printed in the United States of America
04 03 02 01 00 99 98 97 96 95   1 2 3 4 5

ISBN (cloth): 0-226-90422-9

Library of Congress Cataloging-in-Publication Data

Wittman, Donald A.
   The myth of democratic failure : why political institutions are
efficient / Donald A. Wittman.
      p.   cm. — (American politics and political economy series)
   Includes bibliographical references and index.
   1. Democracy.   2. Free enterprise.   I. Title.   II. Series:
American politics and political economy.
JC423.W499   1995
321.8—dc20   94-46186
                                                               CIP

⊗The paper used in this publication meets the minimum requirements of the
American National Standard for Information Sciences—Permanence of Paper for
Printed Library Materials, ANSI Z39.48-1984.

To the memory of my parents

CONTENTS

ACKNOWLEDGMENTS

IN MANY GAMES, FIRST MOVERS have distinct advantages, but in intellectual pursuits, the advantage goes to later researchers who have free rein to criticize those who came before them. In this book I have had a lot of fun criticizing my predecessors. Here, I would like to thank all of the researchers whose ideas were so compelling that I was forced to confront their arguments in a serious way. My glib retorts hide the fact that I worked very hard to undermine their work. I hope that in this sequential knowledge game my work will also provoke reaction. In the age of E-mail, you can send forth your thoughts to wittman@cats.ucsc.edu.

Some of the ideas in this book are based on my previously published work: "Pressure Group Size and the Politics of Income Redistribution," *Social Choice and Welfare* 6 (1989): 275–86; "Why Democracies Produce Efficient Results," *Journal of Political Economy* 97 (1989): 1395–1422; "The Constitution as an Optimal Social Contract," in B. Grofman and D. Wittman (eds.), *The Federalist Papers and the New Institutionalism* (New York: Agathon Press, 1989), 73–84; "Contrasting Rational and Psychological Analyses of Political Choice," in K. Monroe (ed.), *The Economic Approach to Politics* (New York: HarperCollins, 1991), 405–32.

I would also like to thank the series editor, Ben Page, for his support, and those who made comments on various parts of my manuscript.

Finally, I would like to thank the University of California Academic Senate for funding part of the research.

1

INTRODUCTION:
THE MARKET METAPHOR

MOST CONTROVERSIES IN THE SOCIAL SCIENCES are ultimately arguments over the nature of the market. Marxist sociologists believe that both economic and political markets are characterized by poorly informed, possibly irrational consumers and voters who are exploited by monopolist suppliers of goods and policy. Present-day economists, in general, and conservative economists, in particular, claim that economic markets are efficient but that political markets are distorted by indifferent voters, powerful lobbyists, and entrenched bureaucrats. In this book, I argue for a third alternative—both political and economic markets work well.[1]

---

1. This possibility appears to have been, for the most part, overlooked. Adam Smith's most famous passages regarding government are negative ("that insidious . . . animal, vulgarly called a . . . politician), but he did argue that governments would pursue their behavior effectively. McKean (1965) argued that the invisible hand operated in the political sector but claimed that political externalities would cause political-market failure. Tiebout (1956) claimed that competition among localities creates efficient local governments but did not believe that his model applied to national governments. Becker (1983) showed that there will be a tendency for wealth-maximizing outcomes to arise from the behavior of pressure groups, but elsewhere in his article he argued that political markets are very imperfect. Thus some economists have made positive remarks about the efficacy of political markets, but such remarks are hidden in books and articles that are overwhelmingly critical. As is usually the case, it is much harder to characterize the views of political scientists. It appears, however, that earlier writings in the pluralist literature tended to look approvingly upon the workings of the democratic system. Authors such as Dahl (1961, 1966) viewed the outcome of government policy as a bargain between many groups (the bureaucracy, Congress, business, organized labor, etc.). Each group had some veto power over the area that was most important to it. As will be seen, this view is considerably different from that espoused in this book (for example, I do not view the bureaucracy as having autonomous power). Later pluralists argued that power was concentrated in a few hands (corporations and the state), with unfortunate outcomes (see Dahl 1985 and Lindblom 1988 for examples).

I show that democratic markets are organized to promote wealth-maximizing outcomes, that these markets are highly competitive, and that political and bureaucratic entrepreneurs are rewarded for efficient behavior.[2] I demonstrate that nearly all of the arguments claiming that economic markets are efficient apply equally well to democratic political markets; and, conversely, that economic models of political-market failure are no more valid than the analogous arguments for economic-market failure. This book attempts to (1) cure the schizophrenia facing most economists, who believe that economic markets work well, but political markets work poorly, (2) overcome the blindness of many sociologists to the full implications of rational behavior and competition, and (3) help political science (a field lacking in a coherent understanding of democratic phenomena) to develop a consistent theoretical approach. Henceforth, the burden of proof will be on those who argue that democratic political markets are inefficient.[3]

This book also discusses the distribution of political power. While not claiming that there is a uniform distribution of political power among all members of a democratic society, I do argue that the extent of power held by bureaucracies, corporations, congressional committee chairmen, and pressure groups, such as the National Rifle Association, has been greatly exaggerated.

If my thesis is accepted, the nature of economic analysis of political behavior is altered. Instead of looking for examples of political-market failure, intellectual energies should be focused on optimal organizational design. Thus, this book also develops a theory of institutional response. I show how various political institutions, such as political parties, the reputations of candidates, and government structure, arise in order to mitigate the potential for principal-agent problems in a democratic system.

---

2. As in other areas of economics, preferences are given. For our purposes, this means that advertising, political speeches, and so on do not affect voters' preferences; rather, these preferences are embedded much deeper within the culture (e.g., parental values and early religious upbringing) and possibly in the voters' genetic makeups. Preferences may extend to such things as a belief in a "strong" military and hatred of foreigners, although some of these may be explained by more fundamental relationships (economic or otherwise). In addition, many preferences are cross-cultural. Preference for color over black-and-white television is neither due to Judeo-Christian upbringing nor to advertising.

3. I do not discuss totalitarian or other nondemocratic regimes. In general, one would expect these regimes to be less efficient than democracies since competition is thwarted and transaction costs are high.

THE STRUCTURE OF THE ARGUMENT

Efficient markets tend to have informed and rational participants in a matrix of competition with well-defined and easily-transferred property rights. Virtually all models of political-market failure (inefficiency) implicitly or explicitly assume that one or more of these characteristics is missing. In chapters 2–5 (part I), I argue to the contrary—that democratic markets do indeed have the qualities typically associated with efficient markets. Chapter 2 shows how candidates' behavior and voters' response mitigate the problem of "rational voter ignorance." Chapter 3 demonstrates how competition for political office reduces the potential for opportunism by politicians. Chapter 4 shows how political institutions reduce transaction costs, thereby encouraging the efficient exchange of political rights. Chapter 5 argues that the participants in the political process act rationally.

In part II, I consider the organization of particular political markets. I show how Congress overcomes problems of localism (chap. 6), and I demonstrate that the deleterious effects of pressure groups have been overstated (chap. 7) and that bureaucracies neither muddle nor take advantage of monopoly power (chap. 8). In chapter 9, I take a close look at zoning and zoning boards, an oft-used example of political-market failure, and demonstrate why zoning is likely to be efficient. Chapter 10 analyzes the Constitution as an optimal social contract, while chapter 11 suggests that some "problems" in majority rule preference aggregation are easily overcome by political markets. Chapter 12 undermines much of the previous work on "distributive politics."

Part III is devoted to methodological issues. I point out errors in previous empirical tests and reformulate an empirical agenda.

In a nutshell, this book develops an invisible-hand theory of efficient democratic markets and provides an analytic framework for finding errors in models of political-market failure. It attacks the sacred truths of the left, right, and middle and yields a research agenda for the study of democratic markets and their organization.

EFFICIENCY AND WEALTH MAXIMIZATION

Before the analysis proceeds, it is useful to explain what I mean by efficiency and wealth maximization. The concept of efficiency used in this book is that of wealth maximization, or Pareto optimality in the narrow sense of the term, rather than Pareto optimality in its broadest sense. A state of affairs is Pareto optimal if one person's welfare cannot be increased unless another person's welfare is decreased. It is possible to claim that whatever the state of affairs, it is Pareto optimal, rendering the concept virtually useless as a criterion. Consider, for example, a monopolist who artificially restricts output by charging too high a price. Economics texts suggest that the government could force the monopolist to lower her price to a competitive level and at the same time force consumers to pay a lump sum tax to the monopolist equivalent to the excess profits that the monopolist made in the nonregulated regime, thereby making the monopolist indifferent between the two regimes and the consumers better off under the regulation of the monopolist regime (since the tax is less than the additional consumer surplus from lower prices and greater output). On this analysis, unregulated monopoly pricing is not wealth maximizing because the consumers would be willing to pay more in taxes than the monopolist would demand in subsidies if prices were lowered to a competitive level. Equivalently, the original state of affairs is not Pareto optimal in the narrow sense since the consumers would be better off and the monopolist no worse off if the government could institute such a tax-and-subsidy scheme costlessly. However, if we do not observe the monopolist being regulated, we could always say that the transaction cost of organizing such an exchange (determining the appropriate amount that each consumer should be taxed and then collecting it) is greater than the benefit of a lower price, and, hence, restricted output of the unregulated monopolist is Pareto optimal in the broad sense. That is, whatever we observe must be Pareto optimal in the broad sense, for if a change could make someone better off without making anyone worse off, it would have already been undertaken. I do not use this broad definition of Pareto optimality here. Instead, I use the concept of wealth maximization, which in this case means that the monopolist should be forced to charge the competitive price (whether she is compensated or not).

I will now consider wealth maximization in greater detail. Assume that aggregate tastes do not change when the distribution of income changes. This allows me to avoid discussing variations in choice when wealth changes and to ignore those situations where wealth maximization is undefined. Consider the following *possible* states of the world: (A) the firm is not regulated, and it chooses a monopoly price; (B) the firm is regulated, and it is forced to choose a competitive price. I emphasize the word *possible* because I do not want to assume away real-world costs like monitoring since in either state of the world there are transaction costs. Now assume the following hypothetical: There are no transaction costs in going from one of the two states of the world to the other. In particular, there are no organization, bargaining, or monitoring costs in going from A to B or vice versa, but there are, of course, transaction costs within A and B. If in moving from A to B, there exists a set of transfers of wealth from one set of people to another (costlessly administered) that makes at least one person better off and no person worse off, then situation A is not wealth maximizing. If in moving from B to A or to any other state of the world, there does not exist a set of wealth transfers that leaves no one worse off, then B is wealth maximizing. On the basis of these hypothetical transfers, wealth maximization recommends a move from A to B even without actual compensation to the losers.

A rule of wealth maximization may ultimately be Pareto superior if there are numerous decisions and no one is a consistent loser. In addition, wealth maximization does not say that losers are never compensated, only that compensation is not always necessary.

When there is incomplete information, the concept of efficiency is more difficult to pin down and there is less agreement about its meaning (see Holmstrom and Myerson 1983). An omniscient observer could tell when there was no reallocation of resources that could make someone better off without making someone else worse off. But without omniscience, one needs to talk about Pareto optimality within the context of the mechanisms available.

I deal with the problem of incomplete information in two ways. Most of the time, I argue that politicians and voters are well informed. At other times, I accept the impossibility of finding a perfect revelation mechanism. If none exists, then our basis of comparison cannot be with a world that has such a mechanism, but with the best of all possible worlds given the existing technology.

In this book, I use the words *efficiency, Pareto optimality,* and *wealth maximization* interchangeably, but I always mean them in the strong sense of wealth maximization. I do not argue that voters are poorly informed and politicians shirk and that this is efficient because it would be too costly to have it otherwise; but rather I argue that voters are highly informed and there is little shirking. Nor do I argue that because any move is likely to make someone worse off, everything is efficient.

Finally, I do not argue the converse, that democratic governments only make policies that make someone better off without making someone worse off.

Wealth maximization does not mean those with more wealth win in the political process. Nor does it mean that money counts, but not votes. Rather, it means that with the appropriate taxes and subsidies and/or combinations of policies, a wealth-maximizing policy could provide more to voters than a policy that does not maximize wealth.

PART I

FACTORS FOR EFFICIENCY IN POLITICAL MARKETS

2

THE INFORMED VOTER

A CONSTANT CRITICISM OF DEMOCRATIC MARKETS IS that voters are uninformed. Economists have provided a ready explanation: the benefit of a voter's being informed is outweighed by the cost of obtaining information. The benefit is slight since a vote cast by an individual voter is unlikely to have any effect on the outcome; while the cost of obtaining information is high because the ramifications of any policy are complex and rarely fall directly on the voter. Some models have emphasized the differences in information among voters. For example, defense industries are concentrated in a few states. In these states, voters are well informed and sensitive to changes in defense spending since their income is strongly dependent upon the defense industry. In contrast, the cost of defense expenditures is diffused throughout the states, making the tax burden relatively unimportant. According to this model, the net result is excessive defense expenditures, since the benefits, but not the costs, are felt by voters. Other models claim that voters are victims of biased information and that their "[political] 'preferences' can be manipulated and created through information and misinformation provided by interested pressure groups" (Becker 1983, 392). For example, the military-industrial complex may be the voters' prime source of information regarding the appropriate level of defense. Unfortunately for the voters, there are strong incentives for the military-industrial complex to exaggerate its positive role in national welfare. Consequently, voters may vote for too much defense expenditure. As another example, newspapers may be hesitant to publish editorials condemning businesses since this may reduce advertising revenues. As a consequence, their readers may have an overly optimistic view of capitalism.

In the following pages, I show that models of voter ignorance confuse biased judgment with biased information and/or lack of information, overestimate the cost to voters of obtaining information, and underestimate the amount of information that the voters possess. (In chapter 5, I discuss the issue of voter rationality.)

THE AMOUNT OF INFORMATION HELD BY VOTERS HAS BEEN UNDERESTIMATED

The arguments made for the voters' being uninformed implicitly assume that the major cost of information falls on the voters. However, an informed political entrepreneur who provides information to the voters increases her chances of winning an election, and gaining the direct and indirect rewards of holding office. Thus the rewards to the political entrepreneur from discovering and exploiting unknown political demands are analogous to the profits to the business entrepreneur from creating a new market niche.

Party brand names reduce still further the cost to the voter of acquiring information. Parties establish reputations for certain policy positions. The voter can then vote a party line without knowledge of the particular candidates.[1] Numerous studies (see, for example, Hamill, Lodge, and Blake 1985) have corroborated that party cues and ideological labels (conservative or liberal) play an important role in the perception of candidates, allowing the voter to make intelligent inferences.

Voters receive a lot of "free" information—in the news, in the mail, and in ordinary conversations. Arnold (1990, 39) reports that 74 percent of voters remembered receiving mail from their incumbent, 38 percent had seen their incumbent at a meeting, and 20 percent had met with the incumbent personally; while 25 percent of the voters remembered receiving mail from the challenger, 3 percent had seen the challenger at a meeting, and 5 percent had met with the challenger personally.

---

1. Note that this provides a rational explanation for party identification, in contrast to the older sociological literature, which claims that individuals identify with parties for irrational reasons (for example, one automatically votes like one's parents). The rational view would explain the high rate of concurrence between children and parents on party registration by pointing to the likelihood of similar preferences for policies (based on economic class and the like). Furthermore, party *identification* suggests that the person's self-identity is somehow tied in with the choice of political party. The economic view treats choice of party like choice of grocery store. One does not "identify" with grocery stores.

Furthermore, "uninformed" voters may just be storing their information in a format different from that envisioned by the critics of voter rationality. For example, one such critic, Bernstein (1989, 16), reports that 86 percent of the respondents to a 1978 Center for Political Studies survey could not remember how their representatives voted on any bill. But work by Lodge, McGraw, and Stroh (1989) and ordinary intuition suggest that people evaluate evidence and store impressions rather than store information and evaluate at a later date. Hence it is quite possible that voters do not remember how their congressperson voted on particular bills and yet have an accurate impression of their policy stance. This view is corroborated by Erikson and Romero (1990), who showed that despite knowing almost nothing specific about their senators' voting records, over 70 percent of the variation in voters' perceptions of their senators' ideological positions could be explained by their senators' actual voting records and party affiliation.

Aldrich and McKelvey (1977) have more direct evidence regarding the relationship between information and voting. Their study shows that a significant number of voters are able to identify the positions of candidates on issues and that these positions are good predictors of voting behavior.[2] Wright and Berkman (1986) also show that voters vote for the candidate closest to their own position. A substantial amount of learning takes place over presidential campaigns, as Conover and Feldman (1989) show in a panel study of the 1976 presidential election. They observed a considerable increase in voter knowledge about candidates. In February 1976, only 25 percent of the respondents felt that they knew anything about Carter. By April 1976, 79 percent were in this category.[3]

The argument that voter ignorance is rational is based on the assumption that people obtain information about the candidates only to make more informed voting decisions; since the individual vote is extremely unlikely to affect the outcome of the election, it is rational to be uninformed. But there are other important reasons for individuals to be informed. Government policy has economic effects. Therefore, it pays individuals to gain knowledge about government activity in order to make better decisions about consumption and investment even in the

2. There are, of course, a large number of articles "demonstrating" that voters are uninformed, but they tend to be subject to the kinds of criticisms that I have made in this chapter.

3. Unfortunately, the study does not say whether self-reported voter knowledge was correct.

absence of an election. Elections create greater uncertainty and therefore greater rewards to being informed. Candidates have different policies, which potentially impact people in different ways. For example, if elected, the challenger may initiate a low interest rate policy, thereby altering plans in the private sector for investment or refinancing. Or if elected, the challenger may alter defense procurements, making investments in and by certain defense firms more or less profitable. Hence there are economic rewards, not only in learning the policies of the candidates, but also in predicting the outcome of the election. Planning is improved, and investments with higher expected payoffs are made (see Congleton 1991). An interesting corroboration of this claim is found in a study by Roberts (1990), who shows that in the 1980 U.S. presidential election, odds favoring Reagan in British gambling establishments were positively correlated with stock prices in those defense firms likely to benefit if he won the election.

INFORMED JUDGMENTS CAN BE MADE WITH LITTLE INFORMATION

Voters need to know little about the actions of their congressperson to make intelligent choices in an election. It is sufficient for voters to find a person or organization with similar preferences and then ask advice on how to vote. For example, people who like to hunt are more likely to read the literature from the National Rifle Association than literature from an organization attempting to ban guns. And one can always ask advice from a more politically knowledgeable friend with similar tastes.[4] Voters can also look at the list of campaign contributors, who typically make their campaign endorsements public, and infer the characteristics of the candidates' policies, pro or con. That is, endorsements by interest groups are like signals in the market and provide strong cues about candidates' preferences.

Evidence corroborating information shortcuts is found in Lupia (1994), who showed that voter choice on five ballot measures to reform insurance in California was strongly dependent on knowledge of the positions of various interest groups on the measures. Lupia identified fifteen organizations that took positions on one or more of the five

---

4. Thus, voters choose their pressure groups rather than pressure groups influencing voters, as Becker (1983) has argued.

measures. These organizations included the California Trial Lawyers Association, the insurance industry, Ralph Nader, and the Friends of Motorcycling. The first two organizations tried to hide their sponsorship and advertised themselves as proconsumer or procitizen, as did all the other organizations. Despite the fact that there were five complex measures on the ballot and that some organizations tried to hide their true identity, many of those who were otherwise very poorly informed about the substance of the ballot measures were able to correctly identify the positions of the various interest groups and then make the same choice that they would have made if they had been fully informed.

It is not necessary to be extremely knowledgeable in order to make correct choices in the political sphere. Consider the standard Downsian model of a single left-right continuum of voters' preferences. In order for a voter to make a correct choice, she need only know which candidate is closer to her most desired preference. This is especially easy when both candidates are to the left (or to the right) of the voter's most preferred position. In such cases, the voter need not know her own position with any degree of exactitude, nor even the specific stances of the candidates, only their relative positions.

McKelvey and Ordeshook (1986) have taken this argument one step further: If there is a symmetric distribution of voters' preferences, some voters need not know the positions of the candidates, only their own position, which candidate is to the right, and the outcome of voter surveys (where a subset of informed voters register their preference). If polls show a dead heat (and campaign contributions are about equal) and the uninformed voter is to the right of center, then the voter can infer that she should vote for the candidate to the right. A dead heat implies that the candidates are equidistant from the median (see fig. 2.1a–c). The more conservative candidate may be to the left of the voter when the candidates are near the median (as in fig. 2.1a, b) or to the right when the candidates have taken extremist platforms (as in fig. 2.1c), but either way the right-wing candidate is closer to the voter's most preferred position. If the conservative candidate has more than 50 percent in the polls, then the voter again prefers the conservative candidate (see fig. 2.1d). The only time that the decision becomes problematic is when the conservative candidate has less than 50 percent of the poll. Then the voter needs to know the positions of the voters at various percentiles. McKelvey and Ordeshook concede that pressure groups may

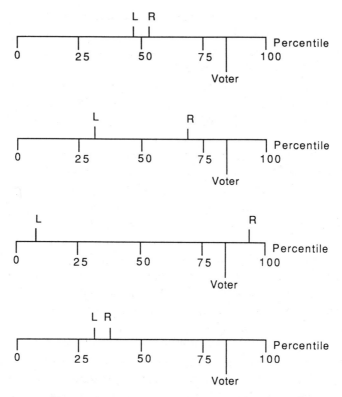

FIG. 2.1. Voters can make judgments based on little information. The voter to the right of the median voter will prefer R whenever 50 percent of the informed voters prefer R.

distort the poll results, but even here one might be able to correct for distortion. It should be remembered that this model is an exercise in demonstrating how little the voter has to know about the candidates. In the real world, individuals have many more clues about the candidates' positions.

It would be foolish to argue that voters are perfectly informed about political markets. However, efficiency does not require perfectly informed voters any more than efficient economic markets require all stockholders to know the intimate workings of the firms in which they hold stock or require all principals to perfectly monitor their agents. Although economists believe that stock markets are among the most informationally efficient markets, arguments can be made that voters are more informed than stockholders. The diversification of portfolios for the purpose of risk spreading makes the average stockholder less knowledgeable about his company than the average voter is about his congressperson or party (voters cannot diversify their locations). In addition, there is a sense of civic duty that encourages voters to obtain costly information even though it is not in their self-interest, narrowly conceived, to do so; no such civic duty exists for the average stockholder.[5] Political scientists have often trotted out statistics showing how few people know the name of their congressperson; probably a lower percentage of stockholders know the names of the CEOs of the firms in which they own stock.

THE DELETERIOUS EFFECT OF BIASED INFORMATION HAS BEEN OVERSTATED

I have never met anyone who believes that the defense department does not exaggerate the need for defense procurement. But if everyone knows that the defense department will exaggerate the importance of its contribution to human welfare, then, on average, voters will sufficiently discount defense department claims.[6] Even when the ruling class has a virtual domestic monopoly on the instruments of information, as was the case in the former Soviet Union, we observe people discounting the information contained in their papers and trusting foreign sources. When the Chernobyl nuclear accident occurred, citizens of the Soviet Union turned to foreign sources for their information. More recently, the Communist party leaders did very poorly in the first elections, although they had been in control of the schools, newspapers, and other sources of political information for several generations. Hence biased sources of information need not lead to biases in belief.

A related problem occurs for those who argue that diffuse taxpayers are insensitive to expenditures on concentrated interests. To be uninformed about a policy does not imply that voters have biased estimates of its effects. For example, to be uninformed about the nature of pork-

5. This and the previous point have been made by Wintrobe (1987). The role of takeovers will be discussed in chapter 3.

6. There is a Nash equilibrium to such a strategy only if greater exaggeration is more costly to the defense department (possibly because its exaggeration is more likely to be falsified) or individuals have other methods of predicting the degree of exaggeration.

barrel projects in other congressional districts does not mean that voters tend to underestimate the effects of pork barrel—it is quite possible that the uninformed exaggerate both the extent and the negative consequences of pork-barrel projects. Furthermore, at some point these diffuse voters should be sensitive to their aggregate tax burden arising from all of the supposed concentrated rent-seekers taxing the unsuspecting, diffuse voters.

I have argued that neither lack of information nor biased information necessarily leads to irrational expectations. However, even if some individuals make incorrect choices, the law of large numbers is likely to yield the correct majority choice.[7] For example, assume that each voter is uninformed and only has a 51 percent chance of voting for her most preferred candidate (the one she would vote for if she were perfectly informed). Even if there were only one hundred voters, there is only a slight likelihood that the majority would vote contrary to the outcome that would result from a perfectly informed majority. While this example assumes that voters' mistakes are uncorrelated, more complicated models yield similar results (see, for example, work by Ladha [1993] and Berg [1993]).

As another example, consider the following situation: if everyone were fully informed, 40 percent of the population would vote for an increase in defense expenditures and 60 percent would vote against; but not everyone is fully informed, and, consequently, each of the 40 percent set of voters votes in favor with a 100 percent chance, while each of the 60 percent set of voters votes against with a 85 percent chance. This is a situation in which there is considerable bias. A voter who should be against has a 15 percent chance of voting in favor, but a voter who should vote in favor will never vote against. However, if there are more than forty thousand voters, the chance that the majority of voters will vote for an increase is less than one out of a hundred.

The law of large numbers may explain the puzzle that the Bill of Rights protects free speech but not commercial advertising. False political advertising may fool a minority, yet it will have no harmful effect since votes for the minority will not be translated into political power. In contrast, a business does not have to persuade a majority of consum-

7. This is a variant of an old argument going back to Condorcet. See Grofman and Feld (1988).

ers, only a few, to have any sales. So the majority may want to protect a minority in the commercial arena.

The theoretical argument that aggregating voters' preferences will tend to cancel out individual voter "mistakes" is corroborated by Page and Shapiro (1992). They demonstrated that aggregate public opinion is rational and well informed and appears to have an important impact on public policy. (For further empirical work showing the positive correlation between voters' preferences and their representatives' behavior, see chapter 3.)

PRESIDENTIAL MANIPULATION OF THE ECONOMY?

Nordhaus (1975), McRae (1977), Tufte (1978), and others have argued that presidents manipulate the macroeconomy in order to stay in office. The basic logic of their models is as follows: During the beginning of the presidential term, unemployment is high and inflation is low. Just before an election, the president turns on the steam and employment increases, but the inflationary impact does not arrive until after the election. Since voters have only short-term memories and a poor understanding of economics, they forget the high unemployment from the first two years of office and fail to anticipate the ensuing inflation. Therefore, they reelect the incumbent on the basis of false economic indicators.

These political business cycle models have two fundamental problems. They rely on voters being constantly fooled and on the failure of the business community to anticipate the behavior of the president, which would undermine his ability to manipulate the economy (the Lucas critique).[8]

8. To get around this critique, Rogoff and Sibert (1988) consider a model where taxation is a measure of competence—the lower the taxes, the more competently run the government. In the period after the election, the voters will be able to observe the competence directly and to see whether the low taxes were achieved through deficit spending. In contrast, the incumbent has contemporaneous information about its competency and policies. But this model assumes that "it is not worthwhile for [the voter] as an individual to monitor the government closely enough to have complete contemporaneous information . . . [and] there is no . . . group which can provide free, complete and unbiased information" (6). The model also assumes parties have finite time horizons and that voters do not punish for past behavior or employ trigger strategies. Not surprisingly, with these assumptions, there is a social welfare loss and a political-business cycle. A thoughtful survey by Nordhaus (1989) shows that the evidence for myopic political-business cycles is inconclusive.

Recent empirical work by Peltzman (1990) shows that the voters do not have such amnesia. Voters base their assessment of an administration on information about both income and inflation over at least the last three years of a presidential term. In addition, they are more savvy regarding the economy, since they are concerned with permanent, not temporary, effects of policy.

Political parties may have different macroeconomic policies, but the voters realize this and separate along lines of those who prefer low inflation and those who prefer high employment. The uncertainty arises because of the uncertain outcomes of elections. That is why the major economic effects of the presidency take place the first two years of a term and not the last two (see Alesina, Londregan, and Rosenthal [1993]; Alesina [1987, 1988b]; and Alesina and Sachs [1988]).

THE UNINFORMED VOTER AND MODELS OF DEMOCRATIC-MARKET FAILURE

In this chapter I have argued that the voter is informed. Those who are dissatisfied with the outcome of majority politics have a vested interest in believing to the contrary.[9] For if the minority holds the "correct" position, how could the majority disagree with the minority unless poorly informed (or the correct position was never an option—a noncompetitive system).

Almost every model of government failure explicitly or implicitly requires biased ignorance of the voters. Marxists are especially in need of the concept of false consciousness of the working class, since the workers are in a majority, yet they don't throw the rascals out. Although economists are generally chary of using such explanations in the economic sector, they do provide such explanations in the political sphere. For example, Goetz (1977) argues that voters suffer from "fiscal illusion" because the tax collection mechanisms cause voters to underestimate the tax burden, while Buchanan and Wagner (1977) suggest that deficit financing causes the public to undervalue the true long-term costs of current expenditures. The fiscal-illusion hypothesis can be traced back to J. S. Mill, who in 1848 argued that direct taxes were more visible and that indirect taxes could be disguised (1970, 220). Perhaps King George

9. On the other hand, those in the majority will tend to think that the system works well.

believed in this theory also when he applied an indirect tax on tea going to the colonies. Unfortunately for him, the colonists had not read the theory and been blinded by its logic.[10]

A model that assumes that voters or consumers are constantly fooled and that there are no entrepreneurs to clear up their confusion will, not surprisingly, predict that the decision-making process leads to inefficient results. In this chapter, I have argued that such assumptions are unwarranted.

10. This insight is due to Mueller (1989, 342). For a recent survey of the fiscal-illusion literature see Oates (1988), who finds that none of it has very compelling empirical support.

3

ELECTORAL-MARKET COMPETITION
AND THE CONTROL OF
OPPORTUNISTIC BEHAVIOR

ELECTED OFFICIALS CAN BE VIEWED AS AGENTS and the voters as their principals. There is always the potential for opportunism by agents—they may be lazy, take bribes, or adopt positions contrary to those that would be adopted if voters were fully informed. Here, I argue that competition, reputation, monitoring, and optimal contract design reduce opportunistic behavior in the political sector and that principal-agent problems may be no more severe than in the private arena.

REPUTATION

Candidates develop reputations. If they have not kept their campaign promises in the past, they are less likely to be reelected or elected to a higher office. In economic markets a firm's goodwill may be capitalized in the value of the firm and ultimately sold. This transferability means reputation will not be inefficiently wasted toward the end of the owner's life. In contrast, the ability of politicians to transfer their reputations is clearly attenuated, thereby creating the possibility of the "last-period problem": in the last term of their finite political lives, politicians may cheat on their promises if there are no costs to doing so. Since voters realize this, they will not elect politicians to their last term in office, making their second-to-the-last term the politicians' last term in office, and on and on. The ability of reputation to constrain the politician unravels. However, the political market has devised substitute methods for preventing the wasting of the reputational asset. The most important role in overcoming the last-period problem is played by the long-lived party. Each political party has a particular ideological stance, and the candidates in that party want to promote those ideological values. Even if it is the incumbent's last term in office, the incumbent wants to uphold the party's reputation so that the party's candidates will continue to win in the future and implement the incumbent's values (see Harrington 1992). Parties can also offer nonideological inducements. The vice president and the political party may "pay" the president not to shirk in his last period by making the former president an elder statesman of the party (see Alesina 1988a). There are other ways of transferring political assets. For example, political dynasties enable politicians to transfer their reputations to heirs. In 1965, forty-five members of the U.S. Congress and over 8 percent of state governors were sons of politicians (Laband and Lentz 1985). The idea of political heirs may be more broadly construed; a representative may be seen as the heir to the senator of the same party, the congressional aide as the heir to the congressperson, and the vice president as the heir to the president.

Political parties develop reputations so that candidates do not shirk on the party's ideology. Other members of the party have strong incentives to maintain the reputation of the party since the brand name is valuable in attracting votes. Especially in legislatures, it is easy for party leaders to monitor fellow politicians' voting behavior. Those legislators who have proven to be reliable in the past are rewarded by being appointed to influential committees (see chap. 6 for greater detail). Unless the person's vote is pivotal, a wayward member without party support is generally ineffectual in a system that requires a majority coalition. The political party is thus the analogue to a franchise in the economic sector. The creation of the party (franchise) brand name allows the voter (consumer) to make more informed judgments about how the coalition of its members will behave. An important activity of the franchise is to prevent shirking that might result in a diminution of the value of the franchise. Political parties are in an especially good position to monitor any shirking.

Note that if a politician's ideological values are consistent with her campaign promises, there is not much impetus to cheat in the first place, and the last-period problem disappears even in the absence of a party. Since elections sort out candidates so that those who get reelected tend to be those whose own ideologies are closest to their constituents, such congruence is likely.

Despite the theoretical concern about the last-period problem, there is little evidence that it is of any consequence. Lott and Reed (1989) have shown that congressmen who do not intend to run for reelection vote less often (possibly due to illness), but not differently. Thus the last period is not associated with increased ideological shirking.[1]

COMPETITION

Monitoring takes place not only within but also across political parties. Competitors can gain great advantage by providing evidence of the opposition's shirking.[2] In this regard, Kingdon's book (1989) on congressmen's voting decisions is insightful. He interviewed congressmen after roll-call votes and discovered that they regularly adjusted their votes in ways designed to forestall electoral problems. When one congressman was asked whether anyone in his district would notice his vote, the congressman replied:

> No, I know that nobody will notice it right now. People never do. But it may be used against you in the next campaign. I learned that lesson in my first campaign for reelection. About 5 days before election day, they hauled out [some charge against me] because I cast a vote against some ridiculous District [of Columbia] bill. You see, most people don't notice it. But your opponent will comb down through every aspect of your record, every vote you've ever cast, looking for dirt and using it. (Kingdon 1989, 60)

In the economic sector, the threat of a takeover reduces opportunism by management, thereby protecting the interests of the diffuse stockholder. Takeovers (losing office) are also an important mechanism for reducing opportunism in democratic political systems. There are differences between political and economic takeovers, but it is not clear that one is a better instrument than the other; indeed, if my argument is correct, each should be best in its own sphere.[3] A corporate takeover need not involve persuasion unless there is a proxy fight; instead a

---

1. Zupan (1990) claims that Lott and Reed's result is due to the fact that quitters are less likely to be shirkers.

2. More egregious behavior by agents, such as accepting bribes, may be sanctioned by law.

3. One difference is that in an election the winner has the most votes, while in a takeover the winner is the side that is willing to pay the highest price. In chapter 11, I show how vote maximization leads to wealth maximization, and thus the result is equivalent to paying the highest price.

higher price may be offered. Unfortunately for the corporate-takeover artist, rules such as "poison pills" are designed for the existing stockholders to capture the benefits from potential takeovers, reducing the return to potential owners. More generally, either stockholders or other investors will anticipate an increase in the value of the stock and the bidder's expected profit will decrease. When much of the return from investment in information is captured by others, there will be less investment in information than otherwise, and ultimately fewer people engaged in takeover activity. In contrast, the candidate with the better ideas does not have to pay a higher takeover "price," but a lower one, since voters will be more likely to vote for him.

One can view elections as a relatively low transaction cost method of exercising political takeovers: the time period between elections is relatively short (legislators are not elected for life), there are no supermajority requirements for being elected, and the opposition participates in the legislature.

Both the far right and the far left view the federal government as an extraordinarily powerful monopolist. On the right, Brennan and Buchanan (1980) use Hobbes's concept of Leviathan. But this view ignores the electoral market, wherein candidates vie for control of the government. If the electoral market is competitive, the fact that there is only one central government may be irrelevant.[4] There is competition between and within political parties. In one-party states the competition takes place at the primary stage or even earlier. Even if the candidate is running unopposed in both the primary and the general election, the theory of contestable markets argues that the threat of competition is as effective as actual competition.[5] One measure of the amount of competition is the enormous amount of money spent on trying to win elections. Approximately $40 million was spent by the two front-runners in the

4. Sufficiently competitive electoral markets also render the goals of the candidates irrelevant, as only those who maximize the probability of winning will survive when one or more of the other candidates have such a goal. Thus political biography and psychological studies of individual politicians add little to our understanding of political outcomes (if we know the market demand).

5. Schumpeter (1950) was one of the first to make an analogy between political competition and business competition. Stigler (1972) argues that political competition has many of the same qualities as economic competition. However, it is evident that Stigler (1971, 1975) finds the effects of political competition less than salubrious. The argument here resonates more with Becker (1983, 1985). However, here the thrust for efficiency is a strong force, while in his work it is a weak force (see chap. 7).

1986 California Senate race.[6] This expenditure is for only one–one hundredth of the voting power in the Senate, which in turn has only a minority share in the power to affect a legislative outcome and an even smaller role in affecting actual policy decisions.

The pervasiveness of competition also undermines the Left's characterization of democratic systems. Miliband (1969) and Domhoff (1967, 1974) claim that the government is run by a relatively unified ruling class. The ability to maintain such a cartel among so many people with so many possible entrants is unfathomable to a student of industrial organization. In economic markets, industrial groupings are relatively small in comparison, yet they have a hard time maintaining cartel pricing against internal and external competitive forces. Difficulty in maintaining cartels also undermines Wittman's model (1973) of party collusion. (We will come back to this topic in greater detail in chapter 12.)

Tullock (1965b) has suggested that there may be serious barriers to entry in plurality elections. In contrast to economic markets, where a firm can survive with 33 percent of the market share, in plurality elections a candidate cannot survive with the second highest market share. Even here, however, a candidate can enter at the local political level and build up a following, and a new "wing" of a party need not win many offices to be represented.[7]

Some might argue that the large expenditures involved in political campaigns make for high barriers to entry, but venture capital from those who expect to profit from a different policy will back a new candidate. In addition, for presidential primary campaigns in the United States there are matching funds for major party candidates who have won in ten primaries and for minor party nominees if the party received at least 5 percent of the vote in the previous election. Furthermore, large amounts of money are not always needed to win an election. While campaign expenditures and votes tend to be positively correlated, the degree of correlation is not very high, and the direction of causation need not be from expenditures to votes.

6. *San Francisco Chronicle/Examiner,* August 31, 1986, sec. A.

7. It would be useful to explore the differences between a concave production function typical of firms and an S-shaped function typical of political parties. Crain (1977) has argued that there are barriers to entry because representatives must live in the district, and successful politicians cannot represent more than one district. However, allies of the successful political entrepreneur can run in other electoral districts, and the successful political entrepreneur can campaign on their behalf.

Fiorina (1981, 1989) has described still another type of barrier to entry. Over time, the reelection rate of incumbent congressmen has increased. Fiorina attributes this to a concomitant increase in funding for congressional staffs, which allows for increased facilitation of constituency interests (for example, making sure that a constituent gets treated properly by the Veteran's Administration). Since these resources are not available to the opposition, entry barriers have been raised.

The logic behind this argument is questionable. Voters are smart enough to know that the opposition is unable to provide the services that an incumbent provides. The voter will ask which candidate will do a better job at facilitation, among other things. Hence, the existence of facilitation does not create a bias for incumbents (unless there is on-the-job learning). Evidence contrary to the incumbent facilitation hypothesis is offered by Jacobson (1987b). He shows that congressional staff, mailings, and paid trips to the district are poorly correlated with the probability that the incumbent will win reelection.[8] State and local elections provide additional evidence against the constituency service theory. Local politics is often facilitation based, but the advantage of incumbency is not nearly as high.

I suspect that there is some incumbency advantage in the House and that this is due to the value of seniority there—the district gains if its representative has been there longer than representatives from other districts. In the Senate, the benefits of seniority are smaller, and so are reelection rates; while in the executive branch, the seniority issue disappears.

The main reason for high rates of incumbent success is much simpler. Incumbents tend to be reelected for the same reason that the winner of the last footrace is likely to win the next one and the head of a corporation is likely to maintain his position tomorrow. They are the best. That is why they won in the first place and why they are likely to win again.

In federal systems, competition also takes place within and across government levels. There is competition between cities and between states. People and businesses choose to locate where their consumer

8. Similar results are found in McAdams and Johannes (1988) and Mann and Wolfinger (1980). The evidence is not all in one direction, however. Empirical support for the Fiorina model is found in Fiorina (1981) and Cain, Ferejohn, and Fiorina (1987).

Jacobson (1987a) has also argued that the "marginals never vanished" since larger margins of victory did not translate into greater frequency of the incumbent winning.

and producer surpluses are maximized. Those cities and states that provide better government will attract more residents (the Tiebout effect).[9] There is also competition between city, state, and federal governments. Citizens choose the arenas where their preferences can be best satisfied. Often one sector has a clear comparative advantage: cities are better at deciding school location, and federal governments are better at deciding defense expenditures. But there are many times when the appropriate arena is not so obvious and the various levels of government are in competition with each other.

Finally, there is competition between these governments and other institutions, such as religious organizations, unions, corporations, and families in trying to satisfy consumer demands.

Competition is like water held in a sieve. To argue that competition does not exist because it is absent somewhere is like saying water is not leaking because one of the holes in the sieve is plugged. Thus the burden of proof in the competitive-versus-noncompetitive debate is on those who would argue lack of competition. The proponents of the noncompetitive view have demonstrated only that a few of these holes in the competitive sieve are plugged.

In economic markets, monopolies (without potential competitors and without the ability to engage in multiple pricing) are inefficient. It is therefore not surprising that monopoly models of government also lead to inefficient results.[10] Thus one-candidate models (e.g., Peltzman's 1976 model of the regulator) and models of government influence that do not have competition for the control of the government (e.g., Krueger's 1974 model of rent seeking) have built-in political-market failure. Even multicandidate models that allow competition only within the

9. Although competition enhances efficiency, it may have undesirable distribution effects (when transaction costs are too high to design a system with the desirable distribution). If there is a consensus about the undesirability of these distribution effects, then voters may choose to limit competition. For example, suppose that people believe that there should be welfare assistance for the poor; but if given the option, they would prefer that others pay for it. Each state might lower its welfare payments hoping that the poor would migrate and be supported by the taxpayers of other states. Voters in all states might agree to federal regulations setting minimum welfare payments.

10. Monopoly power is a prime explanation for economic-market failure. However, it is not clear that government monopoly, even if it existed, would lead to inefficiency. Monopolies are inefficient because they have partial, but not complete, economic power. For example, if monopolies could force some people to buy at a price higher than the average, an efficient outcome might result. The government monopoly may have more instruments available to it than a private monopoly.

imposed structure of the model underestimate competition's inexorable drive toward efficient results.[11] Hence, these models of market failure have failed because they have not accounted for the existence and influence of competition.

OPTIMAL CONTRACT DESIGN

Optimal contract design also reduces opportunism. For example, opportunism by politicians is mitigated when they are paid above-market salaries and then threatened with losing office if they shirk. The fact that candidates engage in very costly election campaigns is consistent with the hypothesis that holding office pays above-market salaries.

In addition, there is usually no mandatory retirement age for legislators, which reduces the severity of the last-period problem.[12]

THE CORRELATION BETWEEN VOTER PREFERENCES AND LEGISLATIVE BEHAVIOR

I have argued mainly on theoretical grounds that political agents represent the interests of their principals, the voters. In this section, I look at some empirical studies. This is meant to be a brief overview within the context of the theoretical structure developed in the preceding pages. A complete survey would be the nucleus of another book.

I start with some negative results. The classic study by Miller and Stokes (1963) found only weak links between constituency preferences and congressional behavior. More recently, Bernstein has devoted his whole book to debunking the "myth [that] constituencies control the behavior of their representatives" (1989, xiii). However, many of my arguments in this and in the previous chapter undermine his results. For example, he presents data showing that only 49 percent of voters know the ideology of their incumbent representative (1989, 17–18), but I have demonstrated that this kind of knowledge is not necessary to

11. This proposition will be more formally demonstrated in chapter 11.

12. However, certain elected positions put a cap on how many terms an individual can serve (e.g., the U.S. presidency). Presumably, if the last-period problem resulted in too much shirking, the restriction on the number of terms served would be removed. Friedman and Wittman (forthcoming) show that voting on term limits aims not to reduce opportunism by politicians, but rather to redistribute power from one district to another, one party to another, or one branch to another.

make intelligent choices. When testing for constituency control, Bernstein looks at roll-call votes when the ideology of the representative and the preferences of his constituency are in conflict. He shows that the ideological variable is more influential than constituency preference in explaining congressmen's decisions. But this leaves out the vast majority of cases where the ideology of the congressman and the preferences of his constituency coincide. This congruence is not mere happenstance— liberal congressmen tend to come from liberal districts, and conservative congressmen tend to come from conservative districts. So Bernstein is looking at the wrong measure (see Wright 1990). In fact, his own data can be used to draw just the opposite conclusion from the one that he is claiming. Bernstein looks at House voting on five bills that advantaged oil companies (1989, 84). In oil-producing districts, congressmen voted in favor 84 percent of the time, while in non-oil-producing districts, congressmen voted in favor only 34 percent of the time.

Before turning to the supporting literature, it is useful to discuss the nature of the empirical problems facing the researcher. Almost all studies that estimate voter preferences will underestimate the correlation (R-square) between voter preference and legislative behavior since there is only an imperfect relationship between constituent preferences and the variables chosen by the econometrician as proxies for these preferences. Even a perfect correlation between constituent preferences and their representative's voting record might yield a low correlation between measured preferences and the voting record. In contrast to the econometrician who throws in a few explanatory variables, legislators spend a great deal of their time trying to get the pulse of their constituents on all kinds of issues. And if our competitive model is correct, only those legislators who are the most skilled at predicting their constituents' interests will survive the electoral competition. Therefore, one would expect that legislators have a much better idea of their constituency's preferences than the econometrician. Although studies that use opinion polls are probably better than the studies that use proxies for voter preferences, the survey data still may not be in the form of the choices faced by the legislator, especially if the legislator has to trade support on some legislation in order to get support on other legislation.

There is a significant body of empirical evidence that supports the argument that voters make informed judgments and that politicians respond. Erikson, Wright, and McIver (1989) showed that 80 percent of policy variation across states could be explained by variation in public opinion.[13] Using survey research data, Powell (1982) found a positive correlation between the stands of members of Congress and the preferences of voters, while Page and Shapiro (1983), also using survey research data, found that changes in congressional behavior *followed* changes in public opinion.

A number of authors have tried to deal with the issues raised by Bernstein in a more sophisticated way. Kau and Rubin (1979) developed measures of the representative's ideology that were orthogonal to the constituency's ideology; that is, they considered only representative ideology not explained by their constituents' preferences. Their method was to regress Americans for Democratic Action scores of congressmen on their districts' economic variables. That part of the ADA score explained by the regression was attributed to the ideology of the constituents; the unexplained variation in ADA scores was attributed to the ideology of the legislator. The role of the constituent's ideology was shown to be far more important than the legislator's ideology. This is a strong result because the economic variables used as proxies for constituency ideology are a very weak measure of constituency preference. Furthermore, this methodology is still likely to overestimate the role of the legislator's ideology, since the measure for the legislator's ideology is unlikely to be orthogonal to the errors in measuring constituent ideology. For example, if voters in a district are more liberal than the economic variables would indicate, and their legislator perfectly represented his constituents' interests, then, using their methodology, the legislator's ideology would appear to be more liberal than his constituency. Numerous other studies have used this two-stage orthogonal procedure. Using district presidential votes as an indicator of constituency preference, Kau, Keenan, and Rubin (1982) demonstrated a positive correlation between voters' preferences and their representatives' behavior. Kalt and Zupan (1984) looked at congressional voting on strip mining. Again their measures of constituency preference (agricultural revenues, percentage of electricity generated from coal, etc.) were highly imperfect, resulting in an underestimation of its true role. However, the data still showed that constituency preference was more important than ideology in predicting the vote. More recently, Kalt and Zupan (1990) were

13. See also Wright, Erikson, and McIver (1987).

able to explain 59 percent of the variation in ADA ratings of senators by constituency characteristics.[14]

It could be argued that voters' preferences are determined by their representatives rather than vice versa. However, the work of Glazer and Robbins (1983, 1985) undermines this counterargument. In their earlier paper, they showed that replacements for incumbents were ideologically further away from the person they replaced when the incumbent had been rejected by the voters than when the incumbent had been promoted to a higher office or had died while in office, implying that voters exert ideological control. In their later paper, Glazer and Robbins showed that redistricting had a direct effect on the behavior of representatives. Those incumbents facing more liberal districts became more liberal in their voting patterns. More recently, Erikson and Wright (1993) have shown that a legislator's voting contrary to constituent interests has severe repercussions on election day.

CONCLUDING REMARKS

Strom (1990) provides three primary requirements for a successful political party: Information about the electorate and its preferences; mobilization of supporters in campaigns; and implementation of party policy in the various institutions to which the party gains access. A party wins elections only if it is effective in fulfilling these requirements. The party organization is designed to limit shirking by its members, to elicit information, and to provide mechanisms that allow party leaders to make credible commitments to their activists and voters.

With monitoring, reputation, competition, and optimally designed contracts, opportunism will be reduced but, possibly, not eliminated. However, this should not be viewed as a political-market failure if there are no superior alternatives because other forms of private and public control are too costly to implement.

---

14. See Kau and Rubin (1993), who argue that the ideology of legislators is of minor importance in explaining their voting patterns.

4

TRANSACTION COSTS AND THE DESIGN OF GOVERNMENT INSTITUTIONS

COASE (1960) AND OTHERS HAVE SHOWN that when there are well-defined property rights and low negotiation-transfer costs, economic-market failures disappear.[1] For example, the ostensible divergence between private and social cost, or "externality," that arises when ranchers have the right to let their cows trample farmers' corn is eliminated when farmers pay ranchers for nondamage. In much the same way, low transaction costs can overcome many of the externality arguments for democratic-market failures.

DEMOCRATIC INSTITUTIONS THAT REDUCE TRANSACTION COSTS

Political markets are inefficient when one group of actors does not account for the costs or benefits to another group of actors. An oft-cited example of the divergence between private and social costs is the majority's shifting of costs onto an unwilling minority. Such a divergence (externality) will exist, however, only when negotiation-transfer costs are high. When political transaction costs are low, any inefficiency is negotiated away. Consider Coase's classic example in the context of a legislature, where a majority represents ranchers and a minority represents farmers. Even though ranchers have the right of the majority to pass laws allowing their cows unlimited freedom to trample farmers' corn, the law

---

1. Transaction, or negotiation and transfer, costs are the costs involved in determining the price and conditions of the exchange. They include the costs of haggling, writing up the contract, and monitoring to insure that the other side has lived up to the terms of the agreement.

will only allow the optimal amount of damage. Of course, part of the legislative deal will require the farmers to pay for nondamage, possibly through higher taxes. The only difference between this version and Coase's is where the deals are made. In his version, they are made in the private sector; in mine, they are made in the public sector. But in both versions the outcome is wealth maximizing.

An independent corroboration of this example has been uncovered by Kantor (1991). He studied the closing of open range in Georgia after the Civil War. The traditional agricultural practice had allowed animals to roam the countryside freely and forced farmers to erect fences around their crops. All unfenced land was considered common pasture and could be used by anyone. According to Kantor's estimates, closing the range would have generated large benefits for many counties in the state, especially those with improved acreage. However, the existence of a commons created high transaction costs, so that voluntary agreements to close the commons were impossible. In 1872, the Georgia legislature partially resolved this problem by allowing county referenda on stock law (closing the range). Voting on the referenda reduced the transaction costs considerably, since the unanimity required in private bargaining to close a commons was no longer required. This still did not lead to many counties adopting the stock law. A majority of voters would lose if such a referendum passed, even though the gains to the minority would be greater than the losses to the majority. In 1881, the legislature passed a law that promised to enforce side payments between expected winners and losers if the new law were adopted at the local (subcounty) level. By law, tenants (who typically used the commons for grazing their cows) were provided free use of pasturage for land enclosure. This changed stock laws from a losing to a winning coalition, and many more stock laws were approved.

Democratic political markets are structured to reduce transaction costs. The small number of members in the House and Senate reduces negotiation costs, thereby creating the conditions for efficient logrolling (exchange). Logrolling occurs only if the parties to the agreement are made better off. Inefficient costs are not shifted onto third parties (other districts) because these third parties would then enter into the negotiations and strike a deal to make all of the participants better off than they would be under an inefficient regime. Although there is an extensive literature arguing that logrolling is inefficient (for example, see Riker and Brams 1973), the arguments are unsound. In order to generate inefficiency, these models implicitly assume that there can be no exchanges between the minority and the majority. But the essence of logrolling is the bundling of minority interests into a majority package. Even when there is intransitivity and inefficient distributions are on the cycle of intransitivity, if there is a cost to forming coalitions, inefficient coalitions will be the least stable and the least likely to be formed. (The formation of legislative coalitions will be discussed in greater detail in chapter 6.)

Representation instead of direct democracy and a federal rather than a purely unitary system are other ways that democracies and other forms of government reduce the cost of political exchange. As Buchanan and Tullock (1962) noted long ago, majority rule instead of a unanimity rule reduces negotiation costs by preventing monopoly holdouts.[2]

Political parties also reduce transaction costs by facilitating trade among their members. Winning coalitions are created within the context of the party platform rather than on an ad hoc basis. In Congress, party organization helps to make commitments credible. For example, party leaders can enforce policy commitments by threatening those legislators who might otherwise be tempted to renege on their promises. The committee structure also facilitates Pareto-improving exchanges. Specialized committees allow those who are most affected by the relevant policy to trade among themselves rather than involving many actors whose interests are only peripheral. Productivity is enhanced when there is specialization, and assignments are made on the basis of comparative advantage.

Pressure groups, too, may be viewed as organizations that reduce the transaction costs of providing information to legislators (see chap. 7).

EFFICIENT SHIFTING OF RENTS

I have already argued that the degree of opportunism by politicians has been greatly exaggerated. In this and the following section, I suggest

2. The fact that people are willing to set up majority rule with its supposed abuses of the minority instead of a two-thirds or unanimity rule suggests that the abuses of majority rule are less than the negotiation costs (and abuses) of a unanimity rule. Majority rule is preferred to a supermajority rule (e.g., two-thirds rule) when the system does not want to give weight to a proposal just because it is the status quo. If there were high transaction costs preventing voters (or congressmen) from making side payments in exchange for votes, then a supermajority rule would favor the status quo. In general, supermajority rules shift wealth toward those in favor of the status quo.

that, to the extent that rent seeking exists, rents will be shifted efficiently and the seeking of these rents will involve minimal social cost.

It is useful to reconsider the farmer/rancher example in the context of political rent seeking. Both sides may try to shift wealth to their own side. But just as in the voluntary transfer case, there is an impetus to reduce deadweight loss. The less the deadweight loss, the greater the gain that rent seekers can extract. Efficient transfers will be chosen over less efficient rules if these create greater net rents. For example, if ranchers had been more politically powerful in Georgia, the commons would still have been closed, even though the closing hurt owners of livestock (albeit less than the gain to farmers). However, if the ranchers had been more powerful, they might have gained special tax breaks in return. Skilled politicians create efficient policy packages with these types of implicit trades.

One might counter with the argument that voters would not accept such blatant transfers and that more subtle, albeit more costly, means would have to be employed. However, this seemingly plausible counterargument is fraught with problems. It assumes that those voters who stand to lose from transfers recognize efficient transfers but not inefficient ones; while those who stand to gain recognize both efficient and inefficient transfers on their behalf. This requires a dual asymmetry. Gainers respond differently from losers; and losers are less responsive to inefficient transfers than to efficient ones. But as shown in chapters 2 and 3, political entrepreneurs have a greater impetus to expose inefficient transfers since the costs are greater.

Politicians have created a number of devices to shift rents efficiently. Grandfather clauses allow rents to be shifted without distorting supply responses to those grandfathered.[3] Farm price supports with acreage restrictions may be a reasonable approximation to an efficient rent redistribution; higher prices would bring forth an inefficient increase in supply. It is easier to monitor acreage responses than to monitor supply responses by individual farmers, so acreage allotments (with their milder form of input distortion) are chosen. As another example of the efficient allocation of rents, the rights to offshore oil are auctioned off.

It is insightful to apply my analysis to "rent seeking" by defense

---

3. Stigler (1971) argued that inefficient forms of rent shifting are provided in order to prevent entry since entry will reduce the rents. But as I have shown here, the more entry is prevented, the less the inefficient supply response. Hence greater rents and greater efficiency need not be in contradiction.

contractors and the possible effect it might have on aggregate procurement of weapons. It should first be noted that much of the lobbying by defense contractors may represent interfirm rivalry, which does not increase the total amount of defense expenditures so much as it results in the allocation of defense expenditures among different firms. The problem of concentrated versus diffuse interests does not apply to such rivalry. While different firms may be more successful than others in the art of lobbying, this may be no more of a problem than the fact that certain firms may have better customer relations. For the sake of our argument, assume that the primary purpose of rent seeking by defense contractors is to collect rents from the general taxpayer and that, contrary to our earlier arguments, they are successful in this endeavor. Assume also that defense contractors have no particular taste for defense. If negotiation-transfer costs are zero, this rent-seeking behavior will have no effect on the number of weapons produced.

The fact that defense contractors want to maximize their income does not necessarily imply that they will try to convince voters to buy too many weapons. It may be easier to convince voters (or Congress) that profit ratios in the defense sector (and possibly wages) need to be twice as high as they are in other sectors than to convince voters that the country needs twice as many weapons as are optimal, especially since it is much less costly to the taxpayer when profit ratios are twice as high than when procurements are twice as large as necessary.[4] A defense contractor could make the following arguments: (1) that high levels of profitability are needed to insure a strong defense industry, (2) that defense contractors should be given special tax write-offs because their capital equipment depreciates rapidly, (3) that they need high profits to promote competition in an industry with high economies of scale, (4) that those defense contractors who have already demonstrated their ability to do defense work should get special performance bonuses (the grandfather clause), and so on. Or perhaps the defense contractors do not need to say anything at all; rather, the defense industry, in its bilateral monopoly position (the rents suggest that it has some monopoly power), negotiates an "optimal" contract with Congress. The

4. Here as elsewhere the rent-seeking theory is undermined by the fact that only relatively fixed factors of production can gain rents. Thus, producing twice as many guns may require twice as many workers, but this helps defense workers little, if at all, when the supply is readily met by recruitment from outside the industry. Even if workers were gaining rents, those in the industry would prefer higher wages to more workers.

more efficient the level of armaments, the greater the monopoly rents the defense industry can extort.

EFFICIENT RENT-SEEKING ACTIVITY

Tullock (1967), Posner (1974), and Higgins, Shughart, and Tollison (1985) have argued that expenditures used in trying to curry government favors will tend to dissipate any rents.[5] However, one would expect that democracies and other governments would make rules so that the activity of rent seeking would involve minimal *social* cost. Government auctions of oil leases and treasury bonds are designed to extract all rents, but the auctions themselves involve relatively low transaction costs. And the standard example in the literature of a complete dissipation of rents (ten risk-neutral players bidding $100,000 each for a one-tenth chance of a monopoly right worth $1 million) involves no social cost. Campaign contributions can also be viewed as efficient transfers. The cost of writing a check is quite minuscule, and the information underwritten by the campaign expenditures is a valuable social product.

The existence of rent seeking may be more in the eye of the beholder than in any objective measure. It clearly has a negative connotation and is typically directed at some government activity that the speaker does not like; its application in the private sector is usually restricted to the internal workings of large firms. However, similar activity in other markets is viewed as value enhancing. Pet stores try to sell you bird feeders (this redistributes income from humans to birds); churches try to convince you to donate food to the poor; gambling casinos provide brochures; and workers search for better-paying jobs. None of these are viewed as rent-seeking activities, even though all involve information costs, some involve pure redistribution, and others may have undesirable effects. In contrast, welfare, environmental legislation, and other legislation is often viewed as the outcome of rent-seeking activity, the implicit assumption being that the majority would be better off without these programs.

---

5. Katz, Nitzan, and Rosenberg (1990) argue that the amount dissipated is much smaller than previously claimed. Most public policy involves some form of public "good." For example, a tariff against cotton imports will benefit all cotton producers. They demonstrate that when there are public goods, the *total* amount dissipated will only be one-half the value to any *individual*.

INEQUALITY OF POLITICAL POWER DOES NOT IMPLY INEFFICIENCY

Certainly, not all interest groups are equally effective in the political sphere. Because of lower organizational costs, it is possible that one interest group can deliver more votes than another and, as a consequence, receive more in the political sector.[6] But, as I have argued here, inequality of political power is no more an argument against efficiency than inequality of income or wealth.

6. In chapter 7, I argue that the power of interest groups is vastly overrated. In chapter 12, I discuss the distribution of political power.

5

HOMO ECONOMICUS VERSUS HOMO PSYCHOLOGICUS: WHY COGNITIVE PSYCHOLOGY DOES NOT EXPLAIN DEMOCRATIC POLITICS

THE CONCEPT OF HOMO ECONOMICUS IS PERVASIVE throughout the social sciences. Sociologists (Coleman 1986; Hechter 1987) and even Marxist theorists (Przeworski 1985) have used the concept of economic man in their analyses of political behavior. The greatest challenge to economic man is provided by a subset of cognitive psychologists who argue that individuals make mistaken and biased judgments because individuals choose schemata that are the most available rather than the most fruitful (Kahneman and Tversky 1984).

In this chapter, I argue that cognitive psychologists, despite their impressive experimental results, have failed to make important contributions to our understanding of political behavior. The psychology experiments that demonstrate mistaken and biased judgments are a hodge-podge of contradictory results rather than an intellectual foundation. Some of the experimental evidence against the economic model of rationality is, in fact, supportive. Finally, their experimental results cannot be applied to the real world since their experiments either underemphasize or ignore entirely the role of incentives, competitive markets, and political institutions.

Before proceeding, it is useful to consider the contrasting views of economists and cognitive psychologists.[1] There are two principal approaches to decision making: global optimization and bounded rationality. Global optimization is usually associated with neoclassical economics. The costs of decision making are either ignored or assumed not to

1. Not all economists are in the "economist" camp, nor are all cognitive psychologists allied with the "cognitive psychology" camp.

distort choice. When outcomes do not take place with certainty, then economists typically assume that individuals maximize *expected* utility as defined by Von Neumann and Morgenstern (1947) and Savage (1954). Others, including Tversky and Kahneman (1974), Fishburn (1988), and Machina (1989), use different criteria than those used by Von Neumann and Morgenstern, but their assumptions are still consistent with utility maximization.

Bounded rationality, on the other hand, stresses the costs in acquiring and processing information and the resulting cognitive shortcuts undertaken to reduce such costs. For economists, bounded rationality suggests that individuals choose optimal rules of thumb. An example is given by traffic lights, which often stay green for longer periods of time on busy streets than on cross streets, insofar as the total value of time is generally, but not always, greater for the drivers on the busy street (Wittman 1982).

In contrast, cognitive psychologists assume that individuals make use of simplifying heuristics without taking note of their instrumental use; hence, from the viewpoint of goal maximization, systematic errors of judgment are likely to arise. For example, in order to save on decision-making costs, a person might make use of only the last (or first) observation, even though optimality might suggest weighting all evidence equally. As another example, depending on the way a question is framed, an individual who employs cognitive shortcuts might choose one option over the other although the underlying meaning in both questions might be the same. Such "framing" violates fundamental notions of rationality because the person makes inconsistent decisions.[2] In a nutshell, cognitive psychologists emphasize the biases and mistakes in decisions, and occasionally argue that individuals are irrational, while economists tend to argue that, given the restraints of bounded rationality, decision-making rules are optimal.[3]

In this chapter, I argue that when issues of bounded rationality arise, the economists' concept of optimal rules of thumb is superior to the

---

2. One could stretch the concept of rationality and claim that such inconsistent choice is rational because the benefit of making a more correct decision is outweighed by the extra decision-making cost.

3. Cognitive psychologists have had a varied response to the concept of irrationality. Some argue that human behavior may be irrational either from a goal-oriented perspective or from the viewpoint of logical consistency. Others argue that behavior is always rational, although there may be systematic judgmental biases.

cognitive psychologists' notion of misleading behavioral rules. Likewise, I argue that the Von Neumann–Morgenstern postulates are superior to other global maximization approaches. I also show how political institutions mitigate problems of bounded rationality, and thus that optimization models may be more appropriate than bounded-rationality models in explaining democratic politics.

In the first section, I consider the effects of framing. Many experiments in cognitive psychology have shown that the response of subjects to questions is greatly influenced by the way the questions are worded (framed). I argue that the relevance of these experiments for explaining democratic politics is nil. In the real world, numerous institutions arise to counteract such errors. Thus the experiments themselves are misleading since they do not account for learning, experience, competition, adequate incentives, or institutional response. The second section deals with risk preference. Experiments in cognitive psychology have shown that people prefer gambles over an equivalent (in expected value terms) sure loss although they will avoid fair gambles when the expected gain is positive. However, such behavior is not the norm in economic and political markets. Indeed, if people adopted such attitudes toward risk, they would make book against themselves. For example, individuals would pay to be in the gamble, but, once in it, they would pay not to be in the gamble, and so on. This is obviously not the case. In the third section, I investigate those psychology experiments that demonstrate biased judgment. I argue to the contrary, that, given the context of the experimental setup, the subjects made decisions consistent with sound scientific procedure. Next I address the function of anomalies. The collection of anomalies discovered by cognitive psychologists is not a basis for a coherent theory but a set of inconsistent results. Although some of this anomalous behavior is consistent with certain cognitive psychological models, normal political and economic market behavior becomes anomalous from the viewpoint of these same models. In the fifth section, I argue that subjective probabilities and other inherent unobservables give the cognitive psychologist unwarranted freedom to make post hoc explanations. In the section on the implications of cognitive-psychology experiments, I consider the claim of many cognitive psychologists that preferences are volatile and dependent on intersubjectively construed meanings. If this were true, then cognitive psychology would not be able to predict democratic behavior, as the relationship between voter choice and objective measures would, of necessity, be unstable. In the section that follows, I suggest that cognitive failures are like optical illusions. Finally, I conclude with an evolutionary argument against the view that cognitive shortcuts are chosen regardless of their implications.

FRAMING

Prospect theory is a set of propositions based on experimental results in cognitive psychology. Components include framing effects, the S-shaped value function, and biased subjective probabilities (to be discussed below). Kahneman and Tversky (1984) view prospect theory as a descriptive theory of human nature, in contrast to economic theory, which they view as merely prescriptive. Arguing that there are biases in human cognition, they assert that their experimental results undermine the economists' notion of rationality.

Quattrone and Tversky (1988) apply prospect theory to the political sphere. They claim that their experimental results demonstrate the superiority of prospect theory over economic theory in explaining political behavior. In this and the following sections, I will argue against this claim and show that economics is much more successful than prospect theory in its description of *actual* political and market behavior.

Several of Quattrone and Tversky's experiments show how people can be mislead by the framing of a question. In one of their experiments, participants found negligible differences between those policies with 92 percent employment and those policies with 98 percent employment even though other participants found significant differences between policies with 8 percent unemployment and 2 percent unemployment (Quattrone and Tversky 1988, problems 9 and 10; see also problems 11 and 12). Since 2 percent unemployment is equivalent to 98 percent employment, the differences are objectively the same. These results appear to violate fundamental notions of rationality.

But do these experimental results have implications for the rationality of democratic politics? No. Mistakes are quite likely to occur when no one suffers from them (and are especially likely when the researcher is searching for ways to trick the unsuspecting subjects). Such is the case with Quattrone and Tversky's experiment. Errors in judgments are costless, not just to some, but to *everyone* in the experiment. No one will lose money, or, more significantly, lose a job if a mistake is made. Furthermore, their experimental framework does not allow for long-term learning or survival. Indeed, their research methodology is more akin to a survey with hypothetical situations (and hypothetical answers) than to a laboratory experiment.[4]

Other studies have incorporated monetary incentives, but these incentives are often minimal. Consider, for example, experiments 7 and 8 reported in Tversky and Kahneman 1987 and reproduced here.

A: 90% win $0; 6% win $45; 1% win $30; 1% lose $15; 2% lose $15

B: 90% win $0; 6% win $45; 1% win $45; 1% lose $10; 2% lose $15

C: 90% win $0; 6% win $45; 1% win $30; 3% lose $15

D: 90% win $0; 7% win $45; 1% lose $10; 2% lose $15

In these experiments, when given a choice between A and B, participants always chose B. However, when given a choice between C and D, participants chose D only 42 percent of the time, although D is identical to option B and C is identical to option A. This experiment does provide monetary rewards for optimal behavior. However, the economic loss resulting from suboptimal behavior is minimal. A calculation made by Harrison (1989) shows that suboptimal behavior in Kahneman and Tversky's experiment results in a loss for the subject of only two cents in terms of expected value. This failure to create viable economic incentives pervades experimental work in cognitive psychology. To frame the argument from a different perspective: given the insignificant economic incentives in experimental work, one should be surprised when experimental results do confirm economic theory.[5]

4. My arguments against this and other experiments in cognitive psychology should not be taken as arguments against experimental technique but, rather, as an assertion that the wrong experiments have been undertaken.

I will not discuss either the Allais paradox or preference reversal. These experimental results also contradict some basic tenets of expected-utility maximization. However, the implications of these experimental results for political behavior are more opaque than the experimental results that I consider here.

The experiments showing preference reversal and the Allais paradox tend to be more immune to some of my criticisms. For example, these experiments often involve monetary incentives (although the amount the subject loses when making a nonoptimal decision is often slight).

5. Kroll, Levy, and Rapoport (1988) performed two identical experiments of the capital asset pricing model, except that the payoffs were ten times as great in the second experiment. The authors found that performance was significantly improved with respect to the capital asset pricing model in the latter experiment.

Suppose that Quattrone and Tversky are correct about voters being susceptible to framing. This still does not mean that voters will make mistaken judgments when casting ballots. If the incumbent politician frames an argument in terms of unemployment, the opposition can, in response, frame the argument in terms of employment or else demonstrate that the two methods are identical. Insofar as elections are a zero-sum game, it will be beneficial for one of the politicians to inform the voters of the mistake. Voters will thus not be persuaded by the frame.

It should also be noted that Quattrone and Tversky's experiment did not allow the subjects to get together and discuss the issue. In the real world, people often discuss politics. If the subjects had discussed the issue together, one of them might have noticed that the two choices were identical and notified the other subjects. Democratic institutions are designed to foster this kind of group discussion and thus to elicit more informed choices. Congress is a good example, as its operations involve specialized committees, large professional staffs, and floor debates between opposing parties.[6]

In addition, in the real world, economic and political institutions help people make their choices by guiding them, even without informing them. Consider the aforementioned lottery problem, where subjects erroneously chose C over D. Both C and D involve an element of risk. Risk-averse individuals might be willing to sell their lotteries. Financiers who know that D is better than C would offer a higher price for D, which might induce these risk-averse individuals to choose D over C in the first place. In this case, uninformed individuals make the right choice, not because they can calculate risk, but because they get a higher price for selling lottery D in the secondary market.

This same type of activity abounds in the political sphere as well. For example, some politicians might promise to insure voters against risk. These politicians need not inform the voters what policy they intend to implement but merely assure the voters that they will have more by choosing them over their competitors. The knowledgeable politicians who choose policy D over C can promise and deliver more, thereby garnering more votes, even though the voters themselves cannot properly calculate the expected values from D and C.

6. For a more extensive discussion of information and democratic institutions see the beginning chapters.

Despite the many experiments in cognitive psychology demonstrating the importance of framing, the framing effect is unlikely to be so powerful in real life. Consider the following "experiments."

1. One group of high school seniors is told that one in five applicants is accepted to the University of California. A second group of seniors is told that four out of five applicants are rejected.
2. One group of consumers is told that a six-pack of Coca-Cola is priced at $2.00 and that a six-pack of Pepsi costs $.11 less. The second group of consumers is told that a six-pack of Pepsi costs $1.89 and that a six-pack of Coca-Cola costs $.11 more.
3. One group of voters is told that 42 percent of the voters favor candidate X and place her two percentage points behind candidate Y. The second group of voters is told that 44 percent of the voters favor Y and place him two percentage points ahead of X.

I have never run any of these experiments. However, I question whether the frames would have any influence on subjects' behavior. The subjects have doubtlessly had previous experience with these situations and are, for this reason, less likely to be influenced by the frame when making their choice.[7] To paraphrase Tversky and Kahneman (1987, 86), subjects are fooled by frames only when they are inexperienced and the framing is nontransparent. Other cognitive tasks generate canonical representations automatically. For example, visual objects do not appear to change in shape, size, or color when we move around them or when illumination varies, and the active and the passive voice are not distinguished by the listener. The key to the existence of the canonical form is the extent of experience. As a political campaign progresses, most people gain familiarity with the issues at hand and the framing becomes more transparent. In contrast, Quattrone and Tversky's tests of framing catch the inexperienced.

7. McNeil et al. (1982) show that specialists are also victims of framing. In their experiment, they asked subjects to decide between two cancer treatments (surgery or radiation). Each treatment had three mortality (or in the reverse frame, survival) rates: death during treatment, death after one year, death after five years. However, doctors have more experience with bivariate choices. I would expect to see much smaller effects of framing if the statistic for death (or survival) after one year were eliminated, and virtually no effect of framing if the only difference in the two methods were survival rates after five years.

0   **INCOME**

FIG. 5.1. CONCAVE UTILITY FUNCTION. Utility (vertical axis) is a concave function of income (horizontal axis). The individual is risk averse (the gamble line is below the utility function), and the function is the same regardless of the person's present wealth (0 on the horizontal axis represents 0 income).

THE S-SHAPED UTILITY CURVE

In standard economics, utility is a concave function of wealth (that is, marginal utility of income is decreasing) and invariant to present position (see fig. 5.1).[8] In prospect theory, the utility function is S-shaped, with the status quo typically being at the origin.[9] Utility is thus convex for losses and concave for gains (see fig. 5.2), which, respectively, imply that the individual is risk preferring for losses and risk averse for gains. In addition, the utility decrease from a loss in wealth is always greater than the utility increase from an equivalent gain in wealth (that is, $U(|x|) - U(0) < U(0) - U(-|x|)$, where 0 is the status quo). This latter relationship is known as loss aversion.

If individuals have S-shaped utility functions, they can rank order their preferences (although these rankings will depend on the status

8. This subsection is more technical and can be skipped without jeopardizing understanding of the remaining subsections.

9. Quattrone and Tversky are more vague. They use the term "neutral reference point." In some of their examples, the status quo is this neutral reference point.

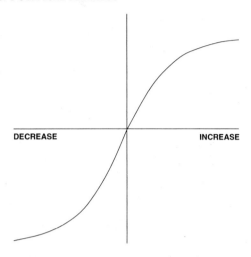

Fig. 5.2. The S-Shaped Curve. Utility (the vertical axis) is an S-shaped function of changes in income (the horizontal axis). The status quo is at the inflection point. The individual is risk preferring for losses (the gamble line is above the utility function) and risk averse for gains.

quo). As will be shown below, their behavior with respect to compound lotteries (lotteries to play lotteries) would violate the Von Neumann–Morgenstern utility postulates, but their behavior would still be consistent with utility maximization and rationality. The conflict between the shifting S-shaped curve of prospect theory and the standard economic assumption of a fixed concave curve thus lies wholly within the boundaries of global utility maximization. The conflict thus takes place at a less fundamental level than the conflict about the existence and effects of framing.

Quattrone and Tversky present several experimental results that contradict the standard economic utility function but are consistent with the S-shaped utility function. For example, they report that most experimental subjects prefer a fifty-fifty chance of losing two hundred dollars or losing nothing to a certain loss of one hundred dollars.[10] These results are consistent with prospect theory insofar as a person with an S-shaped utility curve prefers a gamble to a certain loss. They are not in accord with standard economic theory, which would predict that the risk-averse

10. Quattrone and Tversky report four experiments (problems 1–4) that have political choice rather than income streams, but they are just variants of the choice between one hundred dollars for certain and the zero to two hundred dollars lottery.

individual would prefer a sure loss. On the other hand, both prospect theory and standard economic theory predict that the individual would prefer a sure gain of one hundred dollars to a fifty-fifty gamble between a gain of two hundred dollars or a gain of nothing.

The chief problem with these experimental results is that they are not consistent with real-world behavior. For example, financial markets have developed all kinds of instruments, yet we do not observe financial instruments that exploit the behavior implied by the S-shaped utility function. Perhaps it is time for those who created the S-shaped curve to make money on their ideas and provide the following mirror stock: If the price of stock in IBM increases, the mirror stock will sell at the same price as IBM stock. If, however, the price of IBM drops below the purchase price, say by one hundred dollars, the owners of the mirror stock will be given the opportunity to gamble—50 percent of the time their loss will be doubled and 50 percent of the time they will incur no loss.[11] If, as the Quattrone and Tversky experimental results suggest, people prefer such an option over the sure loss, they will be willing to pay a premium for this mirror stock. Since the owner of the lottery faces many gambles, she is virtually indifferent and therefore will be willing to provide such a gamble. But this is not the end of this winning idea. When the stock actually goes down in price, the status quo shifts and the lottery represents a gain of one hundred dollars or a loss of one hundred dollars. The owner of the mirror stock would now be averse to such a gamble and would be willing to pay the owner of the lottery not to face the gamble! The lottery owner is still indifferent since the outcome of many gambles is equivalent to the sure thing and therefore will gladly take money from the owners of the mirror stock.[12] For a

11. In the United States, gambling is illegal in most states, but one might observe arbitrage over different risk portfolios or other behavior by the individual that yields a similar result.

12. "Making book" against oneself is always possible when individuals have S-shaped curves. Machina (1989) argues that making book against oneself need not arise if history is important (that is, the path to the present state is not ignored). In our present example, the fact that the person chose the mirror stock in round one may influence the person not to choose the sure thing over the lottery in round two, when the price of the mirror stock has fallen, even though the person might have chosen the sure thing in round two if he or she had not purchased the mirror stock in round one. This nonseparability of history (one must even consider outcomes that might have occurred in the past but didn't) creates an enormous cognitive load unknown to expected-utility maximization. For a person who is easily fooled by frames and chooses all kinds of cognitive shortcuts, such

market like the one described above to exist, only a modicum of people need behave in the way that Quattrone and Tversky predict. The fact that such markets do not exist in the real world suggests that the S-shaped curve does not provide an adequate description for even a minority of people.

We next consider the political implications of individuals having S-shaped utility functions. Loss aversion (losses are felt more than gains) implies a strong preference for the status quo.[13] So loss aversion is good at explaining why things remain the same, but less so at explaining why things change. Let's take arms control and arms races as an example. Quattrone and Tversky have given an explanation of arms control through loss aversion theory. I will quote at length:

"Loss aversion may play an important role in bargaining and negotiation . . . each party may view its own concessions as losses that loom larger than the gains achieved by the concessions of the adversary. . . . In negotiating over missiles, for example, each superpower may sense a greater loss in security from the dismantling of its own missiles than it senses in a gain in security from a comparable reduction by the other side" (1988, 726).

Tversky and Kahneman have provided a seemingly viable explanation for why arms control agreements are so difficult to make. However, the same logic would also suggest the counterfactual that arms races are unlikely because the gain in security from building additional missiles would be felt less than the loss in security resulting from an equivalent increase in missiles by the other side.

Another problem arising from loss aversion and preference for the status quo is their implications for welfare theory. If losses outweigh gains in their impact, then the sum total of human utility might be reduced if a rich person gave food or money to a poor person (unless one assumes that the poor people have steeper S-shaped curves).

---

hypercalculation would appear unlikely. Furthermore, making book against oneself is still possible if the person was not aware of the contingency (in this case, the ability to get out of the lottery if the stock does fall) when the first decision was made. This problem can be circumvented if the person contemplates such a possibility when making the original choice. But again the assumption that people who are so easily fooled by frames make such complicated decisions stretches the limits of internal consistency.

13. But this tendency for the status quo is counterbalanced by the variability of framing, which induces changes in behavior even though the objective circumstances do not change.

BIASES FROM PRIORS

Among others, Snyder and Swann (1978) have shown that people search for evidence that confirms preconceptions and ignore disconfirming evidence. In one experiment, they found that subjects were more likely to diagnose X as an extrovert when they were told beforehand that X was extroverted. Rosenberg (1991), applying these results to politics, argues that initial impressions of political candidates could greatly distort voter perceptions.[14]

We should be leery of generalizing from these experimental results to the real world. Such priors lose their significance as the person accrues more evidence. For example, if the subjects had known X for a year, a month, or even a week, the power of preconceptions would be reduced considerably. In politics, competition between the candidates diminishes the role of preconceptions even more. If one side claimed that X was an introvert, then the other side could easily counteract that claim by promoting X as an extrovert if that were, in fact, the case.

In a similar manner one can argue against the claim of Rosenberg and McCafferty (1987) that even a single photograph (flattering or unflattering) could influence a voter's judgment about a candidate. In this experiment, the photograph was one of the few pieces of information supplied to the subjects about the supposed candidate. However, in the real world, voters gain much more information. The influence of one picture or even one interview is rarely as important as the one photograph in Rosenberg and McCafferty's experiment. But even if photographs do influence, this does not mean that voters use inappropriate or biased heuristics. Would you want to have a president who laughed at serious occasions?

From my perspective, the results arrived at by Snyder and Swann are not only in accord with good judgment but are also consistent with sound scientific procedure.[15] It would be foolish to reverse one's views if some new evidence merely hinted to the contrary. In addition, the subjects did not anticipate being lied to by the experimenter. The sub-

---

14. Tversky and Kahneman (1974) have contrary experimental results showing that people underweight their Bayesian priors. Naturally, they present a competing "heuristic" that predicts the outcome of their experiments.

15. Many other experiments "demonstrating" biased choice and irrational behavior by the subject show greater rationality once we consider the overall context of the experiment.

jects might have been too ashamed to report contrary evidence, or perhaps they trusted the opinion of a professional. In the real world, individuals can more accurately assess the reliability of the speaker. A real-world voter might discount a politician's statement when it appears to be self-serving and, at the same time, trust the political opinion of a long-time friend.

THE ROLE OF ANOMALIES

Experiments by cognitive psychologists and economists and some ecological data have highlighted behavior that is anomalous from the viewpoint of economic theory. Although these results are illuminating and should not be ignored, it is important to put them in the context of our overall understanding of human behavior. In this section, I argue the following: (1) anomalies are the exception rather than the rule; (2) some anomalies are predicted by particular hypotheses in cognitive psychology, but standard (normal) behavior is anomalous from the standpoint of these same hypotheses; (3) some behavior is not only anomalous from the viewpoint of economic theory, but from the viewpoint of cognitive psychology as well; (4) the anomalies are, for the most part, second-order effects; and (5) anomalies must remain the unexplained residual until we have a coherent theory to explain a significant portion of both the anomalous and nonanomalous behavior.

A number of empirical studies of financial markets have found anomalies from the viewpoint of economic theory. These studies are often quoted by supporters of prospect theory in their attacks on neoclassical economics (for example, see Frey and Eichenberger 1989; Thaler 1987). However, the evidence from financial markets does not support prospect theory, either. Let us consider the much used example of the January effect.[16] Contrary to economic theory, historical records show that purchases of shares in small businesses made on December 30 yield higher than average returns. Does prospect theory predict this ex ante? If so, does it also predict, in accord with expected-utility maximization, that there is no February, March, April, or industrial-index effect? Should we substitute cognitive psychology for economics because the former might

16. This anomaly is so well known that financial columns are now advising people to buy stock in small firms in December. Of course, if this advice is heeded, the anomaly will disappear. There are other calendar-based anomalies, but they are not consistent with each other.

be consistent with some special case, or should we keep economic theory because it explains the typical case?

Cognitive psychologists have created hypotheses to explain some of the anomalous experimental behavior, but in their models, normal behavior becomes anomalous. Earlier, I argued that if individuals had S-shaped utility functions, they would make book against themselves and strange new financial instruments would arise. Of greater significance, certain regularities of aggregate market behavior, such as stock prices being martingale-like (today's price is an unbiased predictor of tomorrow's price), would most likely not exist if people did indeed behave in accord with the tenets of prospect theory. I write "most likely" because the ramifications of prospect theory for market behavior are not well delineated. Depending on which parts of the theory one emphasized, one might arrive at contrary conclusions. Nevertheless, it seems that concepts such as the representative heuristic and framing would lead to predictable patterns (for example, if the price went up today, it will go up again tomorrow), contrary to the general record of stock prices.

If we subscribe to framing effects and the value of the reference point in determining preferences, observed voting regularities become difficult to understand. Consider the observed positive relationship between income and voting for the Republican Party. Prospect theory emphasizes *changes* in income from the status quo rather than the *level* of income in explaining behavior. For this reason, a prospect theorist would not necessarily expect to find the observed correspondence between income levels and voting behavior.

Despite cognitive psychology's belief in the manipulability of voters, we observe rational voting behavior. After the Civil War, a majority of African-Americans voted for the Republican Party; since the depression, a majority of African-Americans have voted for the Democratic Party. Voters in Wisconsin reelected Senator Proxmire, who relentlessly criticized government expenditures except when they were beneficial to dairy farmers,[17] and voters in Detroit elect politicians who support tariffs on foreign cars. Such regularities are not due to mistaken judgments.

Psychology's shortcomings in explaining aggregate political and economic phenomena should not be surprising. The discipline of psychology is primarily concerned with individual behavior. In contrast, eco-

17. This example comes from Coursey and Roberts (1991).

nomics and politics are concerned with market behavior and the institutions that intervene between individual preference and aggregate outcomes. Markets and other social institutions create outcomes that are not possible when individuals act in isolation.[18] In contrast to the expectations of cognitive psychology, experimental research on aggregate political behavior and on economic markets strongly supports the expected utility-maximizing models. Experiments in politics have shown that voters can make competent judgments with little information (McKelvey and Ordeshook 1985) and that allocations are near the core (Plott 1979). Market experiments show an uncanny ability for market outcomes to aggregate disparate sources of private information (see Copeland and Friedman 1987) and to surmount some of the problems of individual decision-making that occur in experiments without a market setting (see, for example, Duh and Sunder 1985, and Plott and Wilde 1982, who demonstrate that the "base-rate fallacy" and the "representativeness heuristic" no longer hold in experimental market settings).

I have argued that political and economic institutions, both real and those incorporated into the experimental design, tend to undermine many of the previous experimental results of prospect theory. Even with improved experimentation, some anomalies will persist; it would be foolish to believe that economics is so advanced as a science that no real-world anomalies exist. But the anomalies will tend to have second-order effects, so that the transaction costs required to correct these effects will be greater than the distortions from optimality.

Consider the "hot-hand" fallacy. Cognitive psychologists have shown that fans believe that player performance is autocorrelated rather than

18. Arrow (1982), Russell and Thaler (1985), and Miller (1987) argue that markets need not correct irrational behavior. However, Arrow's and Miller's examples are odd. Arrow assumes that rational investors care only about the present but that they irrationally speculate about the effect of expenditures on research and development in the distant future. But, in the real world, different firms have different expenditure profiles on research and development and different horizons for coming to fruition. The rational investor with a short-term horizon can choose firms where the payoff from R and D will be manifest in the near future. Miller argues that because of the high transaction costs of selling short over a significant time period, rational investors could not sell short if they felt that stock prices would fall. However, there are numerous alternatives to selling short, including organized future markets, forward contracts, and an active option market where speculators may buy a put option. Thaler argues that such mechanisms do not occur in other areas (consumer markets and political markets). However, the market for advice is still available: people pay for lawyers, consumers shop at stores with good customer service, voters discuss the issues, and politicians consult pollsters.

based on longer-run averages. For example, fans believe that a basketball player is less likely to make the next basket if the player's recent history is 0101011100 (where 1 indicates a basket and 0 stands for missing an attempted basket) than if the player's history is 0100001111. Evidently, fans believe that the string of successes at the end indicate future success even though the likelihood of future baskets is, according to Gilovich, Vallone, and Tversky 1985, the same in both cases.[19]

Is this effect translated into the betting market? Bookmakers set point spreads (basketball team A will beat basketball team B by ten points) so that equivalent amounts will be bet on each team.[20] An efficient betting market, in which bets reflect the behavior of knowledgeable statisticians, will have teams with win streaks beating the point spread 50 percent of the time. If the distribution is symmetrical, zero will be the average differential between the actual point spread and the betting point spread. Conversely, in a betting market where believers in the hot-hand myth dominate, teams with recent win streaks will beat the point spread less than 50 percent of the time, with a resulting negative average differential between the actual and the betting point spread.

As is typically the case, economic theory has more precision than cognitive psychology. Whereas economic rationality predicts a point (the betting point spread will equal the actual spread), the myth of the hot hand only predicts an interval (greater than the actual spread but without any clearly established upper bound). If the hot-hand fallacy also predicted a point, we would have a clearly defined metric to compare the two hypotheses. In the absence of one, we can substitute a lower bound that would be acceptable to most people: that the myth of the hot hand

---

19. Actually, the "market mechanism" would tend to mitigate streaks even when they exist. Suppose that ceteris paribus a basketball player was having a streak of good luck. Ceteris would not remain paribus. The other team would guard him more carefully or even assign two players to guard him and the streak would be cut short. Thus streaks are less likely for field goal attempts then for foul shots.

Note that if investors believed that the hot hand applied to stock markets, they would want to buy those stocks that had gone up in price in the previous days. This increase in demand would raise prices, thereby turning beliefs into reality. However, there is no evidence for autocorrelation in price changes. Note also that the hot-hand fallacy weights recent observations more than earlier observations; this is somewhat contrary to the work cited by Rosenberg, which argues that first impressions are the most important.

20. The hot-hand fallacy may not carry over to team performance. Unfortunately, there is no well-defined betting market for individual shooting performance.

If individuals have concave utility functions and the Von Neumann–Morgenstern postulates hold, then betting is "irrational" when the expected payoff is not positive.

leads bettors to overestimate point spreads by at least one point. But the observed differential between the actual spread and the betting point spread is only 0.2 (see Camerer 1989). Another metric with an underlying economic rationale is that the extent of the differential between the actual and the betting point spread should be less than the transaction costs. Since the cost of betting (10 percent of the win) is much greater than the advantage of betting against the team currently experiencing a winning streak, there are no profits to be made.

It is much more difficult to make precise predictions for political markets than for financial and betting markets. Riker (1982) maintains that the most established theoretical result in political theory is Duverger's law. Duverger's law states that plurality rule systems (for example, the United States electoral system) will have fewer political parties than majority rule systems (such as France's system until recently) because expected-utility maximization by the voters dictates that they will not want to squander their votes on a hopeless third party when there is plurality rule. What does prospect theory predict in this situation? Basically, it is unclear what, if anything, prospect theory predicts. If the cognitive psychologist seriously believed in the importance of loss aversion, she might predict that all democratic systems would be one-party systems because losses from the status quo are felt more strongly than gains. If the cognitive psychologist believed in the importance of framing, she would predict that the number of parties was determined by the way politicians framed issues rather than the institutional differences in elections. On the other hand, the cognitive psychologist might not have any prediction.

This last example segues to our fifth argument. Cognitive psychology is not a unified theory but a set of often inconsistent descriptive hypotheses. The fact that some experimental results are consistent with certain cognitive hypotheses, while other experimental results are consistent with other cognitive hypotheses, does not imply that there is any consistent subset of cognitive hypotheses that can take over the role of homo economicus as the primary explanation of political behavior.[21] A collection of anomalies does not a theory make.

---

21. Even if we restrict the comparison to experimental studies without market mechanisms, there are numerous "descriptive" hypotheses with strong experimental results contrary to prospect theory (see Camerer [1989], who shows, among other things, that prospect theory cannot explain the degree to which fanning out varies with payoffs).

POST HOC EXPLANATIONS

Although experiments in cognitive psychology tend to be rigorous, the application of these results to real-world events is quite slippery. Cognitive psychologists have too many fudge factors that enable researchers to provide explanations for virtually any real-world event, *after the fact*. These fudge factors arise because, in their theories, subjective beliefs may not coincide with objective reality and utility functions are not stable. Unlike the measurement of blood alcohol, subjective beliefs and utility functions cannot be directly observed but must instead be inferred from behavior. With a sufficiently rich set of subjective possibilities, it is not too hard to discover ex post some set of subjective beliefs that are consistent with a set of observed behavior.[22]

Consider Quattrone and Tversky's explanation for challengers doing better in bad times and incumbents doing better in good times. If voters have S-shaped utility functions, they will gamble on losses and take the sure thing on gains. Thus incumbents profit from good times, and challengers, whose policies are more of a gamble, profit from bad times. But, as the authors argue later in the article, the status quo point is likely to represent the existing economic and political conditions under the incumbent. According to prospect theory, voters feel losses more than gains and therefore would be very averse to gambles. Contrary to Quattrone and Tversky's earlier analysis, this would then imply that the voters do not vote for the riskier candidate if the expected outcome is about the same, regardless of how bad objective reality is.[23] A possible counterargument to this criticism would be that the status quo might be relatively stable and that the voters' frame of reference is based on a longer historical record. But this counterargument reveals a crucial problem in prospect theory. Since the utility function cannot be observed, the researcher is at liberty to concentrate the analysis on any part of the curve. Depending on what outcome the researcher is trying to explain, the researcher will choose a point where the function is locally convex,

22. Do people overuse seat belts because they overestimate low probabilities of bad events, or do they underuse them because they like to gamble on losses (or to avoid cognitive dissonance)?

Of course, economists have their fudge factors also, but virtually all the fudge factors available to economists are available to those who believe in prospect theory, but the reverse is not the case (utility functions cannot shift and biased mistakes do not last).

23. Note that ordinary economic theory predicts risk aversion and hence preference for the incumbent, other things being more or less equal.

locally concave, or locally S-shaped. She is then capable of explaining everything ex post, but incapable of predicting anything ex ante. What we have is an interpretive feat rather than a scientific method.

Subjective probability is another area where the researcher can tailor her theory to the facts. Prospect theory maintains that individuals underestimate very low objective probabilities (the likelihood being viewed as zero), overestimate low objective probabilities, and underestimate both medium and mildly high objective probabilities.[24] The researcher is given a rather large range from which to choose the determining probability, insofar as the extent of bias in estimation is never specified and the terms themselves, *low, very low,* etc., are vague. Consider the following "real-world" experiment: the subject is given a choice between a sure loss of ten dollars and a lottery with a 10 percent chance of losing one hundred dollars and a 90 percent chance of losing nothing. Suppose that most subjects choose the lottery. Cognitive psychologists could claim that the results of the experiment were predicted by prospect theory since the S-shaped curve predicts that people are risk preferring for losses. The issue of subjective probability would probably not arise. Conversely, if subjects choose the sure loss, cognitive psychologists could again argue that the results were predicted by prospect theory, as people overestimate low probabilities and are therefore risk averse.

Standard economic theory does not provide as much latitude for interpretation. A person's subjective probability is generally assumed to be an unbiased estimate of objective probability. And economists generally assume concave utility functions rather than functions that are both concave and convex. Because subjective probabilities and utility functions cannot be directly observed, the scientific researcher needs to be especially cautious so that unseen parameters are not altered to explain outcomes.

---

24. Kahneman and Tversky's experiments demonstrating that people overestimate low probability events is subject to a serious design flaw. Consider the following experiment. Draw a line one meter long and mark a spot at 0.8 centimeters. Ask students to estimate how far the point is along the line in percentage terms (this is the analog to probability estimates). Both the median and the mode are likely to be unbiased, but not the mean, which is the only statistic that is usually reported. The reason for the upward bias on the mean is that there is a lower bound on underestimates (zero) but not such a tight upper bound. Therefore, averages are likely to show an upward bias. While I have not actually run such an experiment, Boyce et al. (1991) have rerun some of the classic tests regarding preference reversal and have shown that the modal response is consistent with economic theory even though the mean is not.

THE IMPLICATIONS OF COGNITIVE-PSYCHOLOGY EXPERIMENTS

> The research in cognitive and social psychology suggests that people do not have the information-gathering, interpretive, or computational skills required to properly recognize, remember, comprehend, and evaluate the circumstances and consequences of choices made under conditions typical of political life.
>
> *Rosenberg (1991, 394)*[25]

Suppose, for the sake of argument, that Rosenberg's characterization is correct. Does this mean that voters will act contrary to their own interests? No. In numerous other areas, individuals do not have the "requisite skills," yet they are able to make the correct decisions. For example, few people know the difference between clidinium and cimetidine; instead, they rely on their doctors and pharmacists for the correct prescription. Weather prediction is another example. Most individuals do not have the highly technical knowledge or even the cognitive capacity necessary to forecast weather. But there is no need to have these skills; all people have to do is tune into the weather report. Likewise, in the political sphere there are institutions that reduce the cognitive work for the average voter. Parties and candidates develop familiar and often stable reputations and interests so that voters will not have to investigate all details in order to make reasonably educated choices. Voters will not confuse Jesse Jackson with George Bush. Also, if voters have specific interests or concerns, they can consult special interest groups for information on the candidates' positions on the issues in question.

There are numerous articles in cognitive psychology demonstrating the limited cognitive abilities of human beings. For example, people have a hard time remembering a sequence of random digits. But what are the implications of limited memory? Not that people do not make use of numerical sequences, but rather that they find substitutes, such as telephone books, for mere memory. If one were to take the experimental results in cognitive psychology at face value, one might claim that an extensive telephone system would be impossible because people do not have the cognitive capability to remember all the necessary numbers. No psychologist would make such a ridiculous claim, although similar

---

25. With this dismal view of human cognition, one wonders how people could have designed democratic institutions in the first place.

generalizations are often made from experimental results regarding the efficacy of democratic institutions.

Again, for the sake of argument, suppose that cognitive psychologists are correct in characterizing voters as being prone to mistaken judgments and having unstable preferences. And assume, furthermore, that there are no intervening political institutions to correct these errors. If such were the case, then cognitive psychologists would be unable to predict real-world outcomes because, in the real world, there would be so many influences, incorrect heuristics, approaches to framing candidates, possible priors, and other ways that actors "infuse the world of choice with their subjectively (and intersubjectively) construed meanings" (Rosenberg 1988, 22) that one would have no hope of determining which was currently influencing the voters.[26] For this reason, cognitive psychology would rarely be of use in predicting any ecological data beyond the obvious extremes, that political outcomes tend to stay the same or that they are random.

IS THERE A VIABLE THEORY OF COGNITIVE FAILURE?

Tversky and Kahneman (1974) argue that people usually choose the most available schemata over more useful constructs. Likewise, Fiske and Taylor (1984) argue that people are cognitive misers who minimize information processing.[27] If such arguments were true, then people would have very strange utility functions: the only costs would be decision-making costs and there would be no benefits to better decisions. As a consequence, people would always choose the first alternative offered to them or else flip a coin. Clearly, this kind of activity is rarely observed in the real world.

---

26. Consider first the issue of framing. "Framing is controlled by the manner in which the choice problem is presented as well as by norms, habits and expectancies of the decision-maker" (Tversky and Kahneman 1987, 73). Since we are unlikely to know what frames the voter has heard or any of the other characteristics, the whole concept is likely to be useless for predicting aggregate voting patterns. Tversky and Kahneman (1974) discuss the following judgmental heuristics that also may lead to biased decision making: judgment by representativeness, judgment by availability, and judgment by adjustment. Each of these depends on the special history of the voter and would in general be impossible to determine outside an experimental setting or large catastrophic events. In predicting voting behavior, all of these factors would have to be considered in addition to the voters' preferences.

27. Lau (1986) also uses the term "cognitive miser."

Cognition is not free, but it is not infinitely costly, either. It is not minimized, but rationed like other scarce commodities. Hence there are trade-offs between time spent cogitating and time spent at other activities. People balance off the marginal expected cost of additional information and cognition with the marginal expected gain in the outcome. When errors involve little cost (for example, answering a survey question incorrectly in a cognitive-psychology experiment), then little cognition will be employed. When errors involve great cost (for example, purchasing unreliable equipment for the military), then greater cognition will be involved: more detailed schemata and complicated heuristics will be undertaken; and there will be more learning, more consulting as well as a greater division of cognitive labor into cognitively manageable tasks.[28] In a nutshell: The more important the decision, the more likely that the actual decision will approximate the decision that would be made if all relevant information were available and correctly processed.

In general, the cognitive heuristic chosen to solve a problem is an unbiased predictor of the desired outcome.[29] If the loss function were symmetric, with an overestimate costing as much as an underestimate, we would observe both over and underestimates and the expected error would be zero. If biases were predictable, then an additional heuristic could account for them, as when a contractor adds up all normal costs and then adds 10 percent for all the costs that were not explicitly considered.

Quattrone and Tversky's experiments demonstrating economic and political irrationality have implications comparable to those experiments demonstrating optical illusions. Yes, it is true that people do make errors

28. See Lodge and Hamil (1986) for a survey of results showing that experts use more detailed and sophisticated schemata. Leland (1988) posits that utility functions are approximated because inexperience and/or cognitive limitations make the "true" utility function inaccessible. Finite resources limit this approximation to N steps in a step-function estimation, with the optimal approximation defined as that minimizing the expected squared error. His theory is able to explain many of the findings of prospect theory for situations of low information and reduces to ordinary expected utility as experience accumulates. Friedman (1989), in a variant of the Leland model, assumes that utility is weighted by sensitivity (a finite resource). For low levels of information, the value function looks like an S-shaped curve. As experience accumulates, the value function looks more like the standard concave utility function.

29. See Beach and Mitchell (1978), who argue that the appropriate cognitive rule of thumb is chosen for the situation, and Christensen-Szalanski (1980) for some experimental confirmation. Thorngate (1980) shows that heuristics often pick the best of several alternatives across a range of alternatives.

in cognition and perception, often because the rule works in general but misguides in the particular situation. For example, the lines converge; therefore, the object looks farther away than it really is. Yet we should not infer that people generally respond to such illusions. Mirages are often seen on hot sand, but no one is going to haul a rowboat to one.

CONCLUDING REMARKS

In this chapter, I have argued that homo psychologicus does not provide an adequate basis for our understanding of democratic politics. Experiments in cognitive psychology do not account for political institutions, competition, comparative advantage, or significant experience and incentives. Although some cognitive-psychology models can explain some market anomalies in a post hoc fashion, they make standard political and economic behavior anomalous by doing so. Ultimately, cognitive psychology is a collection of internally inconsistent hypotheses and results, rather than a unified body of research. It is clearly inappropriate to choose where each hypothesis is successful and then treat the whole corpus of work in cognitive psychology as a single contender with economics for explaining political behavior.

Cognitive psychologists who believe that decisions are irrational or that heuristics lead to biased judgments face a deeper problem. Obviously, the human species is capable of avoiding these errors of judgment. Quattrone and Tversky know that 5 percent unemployment is equivalent to 95 percent employment. Most insurance companies use past frequencies as an unbiased estimate of future probabilities; they do not automatically place higher probabilities on low-frequency outcomes (as prospect theory predicts). If most people's cognitive abilities are so poor that they cannot achieve what they want, why have they been able to survive in the presence of superior beings who occupy a similar ecological niche? Hunters (human or otherwise) who incorrectly estimate the likelihood of finding food in various locations will have a lower chance of survival and ultimately lower reproductive success than those who make correct estimates.[30]

The existence of the human appendix, a useless organ, may serve as a counterexample to my argument for the survival of the fittest. But

---

30. It is possible that more complicated decision-making (of the kind required to resolve the Allais paradox, for example) did not increase survivability.

once again, one should not be misled by the anomaly. Do we really want to rewrite evolutionary theory as the survival of the nonfit? And if cognition is a learned rather than acquired trait, why haven't institutions developed to teach the appropriate cognitive heuristics to those who need to make use of them? Presumably, those oral traditions, schools, and businesses that employ the appropriate cognitive heuristics would have a greater chance of survival than those that choose misleading heuristics. Because information and cognition is costly, cognitive rules of thumb may be employed; but, in general, they will be good guides to the decision that would be made in the presence of full information, and the cost of the expected error will not be greater than the reduction in decision-making costs.

The relationship between cognitive psychology and economics is, then, not in opposition but rather a micro and macro view of the same phenomenon. If my arguments are correct, in the future cognitive psychologists will emphasize cognitive successes rather than mistakes, and political scientists will study how political institutions correct for any remaining biases inherent in individual decision-making.[31]

31. Even at present, there is a growing body of psychological research that supports economic rationality. See, for example, the work by Massaro and Friedman (1990), who show that individuals act as Bayesians.

PART II

THE ORGANIZATION OF POLITICAL MARKETS

6

LEGISLATIVE MARKETS
AND ORGANIZATION

> Congressmen actively exploit the bureaucracy and the
> citizenry. The bureaucracy passively exploits Congress
> and the people.
>
> *Fiorina (1989, 68)*

ONE DOES NOT HAVE TO SEARCH FAR to find complaints about Congress. Scholars have placed the blame on three interrelated structural aspects: Congressmen represent individual districts; committees represent special interests; and voters do not recognize their representative's contribution to legislative output. The result is pork-barrel politics, poor legislation, and weak control over the bureaucracy. In this chapter, I take on each one of these arguments in turn.[1]

PORK-BARREL POLITICS?

Fiorina and Noll (1978), Fiorina (1983), Weingast, Shepsle, and Johnsen (1981), and others have argued that Congress is the source of political failure. Their general argument proceeds along the following lines. Congressmen are completely unconcerned with the welfare implications of their policy decisions on other districts since only their constituents can influence their chances of reelection. Thus each congressperson pushes for policies of benefit to his or her constituency regardless of the financial cost to other districts. The result is pork-barrel heaven.[2] Fiorina (1983, 72) even suggests that representation should be based on a random sample of voters over the whole country to avoid the pork-barrel politics generated by geographically based constituencies.

---

1. Specific discussion of congressional control over the bureaucracy is contained in chapter 8.

2. Economists generally arrive at just the opposite conclusion (efficiency) when they assume selfish behavior in economic markets.

History makes such analysis questionable. The logic used to explain pork-barrel politics does not hold for presidents and governors since they are elected at large rather than representing specified geographical constituencies. Yet there are numerous examples indicating that presidents tend to favor larger expenditures than the legislature desires. Roosevelt, Kennedy, and Johnson requested dramatic increases in domestic programs but received substantially less from Congress. Reagan wanted more spent on defense, potentially the biggest pork-barrel project of all.[3] Cross-national comparisons also undermine the hypothesis that congressional structure induces the size and pattern of expenditures. Parliamentary systems have undertaken large public works projects similar to those labeled pejoratively in the United States as pork barrel. Among the Organization for Economic Cooperation and Development countries, only Japan and Australia now have lower government expenditures. More damaging to the pork-barrel thesis is a comparison of the democratically elected U.S. Congress to its polar opposite—highly centralized authoritarian regimes. The latter are often characterized by extremely wasteful projects.[4] Stalin wanted to reverse the flow of all rivers in Siberia, and the largest Catholic church in the world is in Ivory Coast, a tribute to the regime of Houphouët-Boigny.

Members of Congress tend to represent the interests of their districts, but how does Congress insure that these interests lead to collective efficiency? There are three answers: the small size of Congress, the party system, and the structure of Congress.

As already argued (in chap. 4), the small size of Congress reduces transaction costs, thereby allowing Pareto-improving trades and bargains. An inefficient method of transferring wealth from one district to another can be defeated by an efficient transfer. Politicians do not win reelection by maximizing the amount of pork that comes to their district, but rather by maximizing the welfare of some set of actors (voters or pressure groups). If these actors gain less pork (before-tax income) but at the same time pay much less in taxes so that their after-tax income is greater, the representatives will increase their probability of winning by instituting a lean omnibus bill.

The recent bill closing military bases was designed to facilitate such

3. Party is a better predictor of spending than president versus Congress.

4. Saunders and Klau (1985) have shown that government expenditures are 7 percent greater in unitary systems than in federal systems.

omnibus legislation. Congress delegated the authority to select bases for closure to a special bipartisan commission. The secretary of defense was then given the authority to close all or none of the chosen bases. His decision was final unless Congress passed a joint resolution blocking the entire package.

A number of authors have attempted to argue against the possibility of such an omnibus bill being enacted, but all of their arguments rely heavily on some asymmetry in voter behavior. For example, Fiorina and Noll (1978) assume that the voters are aware of the benefits, but not the costs, of incumbents' facilitation of constituents' needs. Shepsle and Weingast (1981) assume that the voters recognize the job gains from pork barrel in their district but underestimate the job loss from the sum total of pork barrel in all other districts. Clearly, such asymmetry is the driving force for too much pork barrel. But I have argued in the previous chapters that the assumption of voter asymmetry is unwarranted—that is, imperfect information does not imply biased estimates.

Other authors (see, for example, Mayhew 1974 and Holcombe 1985) have argued that politicians can take continuing and full credit for pork going to their district but only partial and onetime credit for getting rid of pork altogether. The argument for getting full credit is that no pork would be given to the district unless the legislator did something, since no district benefits from pork going to another legislative district. Full credit is continuing, since each year the pork is renewed. In contrast, getting rid of pork is a onetime act and is hard to attribute to any one legislator, since it would pass even if the particular legislator were against it. Given these assumptions, the conclusion that there is too much pork is unassailable. But are these assumptions legitimate? It might be possible to give continuing credit to the congressperson for not passing pork during each election period. Or voters could give continuing credit for an act that took place in the past or be antagonistic to the party for continuing pork-barrel policies.[5] While it is harder to assign credit when there are multiple inputs, it is not clear why voters on average would underestimate rather than overestimate their congressperson's marginal contribution to getting rid of pork altogether.

Furthermore, a political party is designed to overcome this problem

---

5. A commitment by the voters to reelect incumbents for undertaking efficient policies in the past may not be credible, but then reelecting incumbents for undertaking inefficient pork-barrel policies in the past may not be credible either.

and to take credit for universal policies (for example, foreign policy). National political parties internalize the negative externalities that might arise from local interests trying to shift costs onto other districts. The political party is a coalition that facilitates Pareto-improving trades within the party and puts restraints on opportunism by its members—party leaders can assign committees, allocate campaign funds, and so on.[6] (These are discussed in greater detail in the next section.)

Although numerous authors have argued for the declining importance of political parties, the party label provides information and has an important influence on the vote tally. Few independents win congressional elections, indicating that the party label is a valuable commodity. In addition, we observe that party identification of the voter is the most important variable in predicting an individual's vote (Jacobson 1987b, 107, 126).[7] Even those voters who are independents may make use of the party label to infer policies of a candidate (Downs 1957; Popkin 1991). A political party that promotes unpopular policies will discover that its candidates lose more elections than otherwise.

Baron (1991) has tried to sidestep some of the problems in the earlier literature on pork-barrel politics. In his model, a legislator proposes a policy. If it is turned down, then some delay follows before another policy is proposed. Since delay is costly, a majority of legislators may vote in favor of an inefficient policy now rather than vote against and implement an efficient policy later.[8] For example, assume that there are three legislative districts and X is deciding between offering the following policies: (200 to X, 100 to Y, 0 to Z) and (200 to X, 109 to Y, 50 to Z). Further assume that if a proposal is turned down today, then another proposal cannot be implemented until a year from now and that the time rate of discount is 10 percent. If X offers (200 to X, 100 to Y, 0 to Z), then the legislature will pass this distribution policy because both X and Y are better off with this plan than they would be if they waited

---

6. Herrnson (1986) has shown how political parties offer valuable organizational resources to congressional election campaigns. Niou and Ordeshook (1985) argue that inefficient universalism may arise. But their model also ignores the role of political parties.

7. Note that this argument also runs the other way. If we observe rational voters choosing to "identify" with a particular party, this must mean that the party label is meaningful. These arguments have been made by Cox and McCubbins (1989).

8. There are other aspects of this model that do not concern us here. For example, if the proposal is turned down, another legislator is chosen randomly to propose an allocation policy. Baron has several variants of this model. Baron (1989) and Ferejohn and Baron (1991) are discussed in chapter 13.

a year to implement the other plan. But why would X offer the inefficient distribution policy discussed in Baron's model in the first place? Although X is indifferent between the two policies, there should exist other policies that make X better off without making Y worse off. If income were perfectly transferable, then X could have chosen the following winning policy (258 to X, 101 to Y, 0 to Z). Perhaps income is not perfectly transferable, so that (220 to X, 101 to Y, 0 to Z) is the best that X can do, given that Y receives 101. Then this is still Pareto optimal (efficient), even though income is not at a maximum. Once again X will choose this outcome over the inefficient distribution (200 to X, 100 to Y, 0 to Z). Thus the original legislator is always better off by proposing an efficient allocation over inefficient pork-barrel policy.

Despite the secular increase in articles on pork-barrel policy, there appears to be a secular decline in geographically based politics. From 1978 to 1988, Congress reduced intergovernmental grants from 17 percent of federal outlays to 10.4 percent, and revenue sharing was completely eliminated. Water projects by the Army Corps of Engineers, "everyone's favorite example of pork-barrel politics," declined from 1.7 percent of federal outlays in 1948 to 0.25% in 1988 (Arnold 1990, 133). A detailed look at their budget will disclose that most of their funds are devoted to maintaining navigation on the major rivers of the United States and not on pork.

PARTIES VERSUS COMMITTEES AND THE ENDOGENIETY OF LEGISLATIVE STRUCTURE

An extensive literature views congressional committees as centers of power and the prime source for political-market failure. For Fenno (1966, 1973), Goodwin (1970), and Price (1972), committees take center stage in the legislative process. For Lowi (1979), McConnell (1970), and Davidson (1981), committees have a more sinister role—they are part of the "iron triangle" of interest group liberalism, pork-barrel politics, and policy reciprocity, while the more recent work on structure-induced equilibria (Shepsle 1979; Shepsle and Weingast 1987a,b) emphasizes committees as agenda setters in the creation of stable but inefficient outcomes.

In this section, I argue to the contrary. Committee structure and assignments are not exogenously determined. Rather, the structure of Congress and the staffing of committees should be seen as efficiency-enhancing arrangements under the control of the political parties and the congressional majority.[9]

Committee Assignments

Shepsle (1978) viewed appointments to committees as predominately determined by individual congressmen's preferences. However, assignments to committees are ultimately the responsibility of the political parties.[10] The majority would not make assignments that would result in negative-sum legislation.

Although the rule is rarely used, congressmen have lost their committee chairmanships for not abiding by party principles. In 1971 the Democratic caucus began allowing separate votes on individual chairs on the demand of any ten members. In 1974 the caucus deposed the chairs of the Agriculture, Armed Services, and Banking committees, replacing them with less senior members. "Thereafter, no chair was deposed until 1985, because it was not necessary" (Tiefer 1989, 82). Chairs yielded to pressure from junior members and party leadership rather than lose their position.

A more important method of party control is to make transfers to major committees partially dependent on past behavior on minor committees. Those who have voted with the leadership on key votes in the past are rewarded with choice reassignments.[11] Empirical support is found in Coker and Crain (1992), who show that House members who have demonstrated more loyalty to the party leaders by voting in agreement with their positions in the past are more likely to obtain assignments on important committees (see also Cox and McCubbins 1990, chap. 6). More important committees also have a greater percentage of members from the majority party, thereby controlling for the possibility of defection.

Because of seniority, committee assignments are stable. The party, however, is still able to influence the makeup of the committee by new assignments. If the present makeup of the committee is to the left of the

9. For an alternative endogenous view of committee structure see Weingast and Marshall (1988).

10. Clause 6(a)(1) of rule 10 of the House: "The standing committees specified in clause 1 shall be elected by the House at the commencement of each Congress, from nominations submitted by the respective party caucuses." The Senate has a similar rule.

11. This is stated policy of the Democratic Party. See Tiefer (1989, 81).

median member of the party as a whole, the party can appoint a new member to the right of the median voter.[12] Evidence that partially corroborates this view of the possibilities is found in Kiewiet and McCubbins (1988, 1991), who show that new appointments tend to move the median committee member from outside the middle 50 percent to inside more than they accomplish the reverse. If necessary, the House can alter the size of committees and/or change their composition (as it did to the Rules Committee in 1961).

Other methods of control include choosing party leaders and members on control committees (Rules, Appropriations, and Budget) to reflect the preferences of the median congressperson in the party, there being less potential for opportunism when the goals of the agent and the principal coincide. Cox and McCubbins (1989) show that these control committees (universal, in their terms) are more representative of Congress than special committees, such as Agriculture.[13]

There is also evidence demonstrating that whips and other congressional leaders tend to be from those districts that represent the median voter in the party. Kiewiet and McCubbins's study (1988) of House leaders showed that leaders gravitated toward the median of their caucus (Jim Wright's score made him the median Democrat). It should not be surprising that party leaders represent the interests of the median party representative, since these positions are elective, and if we have a unidimensional issue space with two candidates, party leaders will converge to the median.[14]

Another method of insuring that party leaders follow the party line is to choose leaders from safe districts. In this way they can afford to toe the party line without risk of defeat even if that line runs contrary to their district's interests. Supporting evidence is found in the fact that party leaders are rarely defeated for reelection to their district.[15] In England, party leaders typically face election in safe districts.

12. The party may also want to take into account the makeup of the other party's membership on the committee.

13. For other work comparing committee preferences to the preferences of Congress as a whole, see Maas (1983, 154); and Hall and Grofman (1990).

14. If the party leader wants to maintain his party position, he needs to promote party policies rather than his own if these are in conflict and to be skilled in creating a viable organizational structure.

15. The causation works both ways. Being a party leader improves one's chance for reelection.

Rules and Procedures

The Constitution grants the legislative branch the right to determine the rules of its own proceedings, so rules and procedures should be seen as endogenous and designed to serve the majority. We should not expect Congress to design a committee system that is inefficient.

While Congress has a committee structure that could be seen as representing special interests (for example, Agriculture), it also has control committees such as Budget and Appropriations that oversee the more specialized committees. Some commentators have argued that the Budget and Appropriations Committees are very weak because they are often a rubber stamp. However, one could use the same evidence to come to the exact opposite conclusion. A well-functioning system of control ensures that gateway committees would rarely need to reject the decisions made by lower levels; when designing legislation is costly, the lower levels should anticipate the ruling of the superior level.

Even after committees have been set up, Congress has considerable power. The House can shift jurisdictions of committees, refer certain bills to several committees, and impose procedural rules (for example, minority members can choose witnesses).[16]

The agenda-setting, structure-induced equilibrium models emphasize rules that enhance the power of committees but ignore other rules that undermine it. As Gilligan and Krehbiel (1990, 535) point out, the work of Shepsle (1979) and Shepsle and Weingast (1981) assumes "gatekeeping power" but ignores discharge powers. Closed rules are assumed (Shepsle and Weingast 1984; Weingast and Moran 1983), even though they are infrequently employed. Restrictive conference procedures favoring committees are assumed (Shepsle and Weingast 1987a), even though less restrictive postfloor procedures are used (Gilligan and Krehbiel 1987). More important, committees have fewer powers in the Senate, where each senator has the right to propose riders for most legislation under an open-amendment rule.

Hence the committees are much less autonomous than previously argued.

More fruitful than merely listing methods available to Congress for controlling committees are the predictions regarding when and where

---

16. Clause 4 of rule 27 of the House has a procedure whereby a bare majority can sign a petition to make it possible to discharge a standing committee from consideration of a piece of legislation.

these controls will be implemented. The following two hypotheses follow directly from maximization when control is costly: (1) the more important the committee, the more control that Congress will exert over it; and (2) the more the committee members' preferences deviate from those of Congress, the more Congress will put controls on the committee.

Turning to confirming evidence, the Budget Committee is very important since it balances all the competing needs by the more specialized committees, and it therefore is a likely candidate for greater control by the party leadership. This is, in fact, the case. Members are handpicked, and tenure and seniority norms observed for other committees do not apply.

We next consider the second hypothesis, regarding preference outliers. The more extreme a committee's preferences relative to those of the House, the lower will be the probability of the committee's operating under restrictive rules for its bills (see Gilligan and Krehbiel 1987, 1988, 1989a,b; Krehbiel 1991, 165–78). And the more extreme a committee chairman's preferences, the greater the restrictions put on the chair. For example, when William Colmer (D-Miss.) became chair of the Rules Committee in 1967, the chair's discretion was reduced, because he was clearly an outlier.

Asymmetric Information

Recently, a spate of papers has modeled the strategic use of asymmetric information by committees and the resulting inefficiencies.[17] There are several problems with such analyses. (1) The degree of asymmetric information is probably exaggerated. Do academic political scientists know that farm subsidies help farmers, especially those with big farms, but the majority of Congress does not? (2) Committees must reconcile conflicting interests among their members. Agriculture pits one commodity against another, small farms against big farms, and farmers with riparian rights against those without (Jones 1962; Weber 1989). (3) If asymmetric information is present, Congress will "buy" less from its committees, not more. That is, when one is less sure about the value of a product and knows that the seller is likely to exaggerate its value, one purchases less of the product.

Congress need not take asymmetric information lying down. Com-

---

17. See Austen-Smith (1990a,b); Banks (1989, 1990, 1991); Gilligan and Krehbiel (1987, 1989a,b, 1990). Asymmetric information between the bureaucracy and Congress is discussed extensively in chapter 8. Many of the arguments used there apply equally well to this section.

mittee hearings are required to be public. If the problem of information is likely to be distorting, Congress can put people with opposite preferences on the committee or create overlapping committees, each with a different viewpoint. If the committee is composed of preference outliers, then others may want to discount information provided by its members. More important, if committee members have been caught being dishonest in the past, they may be disciplined or, at a minimum, distrusted in the future.

Evidence on Outcomes

So far, we have looked at the tools for controlling committees available to Congress and the political parties. Another way to determine the power of committees relative to parties is to look at policy outcomes. We would expect that policies that affect Congress as a whole would more closely represent the preferences of the whole Congress than the preferences of the particular committee. Support for this hypothesis is found in the only study that tries to measure the preferences of the committee members and of Congress. Krehbiel and Rivers (1988) show that the Committee on Labor and Human Resources tailored its legislation on the minimum wage to fit the preferences of the Senate's median voter rather than the preferences of the median committee member.[18]

The greater the extent to which committees are subservient to parties, the less committee structure affects legislative outcomes. Some supporting evidence is found in Stewart's study (1987) of structural change on spending in the House of Representatives during a period of strong party and speaker control (1887–1922). His research found that changing committee structure had little effect on appropriations bills.

The Structure of Committees

Understanding of committee structure is enhanced by looking at the analogous structure for firms. Firms are not unorganized, amorphous blobs. Rather, divisions are created within firms to deal with specific issues. A structure, not ad hoc arrangements, is imposed. The structure facilitates comparative advantage and reduces transaction costs. The upper layers of management provide general direction to the lower levels and deal with the occasional conflicts between departments. Congress is

---

18. See also Cox and McCubbins (1989). Their statistical analysis shows that the power of the legislative committees is much smaller than believed.

structured in the same way. Specialized committees deal with specialized concerns and facilitate trades among the people within the committee. Overall direction is given by the party leadership. It is hard to imagine an effective Congress without a committee structure very similar to the existing one.

THE REWARDS TO EFFORT

Some claim that it is hard to get members of Congress to write bills because doing so is costly in terms of time and the individual is unlikely to get credit because the action is invisible. However, the number and types of bills sponsored by a congressperson is often a salient issue in an election. Furthermore, an effective political party creates the appropriate incentives for individuals to promote party policies. The party may provide positions and even policies to reward those who undertake otherwise undesirable tasks. If the party is effective, both the probability of its members winning reelection and the rewards from winning are enhanced. For example, the majority party gains chairmanships of committees and more influence over policy.

COALITION BUILDING

As the passage of the Tax Reform Act of 1986 and the passage in 1993 of the North American Free Trade Agreement show, legislation may require a long process of coalition formation and extensive trading over different government policies, involving both the legislative and executive branches. The resulting Pareto-improving trades make the constituents of the affected districts better off, thereby increasing the likelihood of their incumbents being reelected.

Members of Congress will try to organize Congress in a way that maximizes their reelection. The structure may grant greater power to some than others (e.g., seniority rules), but, as argued earlier, an unequal distribution of political wealth does not mean inefficiency any more than an unequal distribution of wealth implies inefficiency in the economic sphere. It just means that those members of Congress with greater political power will be able to choose from among the set of efficient policies those policies that deliver more to their constituents.

7

PRESSURE GROUPS

> What happens in other forms of government—namely that
> an organized minority imposes its will on the disorganized
> majority—happens also to perfection whatever the appear-
> ance to the contrary under the representative system. . . .
> This is because the only candidates who have any chance
> of succeeding are those who are championed by organized
> minorities.
>
> *Mosca (1939, 154)*

PRESSURE GROUPS HAVE BEEN VIEWED AS the source of political-market failure
by the Left, Right, and middle.[1] Recently, Becker (1983) has argued that
pressure groups may also create success. Consider the case where there
are two pressure groups with diametrically opposed interests. If the
amount of pressure is a function of their respective utility loss (or gain),
then the net political pressure is in the direction of higher utility. Becker's
model has two limitations, however. It is a black box, and it sidesteps the
issue when pressure groups have orthogonal interests. In this section, I
extend Becker's model by embedding it into an electoral framework.

Consider a two-candidate election. Assume that if a voter votes, he
will vote for the candidate who promises the voter the greatest utility if
elected. The probability of voting is then a function of a voter's utility
differential between the platforms (the greater the utility differential, the
greater the likelihood of voting), the advertising differential, and whether
the voter belongs to a pressure group or not. Belonging to a pressure
group increases the probability of voting. Donations, which are used for
advertising, come from individual voters or, possibly, indirectly through
a pressure group. The amount that the voter (or pressure group) donates
is a positive function of the utility differential to the voter (or members
of the pressure group) times the probability of the candidate's winning.
It is further assumed that, other things being equal, pressure groups donate

1. For a general survey on pressure groups, see Mitchell and Munger (1991).

more than individual voters and that some pressure groups may be more successful than others when their organizational costs are lower.

This model obviously elevates the importance of pressure groups. Other things being equal, vote-maximizing candidates will tend to weight the interests of those who belong to pressure groups more than those who act as individual voters. Furthermore, candidates will trade off votes gained directly from policy differentials for votes gained through advertising differentials, and pressure groups have a comparative advantage in raising the money for advertising. Even though I have intellectually boxed myself in, I will now argue that the distortion caused by pressure groups is limited.

CONCENTRATED VERSUS DIFFUSE INTERESTS

> The steel industry and its workers . . . are willing to act because the benefits from protection are concentrated on the relatively few who invest and work in the industry. Their incomes are significantly affected. The larger costs of their protection are borne in dispersed fashion by the much more numerous population of taxpayers and consumers. The dilution of costs renders its bearers politically ineffective.
>
> *Demsetz (1982)*

> [A democratic] system tends to give undue political power to small groups that have highly concentrated interests. . . . Consider the government program of favoring the merchant marine by subsidies for shipbuilding. . . . The estimated cost . . . is 15,000 dollars per year for each of the 40,000 people actively engaged in the industry. Ship owners, operators and their employees have a strong incentive to get and keep these measures. . . . On the other hand [these subsidies] only come to about 3 dollars a person per year. Which of us will vote against a candidate because he imposed that cost on us?
>
> *Friedman and Friedman (1980)*

> Politically successful groups tend to be small relative to the size of the groups taxed to pay their subsidies.
>
> *Becker (1983)*

These quotes represent only a small subset of the numerous authors who have argued that those who have concentrated benefits (e.g., the defense industry) will have an upper hand in the political process over those who face diffuse costs (the taxpayer). The logic is that it does not pay to enter the political arena when only small amounts are involved. However, this argument confuses individual motivation on one issue with overall political effect. In fact, quite plausible arguments can be made that concentrated interests are at a great disadvantage in majority rule systems. Consider the case in which a candidate's policy would result in taking a dollar from a million voters and distributing the proceeds to one thousand members of a pressure group. Obviously, the probability that each of the thousand members of the pressure group votes for the candidate is a lot greater than the probability that each of the one million voters (most of whom may not even be aware of the policy) votes against the candidate. But even if this policy reduces the probability of each of the million voters voting for the candidate by only .005, such a redistribution will not take place, for it involves a loss of five thousand votes from the diffuse majority in return for a thousand more from the pressure group. And even if the pressure group donates $500,000 and the resulting advertising reduces the probability loss from .005 to only .002, the candidate would lose undertaking such a policy. Indeed, given these stylized facts, we would observe the diffuse majority taxing the concentrated minority.[2]

Despite the widespread arguments claiming that the concentrated interests of a minority will override the diffuse interests of the majority, the contrary theoretical results presented here should not be surprising. As in other areas of economics, some people are at the margin, and thus very small changes will have an effect. This effect multiplied times the very large number of voters with diffuse interests may be very substantial. There is also an inherent logical problem that occurs if minorities have a natural advantage over larger groups—it is easy to make a group smaller, and everyone is a concentrated-interest minority of one.

The historical evidence also appears to support my conclusions. Cultural, religious, and ethnic minorities are more often victimized by the majority than the reverse.

THE ROLE OF COMPETITION AND RATIONALITY

I have argued that the concentrated-benefit versus diffuse-cost explanation for pressure group success is problematic; however, there may

2. A more general and more formal argument is found in Wittman (1989).

still be other valid explanations for their success. I will now show that any economic distortions are limited by competition between the participants and rationality of the voters.

Pressure groups compete for their policies to be adopted. The politician chooses policies until the gain in his/her expected plurality coming from an advertising dollar equals the decrease in plurality that results from the policy undertaken to gain that advertising dollar. Obviously, the best choice for the politician is where there is little or no conflict between the two. Since legislative districts vary in their characteristics, the success of the pressure groups will depend on the relative costs in policy to the voters in the district—the soybean growers association will gain a more sympathetic ear in those districts where soybeans are grown. Hence, competition may mitigate any losses that might arise from service to pressure groups, and there may be a very close congruence between the preferences of the voters in a district and the pressure group support of the incumbent (see Denzau and Munger 1986).

Advertising is informative. Other things being equal, the more advertising, the less uncertainty about the candidate's position and the more likely that risk-averse voters vote for the candidate. For example, in the absence of advertising, voters might believe that the distribution of possible choices by candidate X is uniformly distributed between $m - 10$ and $m + 10$; with advertising, the distribution might shrink to $m - 5$ and $m + 5$. This reduction in uncertainty would encourage risk-averse voters to vote for X. Other things might not be equal, however. Suppose that m stands for the preference of the median voter and that a person on the right is willing to donate to candidate X if X moves his position to $m + 1$. Then voters would perceive the distribution of possible choices by X as ranging from $m - 4$ to $m + 6$. In this case the candidate is faced with a trade-off between the vote gains from greater certainty and the vote losses due to a less popular expected position.

For both businessmen and politicians, advertising is not costless. Politicians may give preferential treatment to pressure groups that provide campaign contributions (Peltzman 1976), but the degree of distortion that arises from such contributions is limited.[3] If in order to attract

3. Campaign contributions are not distorting from the optimal if contributions are proportional to the costs and benefits of policy to the donors.

A believer in imperfect political markets could interpret contributions by corporations and other pressure groups as a sign of weakness rather than strength. Assume that politicians were acting as a cartel. They could threaten to write legislation or enforce laws that

campaign contributions the candidate takes a policy position far from the median voter, the number of votes captured from uninformed voters via increased advertising will be less than the number of votes lost from informed voters. This potential for loss is especially acute in political campaigns since there is so much more comparative advertising in political markets than in economic markets. A politician's claim that "the other side is a captive of special interests" need be directed to only a small subset of voters (say, ten thousand) in order to be politically effective.

One reason for greater comparative advertising in politics is that elections are zero-sum games (a greater plurality for one candidate is a lower plurality for the other), while comparative advertising in the private sector may be negative sum (e.g., "our chickens have less salmonella than others" is not a viable marketing strategy).[4] Bad policy increases the marginal productivity of advertising by the other candidate and will be pointed out.[5] Advertising does not make up for severe product deficiencies in either political or economic markets. If there is any policy distortion, this is the cost of information, just as consumers absorb the cost of advertising in the products they buy.

To the extent that pressure group models rely on the voters' ignorance of pressure groups' influence, we have a metatheoretical inconsistency—the more people believe in the validity of the model, the less true it can be. If everyone believes that pressure groups are pulling the wool over people's eyes, then who is being blinded?

Consider the work by Magee, Brock, and Young (1989). They have a very complex model of tariffs with two lobbies, two goods, two political parties, and two inputs. In their model, the majority of voters are ignorant of, or not very sensitive to, the consequences of trade policy. Implicit in their model is the inability of voters to first understand that campaign contributions come at the expense of the majority and then vote against the party on the basis of its campaign contributors. Not surprisingly,

---

hurt corporations (even though the voters were not interested in such legislation) unless the corporations donated money to them. For example, the threat of enforcing the Sherman Antitrust Act could be viewed as a credible method of extracting tribute from large firms.

4. Another reason is that candidates tend to represent different interest groups. Rarely does one interest group contribute to both campaigns. Note, however, that the candidate not receiving funds can alter the amount of funds going to the other candidate by taking differing stands on the issues important to the interest group.

5. This self-correcting mechanism also exists for news organizations. The greater the number of newspapers that refrain from reporting disparaging information about business because they fear losing advertising dollars, the greater the demand for those that do not.

under these assumptions, they find that tariff policy may be a black hole, swallowing up ever greater amounts of productivity. However, contrary to their model, it is quite common for electoral campaign literature to highlight excessive campaign contributions to the opposition (for example, the antismoking lobby typically advertises the contributions by the prosmoking lobby when there is an antismoking referendum in California). Evidently, Magee, Brock, and Young believe that only economists understand that pressure groups try to promote policies beneficial to their members.[6] This is not the only unrealistic assumption in their model. They implicitly assume that neither party has squealed on the other and that consumers do not realize that a higher tariff means a higher price for goods. They also assume platform rigidities, so that neither party can emulate the other party's position. Why did they make all of these strong assumptions? Not because they are stupid, but because they are so smart. They knew that without these assumptions, their results would no longer hold.

ORGANIZATION, TRANSACTION COSTS, AND INFORMATION

Pressure groups perform a valuable function by reducing the costs of transmitting information from individuals to politicians, and vice versa. Politicians are informed of various constituencies' preferences in a relatively low-cost way.[7] Politicians may also gain information from the existence of the lobbying activity itself. Other things being equal, politicians can infer strength of preference from the strength of lobbying efforts. The more spent on lobbying, the more important the policy is to the group. Of course, other things may not be equal. Congressmen and their constituents know that certain groups have lower organizational costs and that greater lobbying need not reflect more votes at the ballot box. In such cases, politicians take into account these biases and discount the effect of organizational advantages. Congressmen know that unorganized voters will not fly out to Washington to lobby against a bill, yet they will vote against the congressmen if the congressmen support the legislation.

6. See Austen-Smith (1990) for an extensive review of their book and Morton and Cameron (1991) for a critical analysis of the campaign contribution literature.

7. Coughlin, Mueller, and Murrell (1990) use this insight in developing a formal model of interest group politics. In their model, pressure groups reduce the uncertainty that politicians have about the preferences of members of the groups. The politicians respond by weighting their (known) preferences more than the less precisely known preferences of other unorganized groups. The outcome is Pareto optimal.

Seeing pressure groups as institutions that reduce transaction costs rather than as institutions that distort democratic decisions suggests an entirely new research agenda—discovering the optimal method of organizing information networks to elicit preferences and transmit them to politicians. Pressure groups are part of the solution. Their scope depends on the optimal division of labor and comparative advantage within the context of the political structure. Consider the following thought experiment: Suppose that you were designing a method to elicit and transmit preferences and that you had limited means to do so. Would you organize by first letter of a person's last name or by certain interests, such as job and religion? Clearly, the latter. How fine a division would you create, and would the structure be parallel or overlapping? The answer depends on the span of differences and whether the added information from parallel networks overcomes the cost. Thus in the United States, Orthodox and Reform Jews are more likely to work together under one umbrella when lobbying Congress than they are in Israel when lobbying the Knesset. What would be the extent of vertical integration? That is, which information gathering tasks would be allocated to the legislator's office staff, which would be allocated to an independent organization (such as a polling firm), and which would be allocated to externally organized groups? Again comparative advantage would provide the answer. The actual solutions to these and the previous questions are not determined by one person setting up the overall structure, but by individuals trying to achieve their own particular needs.

IMPROPER EXAMPLES

One of the oldest, and unquestionably one of the most powerful, single issue groups is the National Rifle Association, which has zealously defended the right to bear arms against almost perennial legislative efforts to impose gun control. Despite public opinion polls that show a majority of Americans favor some kind of gun control, Congress has consistently defeated such efforts in large part because of the power of the NRA.

Peter Navarro (1984, 49)

Large numbers are not, however, essential for groups to be influential. Organization and money also matter. . . . Some of the most successful groups—the National Rifle Association . . . win by the implicit threat to finance and work for the opponents of members [of Congress] who do not support their positions.

Jacobson (1987b, 194)

Congress serves the vocal and the organized. . . . The best examples are veterans (widely distributed, well organized).

Jacobson (1987b, 193)

"The Veterans' Lobby as an 'Iron Triangle.' "

Keller (1987)[8]

Commentators have routinely assumed that pressure groups have extraordinary powers. The NRA is probably the pressure group most commonly cited by those who believe that Congress is controlled by special interests to the detriment of the majority. A standard argument is that this organization perverts the will of the majority by intense lobbying of Congress. But it is silly to blame Congress in this way, when ballot initiatives to control guns don't pass either. For example, in 1982, 63 percent of California voters voted against handgun control and only 37 percent voted in favor. So congressional inaction on gun control may reflect the will of the majority rather than result from the National Rifle Association's lobbying Congress. If one ignores the arguments of chapter 2, it is possible to believe that the majority has been bamboozled by the NRA. However, the voters have had many opportunities to hear the arguments in favor of gun control, and, hence, such market failure explanations should be taken with a grain of salt.

The cozy relationship between Congress and veterans' groups is also used as a prime example of the failure of Congress to reflect majority opinion. The explanation typically proceeds along the following lines: The diffuse voters are unlikely to be aware of the legislation in favor of veterans because it has so little effect on any one of them. The veteran's group will strongly support the campaign of the congressperson via votes and campaign contributions. Hence, the congressperson's need for contributions will result in her sacrificing the interests of the uninformed majority.

Again one needs to ask whether Congress is succumbing to special interests or is reflecting the will of the majority. Again an important test

---

8. This is the title of an article showing the close relationship between the veterans' lobby and Congress.

of this proposition is to look at referenda. In California and numerous other states there are often referenda that give special advantages, such as low-cost home loans, to veterans. A very high percentage of voters vote in such referenda, and in California, at least, the propositions typically pass. Not very much advertising one way or the other is aimed at the general voter, and the ballot is not so complicated that the average voter cannot figure it out. In other words, those who voted in favor of such an initiative knew that it was helping veterans who were buying homes.[9] While pure self-interest might suggest otherwise, what these voters do is consistent with what economists view as rational. The voters have a set of *clearly defined* preference rankings and they choose the most preferred.[10] Thus we cannot explain this behavior as a political-market failure. But if legislation benefiting veterans is enacted by the legislature, it tends to be treated so by the critics. Perhaps people are too quick to label legislative outcomes as political-market failures.

EMPIRICAL EVIDENCE

Empirical studies that try to directly measure the effect of lobbying on policy are plagued with methodological difficulties. The most critical problem is the direction of causality. The legislator's voting record may be solely a function of her preferences and the preferences of her constituents. Nevertheless, if contributions by political action committees were also based on voting records, researchers would find that PAC contributions determined legislators' votes. Attempts to control for the preferences of constituents also have problems. The measurement of voters' and legislators' preferences is inevitably imperfect. Attributing to lobbying those votes that are not accounted for by preferences is inappropriate, since it may be merely measurement error. Not surprisingly, the empirical results are often not convincing.

Some empirical studies suggest that the influence of pressure groups is modest. Bronars and Lott (1993) tried to get around the issue of the direction of causality by looking at the voting records of congressmen who had announced that they would not seek reelection. Under such

9. Of course, there is heavier voting in favor by those who are veterans.
10. A diehard would say that they were propagandized subtly in the schools to be in favor of veterans. See Hochman and Rodgers (1969, 1970) for Pareto-optimal explanations for income redistribution.

circumstances, pressure groups could no longer threaten to reduce campaign contributions to the incumbent or to increase campaign contributions to the challenger in the next election.[11] Lott and Bronars found no change in congressmen's voting records. Politicians did not vote differently on those issues for which they had been receiving contributions, nor did those who had been receiving the largest contributions change their position relative to others, suggesting that campaign contributions had little effect on incumbents' behavior.[12] Wright's study (1985) of political action committees showed that receiving a contribution increased by only 1 percent the congressperson's probability of voting in the way favored by the PAC. In none of the cases studied by Wright did contributions determine the ultimate fate of the bill. Similarly, Grenzke's study (1989) of 120 PACs showed that contributions did not change House members' voting patterns.[13]

This lack of success may explain why corporations contribute so little to congressional candidates. Kosterlitz (1982) reports that corporate PACs contributed only $19.2 million during 1979–80. According to Weinberger and Greevy (1982), a congressperson sitting on the House Armed Services Committee received on average about one thousand dollars total from all defense contractors. And it should be remembered that some of these contributions may cancel each other out if different defense contractors are vying for the same contract. The natural retort to this evidence is that the contributions are small because members of Congress can be bought cheaply, but this ignores the effect of competition. If a few thousand dollars in influence peddling can mean millions of dollars in extra profits, then many more firms will start to lobby Congress, and the price will be bid up until the marginal cost of lobbying equals the marginal benefit.

11. However, pressure groups could threaten to withdraw promised positions with their organizations after retirement from Congress.

12. This result does not imply that campaign contributions have no effect on who gets elected in the first place.

13. The question then becomes, why did the PACs contribute money? Again, I would suggest that contributions provide information to the representative regarding his constituency's intensity on the particular issue. Although PACs can contribute to anyone's reelection campaign, the great tendency is for PACs to contribute to their natural representatives (for example, dairy PACs contribute to representatives from dairy-producing states; see Chappell 1982). Furthermore, contributions provide access to the congressperson, thereby improving channels of communication. The congressperson can be informed of problems in the design of legislation and the industry can be informed about the possibilities of proposed legislation.

Finally, voters always have the option of imposing limits on rent seeking. For example, civil service limits patronage, blind bidding for government contracts reduces bribes, and campaign financing laws reduce monetary inequalities.

CONCLUDING REMARKS

Downs (1957) demonstrated that candidates' policies converge to the median voter's most preferred position when preferences are single peaked. There have been numerous extensions of his spatial model, but they all show the power of the majority. In contrast, pressure group theories claim that it is the small, organized groups with concentrated interests that get their way in the political process. In this chapter, I have combined the two approaches and have demonstrated that even in nonspatial political arenas, the majority's diffuse interest dominates.

8

BUREAUCRATIC MARKETS: WHY GOVERNMENT BUREAUCRACIES ARE EFFICIENT AND NOT TOO LARGE

SINCE WEBER (1947), NOBODY HAS HAD a kind word to say about government bureaucracies.[1] A legion of commentators has found that the bureaucracy serves the public very poorly. The literature provides two contradictory explanations for this view: (1) government bureaucracies lack direction, are ineffectual, and are characterized by inertia (Lindblom 1959; Downs 1967; Wildavsky 1979), versus (2) bureaucracies are extremely sophisticated at promoting the self-interest of their members (Niskanen 1971).

In this chapter, I argue to the contrary. Government bureaucracies engage in economically efficient behavior, they are not too large, and their principal-agent problems have been greatly exaggerated. I demonstrate that much of the evidence marshaled against government bureaucracies is methodologically flawed and that the prevailing theories are empty of empirical content. The efficiency argument is interwoven with the question of institutional design. I show how various institutional arrangements, such as oversight committees, civil service, and competitive supply systems, are devised in order to reduce opportunism by either the bureaucracy or its principals, Congress and the president.

The chapter is organized along the following lines. I argue in the first section against the incrementalist and rule-of-thumb approaches. In the next section the budget-maximizing and bureaucratic-power models come under scrutiny. I then concentrate on research that is derivative of the principal-agent approach. In the following two sections I present some propositions regarding the choice of institutional design and

---

1. Although Weber admired bureaucratic effectiveness, he was quite concerned about the threat of bureaucracies to democratic systems.

briefly discuss the issues that arise because government bureaucracies have two superiors, the president and Congress.

Incrementalism, "Satisficing," and Rules of Thumb

A large body of literature has argued that bureaucrats do not optimize but instead use simple, myopic rules to reduce decision-making costs. This literature, also known as the behavioralist approach, claims that bureaucrats make limited and incremental comparisons (Lindblom 1959), "satisfice" (Simon 1957; Wildavsky 1979), ignore the full range of consequences (Braybrooke and Lindblom 1963), choose simple rules (Bromiley and Crecine 1980) and heuristics (Newell and Simon 1972) rather than pursue goals, make only small changes (Wanat 1978), and determine current budget expenditures almost wholly on previous expenditure levels (Sharkansky 1968).

The first order of business is to argue that the optimization approach is superior to other models of bureaucratic behavior.[2] I demonstrate this by showing that (1) much of the evidence and theorizing in favor of the behavioralist model is consistent with optimization; (2) when the approaches differ, the behavioralist model tends to be ad hoc with limited generality, (3) the incrementalist view is a very low-level theory, and (4) optimization is much more powerful in explaining empirical phenomena.

A number of people have argued for bounded rationality as an alternative to optimization (see Cyert 1988 for a recent example).[3] But these two concepts need not be in opposition. Firms and people can optimize in the presence of bounded rationality. For example, contracts between firms do not account for all contingencies, and rules of thumb may be chosen. Rules of thumb economize on decision making but may distort goals. The optimization approach suggests that those rules of thumb that minimize the sum of goal distortion and decision-making costs will be implemented.[4]

---

2. There are other arational models of bureaucratic behavior. For example, Ripley et al. (1975) have argued that agencies have life cycles. Some of the same arguments that I use against the incrementalists can also be used against the life cycle hypothesis and other arational theories.

3. Bounded rationality is also discussed in chapter 5.

4. See Wittman (1982) for an analysis of the optimal rules of thumb for highway and sports rules.

Simon (1957) has argued that bureaucrats "satisfice" rather than optimize. But what determines the satisficing level? If people stop searching when the expected marginal returns to information go below the cost of acquiring the information, then we are back to the optimization model. Even if people do not optimize, an optimizing model will yield good predictions if the satisficing level of performance is close to the maximum level.

Davis, Dempster, and Wildavsky (1974) provide evidence showing that bureaucratic behavior is incremental.[5] But optimization does not mean constant global searches or frantic changes from day to day. The method of production that maximized profits yesterday is likely to be the same method that maximizes profits today. The fact that behavior is often incremental is thus entirely consistent with optimization (especially so when the exogenous changes in factor prices and competitors' prices are also incremental). Furthermore, long-term planning often leads to smooth changes over time rather than chaotic irregularities.

Bendor (1988) has pointed out that "behavioral" models tend to be backward looking while rational-choice models tend to be relentlessly forward looking. But certainly, rational people use the past to predict the future—either through econometric estimation or by updating Bayesian priors. And what determines the bureaucracy's rate of adjustment? Is it just an inherent rate of sluggishness or an optimal rate of change?

Bendor suggests that there are two central premises of bounded rationality: a limited number of alternatives are generated, and a simple test will be applied to end the search. But these central premises are too open-ended to yield any predictive power. At one end of the spectrum, these premises are perfectly consistent with maximization in the presence of *perfect* information. For example, consider the behavior of the for-profit firm in the presence of "bounded rationality": estimate the cost and revenue curves facing the firm (this estimate may be imperfect), and use the "rule of thumb"—quantity should be increased until marginal revenue equals marginal cost. This rule maximizes profits. It also satisfies the major tenets of bounded rationality, as only a limited number of alternatives are generated, and the decision-making process may be incremental and myopic. Production can be changed in one-unit increments; over time, the firm will converge to the optimal. In addition, the

5. Other works in this genre include Fenno (1966) and Sharkansky (1968).

firm considers only two variables, supply and demand, and there is a simple stopping rule.

Unfortunately, these central premises are perfectly consistent with a wide variety of other behavior. Even looking at the astrological chart in the paper for guidance is an application of a simple rule. What rule of thumb does the bureaucrat employ in choosing a rule of thumb? This question plagues the rule-of-thumb literature that is not embedded in optimization theory. For example, Padgett (1981) models an Office of Management and Budget manager who cuts more or less randomly until the total cut in the budget equals a certain number. Unfortunately, the possible rules of thumb, if not infinite, are quite high. Rules of thumb might be to reduce budgets for those bureaus with the largest budget first, reduce budgets for those bureaus with the smallest budgets first, reduce budgets for all bureaus by the same percentage, or reduce the budget for those bureaus whose clientele voted against you in the last election. Unless we are willing to be drowned in a sea of special cases, we will have to decide which rule of thumb is chosen. So how do we predict which rule of thumb an individual or bureau will choose? The best answer going is maximization.

There is another related problem. How simple is a simple test? When individual outcomes are unimportant and choices nonrepetitive, one might choose a simple rule of thumb. When they are more important, the simple rules become more complex. This poses a serious problem for the social scientist who wants to explain behavior by nonoptimizing rules of thumb. Each change in complexity will change behavior, and there is no convergence (as there would be if rules of thumb were shortcuts to optimization).[6]

Thus the key difference between the optimization and "behavioralist" approaches is that optimization-based models of bounded rationality argue that the rules of thumb chosen will optimize, while sui generis models of bounded rationality incorporate some rule of thumb with little justification. Optimal rules of thumb also have a greater chance of survival, since competition between bureaucrats (and/or bureaucracies) would tend to eliminate those who employed inefficient rules. (This argument will be discussed at length in later sections.)

---

6. One might counter that there are an infinite number of things to maximize. But often the comparative statics results are the same regardless of the maximand (within reason), and furthermore there are some very prominent choices for maximizing.

Related to the incremental model is the lagged-adjustment model. Leibenstein (1989) and March and Olsen (1989) have argued that bureaucrats are highly routinized and hence slow to adjust to new circumstances. Thus bureaucratic behavior falls somewhere between what was optimal ten years ago and what is optimal today. The lagged-adjustment, or inertia, model, like other disequilibrium models of human behavior, fails to account for rational expectations. In contrast, equilibrium models predict a system that is ex ante optimally responsive to new circumstances. While mistakes could be made, there would be no predictable biases for the system as a whole. That is, sometimes the bureaucracy would react too rapidly (because the external circumstances did not change as rapidly as predicted); while other times the bureaucracy would react too slowly because it had underestimated the change in external circumstances.[7] This does not mean that every bureaucracy moves rapidly but that those bureaus with a comparative advantage in dealing with new circumstances will make up for those bureaus that are set up to handle changing events less quickly. Indeed, if there are other organizational forms, such as markets, that deal with new circumstances more efficiently, then the tasks will be shifted to these organizations. To the degree that inertial systems are set up, they are developed to maximize over time, not just to maximize the output in the initial period. Any inflexibilities in the system mean that part of the time the system leads and part of the time the system lags. A concrete example would be the building of a warehouse. If the system is growing, the warehouse would initially be too big and later be too small (even if it were the optimal-size warehouse). If there are many warehouses being built during a period of anticipated growth, the average warehouse is neither too small nor too large. The same holds for routines and procedures. If change is very rapid, so that certain routines are quickly made obsolete, one creates flexible routines that are designed to deal with change.

The view that bureaucracies are headless organizations greatly exaggerates the cost of coordination. There are costs of coordination in any market, including the abstract markets envisioned by Arrow-Debreu (someone has to pay the Walrasian auctioneer). If the invisible hand can coordinate a hundred million producers and demanders in the market-

7. If the costs of overreacting were greater than the costs of underreacting, then optimal behavior by the bureaucracy would result in a higher probability of underreacting. Either way, under- and over-reacting are responses to uncertainty, not responses to predictable circumstances.

place, it would be hard to explain why some combination of invisible and visible hand could not achieve a similar result in a system involving only thousands of people. There are large bureaucracies in the private sector, and their survival suggests that any bureaucratic inefficiencies are at most relatively minor.

The "muddling-through" literature claims that incrementalism is the only way to deal with the conflicting and complex goals imposed on the bureaucracy, but constrained optimization is a standard technique in handling complex management decisions. Utility maximization has been a very rewarding approach to understanding individual behavior, even though one could argue that individuals have conflicting goals (after all, that is the essence of scarcity—all wants cannot be achieved).

The incrementalist theory is an extremely low-level theory with little power. Saying that the sun will rise at about the same time this morning as it did yesterday morning because it is too costly to optimize and consequently the sun muddles through the day will give us a reasonably good prediction, but such a theory will never supplant Kepler's. Saying that the businessman chooses the same price today as yesterday or that the bureaucrat asks for the same or a little bit more than yesterday because it is too costly to do constrained optimization does not get us very far either, since the exogenous variable, yesterday's price or quantity, is only a lagged dependent variable.

Ultimately, there is very little predictive power in the incrementalist approach. Consider, for example, the methodology of Dempster and Wildavsky, who take almost all theoretical justification out of their model by defining an incremental process [as] one in which the relationships between actors are regular over a period of years and a nonincremental process [as] one in which this relationship is irregular" (1979, 375). They even allow greatly different patterns (particularly in the amount of change) from one bureau to another, as long as the pattern within the bureau is regular. The problem with this approach is that it does not explain the pattern of regularity (for example, why one bureau would grow at 2 percent annually and another at 10 percent annually), when or why the pattern of regularity changes, or what variables we should look for when trying to discover regularities (is the regularity found in the relation between this year's budget and last year's budget or between the median senator's preferences and this year's budget?).

Empirical evidence has not been very kind to the incrementalist literature. Its heyday was in the 1960s and early 1970s. But when Ronald

Reagan came to power, he had an ideological agenda that differed greatly from his predecessors, and, not surprisingly, there were nonincremental changes in the government bureaucracy (see empirical work by Kamlet and Mowery 1983, 1987; Auten, Bozeman, and Cline 1984; and Strauss-man 1988). Moreover, there is serious question whether incrementalism ever existed. Gist (1977) showed that the controllable portion of the federal budget actually declined 15 percent between 1968 and 1974; while Gist (1974) showed that the pattern of defense procurement, re-search, and development (between 30 and 50 percent of the defense budget) did not coincide with the Davis, Dempster, and Wildavsky incre-mentalist rules (see also Kiewiet and McCubbins 1985, 75).

As argued earlier, one expects regularities in budgets when the un-derlying demand does not change much from year to year (and, con-versely, a greater fluctuation where the underlying demands themselves fluctuate). For example, agricultural productivity varies greatly from one year to the next due to fluctuations in the weather; in turn, there should also be fluctuations in the demand from the Commodity Credit Corpora-tion, which services agriculture. In contrast, the Federal Aviation Admin-istration should have relatively constant demand, since the need for inspectors and airport administration is not that cyclical. This is in fact the case, as can be seen in figure 8.1. The graph also suggests that the incre-mental model makes no sense for the Commodity Credit Corporation.

Figure 8.1 is very enlightening in other ways as well. Regressing present Veteran's Administration expenditures against past VA expendi-tures (or regressing change in VA expenditures against level of VA expen-ditures), one gets a high R-square (.92 and .63, respectively) and very significant coefficients. This may seem to be strong support for the incre-mentalist view.[8] But why is the absolute change large and increasing toward the end of the 1960s? One does not need to be a student of history to understand that appropriations for the Veterans Administration would increase rapidly as casualties from the war in Vietnam increased. The war shifted defense priorities from space to conventional and guer-rilla warfare. Hence, expenditures on the National Aeronautics and Space Administration decreased. A concentration on the incrementalist mode would miss and possibly mask this result.

---

8. Actually, serial correlation of the error terms biases upward the apparent significance of the results. This problem undermines much of the econometric work done to support the incrementalist view. The ocular test also seems to violate the incrementalist view.

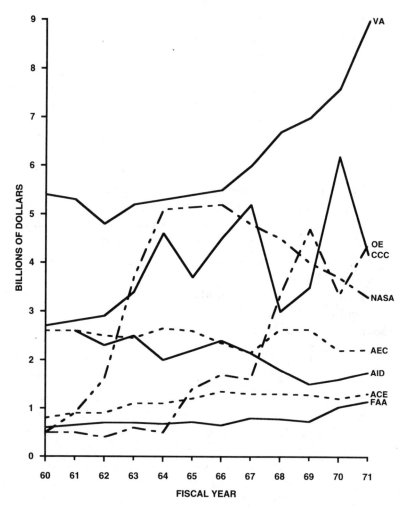

FIG. 8.1. Appropriations for Eight Agencies, Fiscal 1960 through 1971 (from Leloup 1975, 75)

BUDGET MAXIMIZATION AND RELATED THEORIES
OF BUREAUCRATIC POWER

The second view of bureaucracies has more of an economic flavor. The players now optimize, but as we shall see, the rules of the game are nonoptimal and the players may not have rational expectations.

We start off with Niskanen's model, since those that follow are just variants on a theme.[9] Niskanen argues that government bureaucracies, such as the defense department, are better informed than those who are supposed to oversee them. Since the utility functions of the bureaucrats tend to be positively correlated with size (income, power, prestige, and opportunity for advancement tend to increase as the size of the bureaucracy increases), bureaucrats will exaggerate the need for their services. Congress will be at the bureaucracy's mercy (congressmen don't have enough time to devote themselves to such intricacies), and hence the bureaucrats will tend to get their way.[10]

Once again, competition undermines the argument.[11] Even if it were true that each bureaucracy were trying to maximize its size, that would not make each bureaucracy too large. Competition for funds between the bureaucracies would tend to create information and force bureaucracies to be an optimal size. When a government program might be undertaken by several agencies, the agency with the most persuasive argument and/or lowest expenditures would get the funding.[12] This is similar to an English auction (which eliminates all rents when the two highest private values are the same) and to the adversarial system used by courts to elicit information. More importantly, bureaus compete against each

9. For example, see Breton and Wintrobe (1982); Orzechowski (1977), who argues that bureaucrats have a preference for labor intensity (in order to maximize the number of voters the bureau has); Spencer (1982), who allows for a sequence of bureaucrats; and Wyckoff (1990), whose model assumes that bureaucrats have a taste both for slack and for size, with their trade-off being characterized by a homothetic production function. Niskanen (1975) altered his model so that the degree of discretion by bureaucrats was reduced, and he put more of the blame on Congress.

10. This is quite similar to the early works of Marx, who saw bureaucrats as furthering their own interests (only later did he claim that they served the interests of the ruling class). Bureaucrats were able to maintain their domination via their monopolization of knowledge. Weber (1968, 993) also argued that the bureaucracy could overrule its master by maintaining secrecy.

11. Niskanen viewed the situation as being a bilateral monopoly between the supplier of the service (bureau) and the demander (Congress). But if his model is true, why would Congress and the presidency be so stupid as to set up such a monopoly supplier? One possibility is that these bureaucratic costs are minor in comparison to the benefits from scale economies. A second possibility is that Congress and the presidency really wanted it that way, but then there is no conflict between the bureaucracy and the legislature and consequently no bureaucratic failure. Niskanen also considered a variant of this latter case and suggested that bureaucracies be split up into competing parts.

12. See Neustadt (1980), who argues that skilled presidents will have secretaries of state and defense in opposition, so that each will present different sides of the story. Also see Breton and Wintrobe (1982).

other for budget dollars for different outputs (cross elasticities). The analogy to the consumer may be enlightening—everyone wants to sell you something (cars, food, exercise equipment), but does that mean that you buy too much of everything?[13]

There is also competition for managing the bureaucracy itself. Potential managers compete for the job not only in salaries but also by the quality of their performance and the extent of information they provide their principals. If they successfully reduce a small bureaucracy by 10 percent, perhaps they may be appointed to manage a bureaucracy twice as large.[14]

Alessi (1969) has argued that voters monitor the performance of politicians less than stockholders monitor the performance of firms because voters cannot capture the benefit of improved political performance. In turn, politicians will be less inclined to monitor their bureaucracies. Hence government bureaucrats and employees (via their unions) will have a greater incentive and opportunity to increase their own utility at the expense of their employers. In earlier chapters, I have argued against the first point. Here, for the sake of argument, assume that politicians are not controlled by the voters. This still does not mean that bureaucrats will have their way. If politicians have greater freedom to neglect the interests of the voters and to pursue their own objectives, why should they cede any of this freedom to the bureaucrats under them?[15] If politicians have greater discretion, bureaucratic behavior will reflect the preferences of politicians rather than those of the voters, not the preferences of bureaucrats rather than those of the politicians. While it is possible that politicians may use their discretion to pursue the quiet life, thereby leaving the bureaucracy to its own devices, the reverse is also quite possible. For example, politicians could fill the bureaucracy with their friends and encourage policies that erected barriers to the entrance of opposition parties. Real-world evidence suggests that political dictators, who have a great deal of discretionary power, do not cede their power to bureaucracies.

Even if I am wrong about the quality of information that legislatures have about bureaucracies, it is unreasonable to believe that bureaucrats

13. See McGuire, Coiner, and Spancake (1979).

14. The possibility of advancement has been pointed out by Breton and Wintrobe (1982); however, they argue that trust between members of the bureaucracy prevents such behavior.

15. This point has been made by Wintrobe (1987).

would extort their monopoly power in the form of excessive production. If bureaucrats are so capable of pulling the wool over their clients' eyes, why bother with making the firm too large? The share of the output that bureaucrats get from such a policy is certainly very slight. Couldn't they just persuade Congress, or whomever, that the bureaucracy could not function without them and that they therefore deserve twice as much pay? Furthermore, it is not clear that the heads of the bureaucracy benefit from lower-level bureaucrats' functioning in less than an optimal way, for then the rents that the head bureaucrats collect are of necessity much smaller. And competition for lower-level jobs within (and outside of) the bureaucracy keeps excesses by lower-level bureaucrats in check.[16]

We next turn our attention to the more detailed aspects of the Niskanen-type model.

The mathematical model that Niskanen used to demonstrate his thesis assumed that the legislature reveals an offer curve to the bureaucracy: For each level of output, Q, the legislature states the maximal budget, B, it is willing to provide. The bureaucrat then chooses that B, Q combination from the offer curve such that B is as large as possible given the constraint that the cost of providing Q is less than or equal to B (this cost function is known only to the bureau). Not surprisingly, this leads to larger budgets and outputs than would be the case if the legislature were provided information concerning the cost curves or if the legislature took a more active role in the process.[17]

Miller and Moe (1983) argue that such a characterization of the budgetary process is inappropriate. They develop a model that is virtually a mirror image of the Niskanen model. The bureau reveals an offer curve to the legislature: For each possible P, price per unit of output, the bureau states the Q that it will deliver. Miller and Moe assume that

16. See Posner (1974) and Tullock (1965), who have made the same point.

17. Chan and Mestelman (1988) argue that this is not overproduction because the utility of the bureaucracy is reduced if the budget is reduced. They also consider several other models that produce results on the contract curve.

Given my comments, a systematic survey of the empirical research on the budget-maximizing hypothesis is probably not productive. The reader may want to consult McGuire's survey (1981). He found little empirical support for the budget maximization hypothesis. His explanation for the lack of support is that most of the studies were concerned with local governments. More recently, Brueckner and O'Brien (1989) test the Niskanen model against the bureaucrat as perfect agent of the voter model by looking at collective bargaining outcomes for police, for firefighters, and for sanitation workers. Their results showed an absence of an effect of self-interest by bureaucrats. They also provide a short survey of recent work in the genre.

the bureaucrat does not know the legislature's demand curve and treats P as fixed. With a fixed P, the bureaucrat will choose the largest zero profit output ($B = P * Q = $ cost), thereby revealing the true cost. The legislature can then choose that budget which maximizes social welfare.

Both models employ extreme myopic behavior. In the Niskanen model, Congress submits an offer curve without anticipating that the bureaucrat will want to maximize the budget. The legislature has no Bayesian priors regarding cost curves and does not try to manipulate the bureaucrat's choice. In the Miller and Moe model, the bureaucrat treats P as given when it is not and therefore does not try to manipulate the legislature's choice.

In the latter part of their article, Miller and Moe consider the case where the price is not fixed and the bureau or Congress can consider any functional form linking budgets and outputs; the interaction between the bureaucracy and Congress is a two-sided game. In comparison to the pure Niskanen model, the ability of the bureaucracy to manipulate information is reduced but not eliminated.

However, even Miller and Moe's characterization gives too much autonomy to the bureaucracy. They have chosen the wrong economic analogy. Their analogy is to a consumer who is trying to elicit truthful information from a monopolist supplier of automobiles.[18] But certainly the degree of difficulty in obtaining the truth is considerably less if the owner of the automobile company is trying to get information about a car her firm has produced. This latter principal-agent model seems more appropriate than the monopoly/oligopoly model from industrial organization. The president and/or Congress has considerable control over the government bureaucracy.[19] Congress or the president, like any consumer, can discount the self-serving statements by bureaucrats, but, more important, they can direct bureaucrats to reveal information. (We will consider principal-agent models in the following section.)

More recently, Bendor, Taylor, and Van Gaalen (1985) consider the case where the bureaucrat has programmatic preferences and wants to

18. Even here, a true monopolist is likely to extort her monopoly position via higher prices rather than create needless uncertainty, which lowers demand from risk-averse consumers.

19. Some authors have argued that it is Congress in cahoots with the bureaucracies that make the bureaus too large. See Fiorina (1983) and Weingast and Moran (1983, 1986). In the previous chapters I have argued that Congress does not distort the interests of the people.

rig his superior's agenda to boost the odds that his preferred program will be selected. He does so by allocating more design time to his preferred program. But if their model is correct and even outsiders like Bendor, Taylor, and Van Gaalen know that the bureaucrats are manipulative, then surely the president and Congress should also be aware of this bureaucratic strategy (if not, someone should send them a copy of the Bendor et al. article). Hence the president or Congress should be able to infer the bureaucrat's preferences by the quality of the presentation and discount it. If this were a serious problem, Congress and/or the president might install an outside monitoring agency or have several agencies each design and be responsible for a single plan.[20]

Banks (1989) and Banks and Weingast (1992) have still another variant of the Niskanen model. They assume that the bureaucrat wants to maximize surplus between revenues received and costs. This assumption is more appealing than budget maximization since it means that the bureaucrats are trying to maximize rents in general, and the exact form (excessive salaries, staff, etc.) of these rents need not be specified. Their model once again assumes that the legislature's demand function is common knowledge, that the bureaucracy's cost function is known only to the bureaucracy, and that the bureaucrats present the legislature with an all-or-nothing-at-all choice. They complicate their model by allowing for triggered audits and potential competition, but they use the simplifying assumption that the good will be supplied at one level only. Not surprisingly, competition and audits move the outcome closer to the optimal. In their model, the move is not complete. However, if the good can be provided at more than one level, then a simple analysis employing supply-and-demand curves will show that the bureaucracy will always supply the optimal amount, and that when there is competition, all the bureaucratic rents will be competed away.

Assume that the legislature's demand curve is known to the bureaucracy and that the legislature's demand for the nth good is independent of the price paid for the previous goods. Further assume that the bureaucracy can offer a "supply" schedule (the first unit will be sold at price p1, the second unit will be sold at price p2, etc.) to the legislature and that the legislature must choose a point on the schedule (which includes

---

20. Bendor, Taylor, and Van Gaalen (1985) present several models in their paper. Their model 3 does incorporate monitoring. Such principal-agent models will be discussed in the section devoted to them.

the possibility of zero supply). The surplus-maximizing bureaucracy will choose a price schedule to exactly emulate the legislature's demand curve except within epsilon of the intersection of the bureaucracy's marginal cost curve and the legislature's demand curve.[21] There the supply schedule will be delta below the demand curve but still above the marginal-cost curve. The legislature will choose this point since it is gaining a surplus of epsilon, whereas elsewhere it is merely indifferent.[22] At the intersection, the bureaucracy has maximized surplus. It is the entire triangular area between the supply curve and demand curve. Note that by giving the bureaucracy more power (allowing the bureau to sell units at different prices), efficiency is gained.

Now suppose that there is competition between bureaus. If they have identical cost curves, the value of delta will equal the surplus triangle. That is, the legislature will capture all the surplus. If the cost curves are not identical, then the legislature will capture a surplus equal to the second-highest bureau's surplus. The bureau with the highest surplus will capture the difference in surplus between it and the second-highest surplus.

Note that if Congress truly does not know anything about the bureau's cost function, even to the extent of whether it is monotonic or continuous, then this revelation mechanism is cheat-proof in the following sense. In the next budgetary session, the legislature will play the game all over again. It has not gained any valuable information from the bureau that allows it to take advantage of the fact that the bureau has revealed the truth about the point of intersection. So this limited truth-telling by the bureau and the resulting efficient outcome will not be undermined by potential exploitation of the information by the legislature in future rounds.[23]

Niskanen's model is an elegant representative of an extensive, but less formal, literature on bureaucratic power. Since theories of power are popular alternatives to economic-efficiency explanations, it is useful to close this section with a brief discussion of the inherent limitations in such power explanations. The first question is whether bureaus have

---

21. Beyond the intersection, the schedule is either not defined or it follows the bureaucracy's cost schedule.

22. Actually, the schedule could be above the demand curve every place except at the intersection.

23. Surplus maximizing does not have the same problems as budget maximizing. See Mumy and Turnbull (1992).

any monopoly power to exploit. I have already argued that the position of the government bureaucracy as compared with Congress and the presidency is considerably weaker and less autonomous than the position of Coca-Cola vis-à-vis the unorganized consumer. Hence the basis for autonomous power may be missing. Even if we treat the bureaucracy as autonomous, the monopoly or oligopoly model may not be appropriate. While one can view the government bureaucracy as a monolithic organization, in reality there are numerous bureaus competing with each other and with institutions outside the government. More important, the people who staff these bureaucratic organizations have virtually no monopoly power. There are simply too many competitors for these positions. An extensive sociological literature has tried to build models of collusion. Collusion may arise by building professional norms or by informal agreements built up by members of the bureau.[24] But Congress and the president want to promote their own interests over the bureaucracy's and would create incentives to undermine such collusion. Hence, coalitions might arise between members of Congress and members of the bureaucracy that defeat pure bureaucratic coalitions. Furthermore, the ability to create a cartel on such a grand scale is highly questionable. Consider how difficult it has been for OPEC to exploit its potential monopoly power via cartel behavior. OPEC involves only a few sovereign countries (in comparison to the number of bureaus or bureaucrats); the main item on their agenda, to maximize profits, is a relatively simple goal compared to the type of agreements that might have to be made regarding bureaucratic collusion; and the agreements between OPEC members are legal and can be made public. If OPEC has problems maintaining cartel pricing, then bureaucrats should find it impossible to establish an informal cartel.

Even if bureaus had monopoly power, it would be highly unlikely that they would exploit it in the way envisioned by the proponents of the bureaucratic-power theory. Economic models of monopoly in the private sector predict that monopolist output will be too small, not too large. For similar reasons, one would expect monopolist bureaucrats to use their monopoly power to extort higher wages rather than squander it on excess production. Certainly, our knowledge of dictators

---

24. But then again, professional norms may be developed so that bureaucrats are more trustworthy and less likely to collude, thereby increasing the overall demand for bureaucrats.

shows that they use their monopoly power to garner great personal wealth.

Another problem with the theory of bureaucratic power is that the concept of an equilibrium is often missing. Even if bureaucrats have power, this does not explain bureaucratic growth or change. A powerful bureaucracy that wants to grow should have already expanded to its limits. Change in bureaucratic output then represents changes in power at the margin. Unfortunately, change in power is not typically measured directly, but rather by result. Thus the "evidence" is often true by definition and does not satisfy the requirements of a scientific test.

Finally, the evidence for bureaucratic power is often perfectly consistent with the theory that the bureau has no power. If researchers observe that Congress always accepts bureaucratic decisions, this need not mean that the bureau is powerful; it may just mean that the bureau has anticipated the desires of Congress. In order to disentangle these two possibilities, one should look at changes in congressional committees brought about by election turnovers. If bureaus are all-powerful, then differences in the makeup of Congress should have no effect on bureaucratic behavior. Weingast and Moran (1983) were able to demonstrate to the contrary. They showed how the Federal Trade Commission became more consumer oriented when more liberal members were elected to Congress.

Principal-Agent Models and Games Bureaucrats Don't Play

Niskanen-type models typically have optimizing behavior by the bureaucrat, but the behavior of the superior is often reduced to an exogenously given parameter rather than characterized as that of a strategic participant, while the rules of the game are exogenous and not designed to produce optimal outcomes. In this section, I consider games where both sides may act strategically, and where some of the rules of the game are endogenous and chosen to encourage Pareto efficiency. Congress (and/or the president) are viewed as having a much more decisive role than the bureaucracy. They are the principals, and the bureaucracy is the agent. They create rules, procedures, and contracts with the bureaucracy that are optimal.[25] Not surprisingly, this view undermines some of the more egregious results of the Niskanen-type models.

25. Applications of the principal-agent literature to bureaucracies include Weingast (1984); Bendor, Taylor, and Van Gaalen (1985, model 3); and Tirole (1986).

If the participants engage in maximizing behavior, it would be strange if the rules of the game were not, at a minimum, organized to produce Pareto optimal outcomes for the participants. The bureaucracy and its superiors have a long-term relationship, and transaction costs are relatively low. Rules that produce inefficient transfers should have been replaced by those that produce more efficient transfers. Even if the system is not in perfect equilibrium, there should be no obvious biases in any one direction, since obvious biases should be accounted for by the participants.

A natural objection to my thesis is that numerous game theory representations of congressional-bureaucratic relations (including some principal-agent models) yield inefficient-equilibrium outcomes. My counterarguments are that these games do not accurately represent the situation: (1) the payoff matrices can be altered, (2) the actual interactions are often cooperative rather than noncooperative, and (3) the metagame of choosing a game is likely to reduce the inefficiencies to lower levels.

I illustrate with game theory's most famous example, the prisoners' dilemma, where the dominant strategy is for each prisoner to squeal even though both would be better off if neither did. From the viewpoint of this book, the most interesting aspect of this game is not that the prisoners have chosen a suboptimal equilibrium from their perspective, but rather that the district attorney has devised an institutional arrangement to make each criminal squeal, thereby overcoming the problem of asymmetric information. So while the predominant focus of the game theory literature has been on how to resolve the prisoners' dilemma (via different strategy concepts, viewing the game as infinitely repeated, etc.), our focus, here, is on how the principal structures the game to achieve his/her own ends.

Now the key to the prisoners' dilemma is that there should be gains from trade, but this does not take place because contracts between the criminals are not enforceable by a third party. Of course, in real life, one prisoner might have his friends kill the other prisoner for squealing. In other words, it is in the interest of the prisoners to alter the game from one form to another. But the gains from trade are not all in the hands of the prisoners. The DA and one of the prisoners may gain by making an agreement with each other. Thus, in serious cases, the criminal may be given a new identity if he testifies against his former cronies.

The focus has shifted, not only within game theory, but also on a deeper level. One could say that criminals (politicians or bureaucrats) will lie and cheat and hence truth is impossible. But where does this get us? The more interesting question is how the criminal justice (political or bureaucratic) system is organized in order to obtain as much truth as possible. In its most abstract form, this is the field of optimal mechanism design. While there may not always be a truthfully implementable mechanism or even an implementable (albeit untruthful) mechanism, the focus is shifted to the design of such mechanisms.[26]

Getting back to Congress, the presidency, and the bureaucracy, one might use a prisoners' dilemma model to characterize their interaction (see Miller 1977 for an example). But this means that there are gains to trade. Before accepting such a model, one should ask why the parties did not enter into a more cooperative binding agreement or design an incentive structure that did not lead to the dilemma. Perhaps the costs of doing so outweigh the gains; perhaps there are no credible commitments. But the thrust of the argument here is that one should ask how the participants could change the payoff matrix so that the game is no longer a prisoners' dilemma or how they could make credible commitments. Then look at the real world and see if these institutions exist. My priors are that we will observe such institutions.

Congressional-bureaucratic relations are typically characterized as a one-shot game. But Congress and the bureaucracy have an ongoing relationship. Even prisoners' dilemma games may yield optimal outcomes if there is an infinitely repeated sequence and the player's time discount is not too great.[27] More relevant for our argument is that an ongoing relationship undermines much of the canonical characterization of the principal-agent problem. The standard representation is that the principal can observe outcomes but cannot disentangle the separate effects of the environment and the agent's effort. But in a repeated game, the principal could rely on the law of large numbers and estimate the mean state of the world facing the agent and thus infer the agent's behavior.[28] The canonical problem of asymmetric information becomes smaller as the game is repeated. Of even greater impact is the fact that

26. See Green and Laffont (1979) for an example.

27. There may also be multiple equilibria; see Fudenberg and Maskin (1986).

28. Bureaucrats may work as a team. Hence it may be hard to infer individual contributions even in repeat play. However, the superior should be able to judge the team as a whole in repeat play.

an ongoing relationship allows the principal to devise a series of different games, where each game played is conditional on the outcome of the previous game if it yields better payoffs than the simple repeated game.

The principal-agent problem also occurs in private markets, even in private markets where no bureaucracy is involved. For example, individuals are uninformed about their lawyers, managers are unaware of workers shirking, and individuals cannot judge the durability of an appliance. In the private market, numerous institutions arise to mitigate possible problems. For example, the risk is shifted onto the potential shirker by making him the residual claimant, workers are given above-market wages with the threat of being fired if performance is not satisfactory, and department stores establish reputations so that one can rely on the store even if one does not know anything about the particular item it sells.[29] In a similar fashion, Congress and the presidency can provide optimal contracts for bureaucrats and develop different organizational forms that reduce the potential for opportunism.[30] Vertically integrating bureaucracies reduces the opportunism that might arise between bureaus if there were horizontal integration; making the head of the bureaucracy a political rather than a civil service appointment insures proper direction; and monitoring by OMB, the Government Accounting Office, and various congressional oversight committees reduces the potential for opportunism (these will be covered in greater detail in the next section).

Although civil service has been characterized as a method of creating monopoly power for slothful career bureaucrats, the historical explana-

29. If the agent is risk averse and shirks, there may be no contract, which makes both the agent and the principal as well off as they would be if monitoring of the agent were costless or the agent did not shirk. But such a situation is, alas, impossible.

30. Lindsay (1976) argues that Congress only rewards things that it can measure and that somehow Congress is not able to measure things like delay and rudeness of bureaucrats. Therefore, bureaucrats are rude and make people wait. But clearly this measurement problem is no more serious for government than for business. Furthermore, one could have a measure of waiting time (e.g., a sample survey of patients' waiting time, or a test of lengths of lines), and both business and government bureaucracies could measure the overall decrease in consumer demand. In addition, it is not clear that bureaucrats are uninterested in directly satisfying their customers, since their customers may create the political pressure for expansion of the bureaucracy. Finally, to the degree that waiting time in lines is longer for government bureaucracies, this may just reflect the fact that they cater to lower-income people (including charity cases), whose shadow price of time is lower.

tion is that it was a method of reducing opportunism by politicians, especially the executive branch. This enabled the development of a professional class of bureaucrats whose livelihood was not subjected to the caprice of changing electoral majorities. Civil service is part of the optimal contract passed by Congress and is designed to make their commitments to bureaucrats credible.

I will now argue that there is even a stronger result: the rules are not only Pareto optimal but also keep bureaucrats at their competitive wage. That is, bureaucrats have no rents to exploit. Congress and the president have considerable control over the rules of the game they set out for bureaucrats. Pay scales and rules for bureaucrats are determined by competitive market mechanisms. It would be hard to argue that the supply curve of potential bureaucrats is vertical and that they can determine how much rent they collect. Congress need not pay above-market wages either explicitly through excessive salaries or implicitly by excessive perquisites, such as large budgets.

The preferences of bureaucrats may differ from those of their superiors. Even when their preferences are met, however, this does not imply an inefficient outcome. Consider the case where government bureaucrats like thick rugs.[31] Like other job characteristics, amenities are paid for by the employee; in this example, those bureaucrats who work in offices with thick rugs will receive lower salaries. If government bureaucrats truly prefer thick rugs, then it is not inefficient to provide them. This analysis can also be used in determining an upper bound on budget excess. First note that amenities are substituted for salaries only when the benefit of the amenity to the bureaucrat (and to Congress when Congress gets value from the amenity also) is greater than the benefit to the bureaucrat from an increase in salary equivalent to the cost of the amenity. That is, the total budget is less when the amenities are provided than when they are not (if Congress does not value the amenity). It is hard to believe that many bureau heads would prefer a budget increase of $5 million over a salary increase of $50,000 (possibly in terms of expected promotion), let alone $5 million. For all but cabinet level posts, budgetary excess is unlikely to be of the magnitude envisioned by the bureaucracy's detractors.

---

31. I am not aware of any empirical studies that show that government offices have thicker rugs than private firms.

I have argued that the principle-agent problem of bureaucracies has been greatly exaggerated since there are numerous methods of reducing the potential for opportunism. However, not all methods of reducing opportunism are costless, and some opportunism remains; but this still does not mean that bureaucracies are inefficient. If it is truly impossible to find any alternative structure that is more technically efficient because individuals lie and shirk and monitoring is costly or because any structure has inherent problems of coordination, then the bureaucratic form is, in fact, efficient. It is inappropriate to assume away the costs of shirking if there is no economically superior solution, just as it would be inappropriate to assume away the shirking by draft animals in doing farmwork. And even if other forms of organization have higher-powered incentives and less opportunism than government bureaucracies, government bureaucracies are still efficient if these costs are less than the benefits (such as economies of scale) accruing from the bureaucratic form.

Furthermore, the existence of principle-agent problems does not imply that the agency will be too large. Asymmetric information and inability to monitor opportunism does not imply that principals on average underestimate the opportunism by their agents or overestimate the quality of services provided. Rather, principals are likely to have unbiased estimates of the degree of opportunism by their agents. Some principals will underestimate the degree of opportunism by agents, but this is likely to be balanced by others who overestimate the degree of opportunism.

More important, the potential for opportunism creates a tendency for bureaucracies to be smaller than they would be otherwise, not larger. When an agent engages in opportunistic behavior, the marginal value of the output per dollar spent on the input is less than it would be otherwise. In such a situation, the demanders of the input are likely to substitute away. If workers shirk, the response may not be to employ more workers but fewer workers and more machines. And since the production of this good is now more expensive than it would be in the absence of opportunism, the demand for the product or service may also be reduced if there are substitutes. Indeed, if the shirking or moral hazard is sufficiently severe, the market for the good or service may fail altogether. Thus the potential for opportunistic behavior by a bureaucracy may encourage the executive branch to substitute outside contractors or to reduce the overall demand for the kinds of services the bureaucracy provides. The same holds true when we look at representatives as agents for voters. If voters can only monitor the extent of expenditures but not their content, and if their agents choose inefficient allocations, then voters may vote for lower levels of government expenditures than otherwise by substituting private for public expenditures.[32] Arguments that governments and bureaucracies are too large fail again.

Finally, much of the empirical evidence for bureaucratic failure is flawed on methodological grounds. Many models of bureaucratic failure rely on the inability of the principal to monitor the bureaucracy. If the principal cannot observe the agent, then the researcher cannot either; conversely, if the researcher can observe empire building by government bureaucrats, then the principal can also. And since we are looking at long-term relationships with credible commitments, the principal could correct for such problems. For an example of measuring the agent's behavior, consider the work by Staaf (1977). Staaf shows empirically that the larger the school district, the greater the bureaucratic fat. But if this observation were truly the result of opportunistic behavior, then voters and politicians in large school districts could make use of this cross section study (or make their own) and reduce either the salaries of administrators or the size of the administrations. Measuring this type of opportunism involves an internal contradiction. When recontracting is possible, the potential for shirking is best measured indirectly, by observing changes in the institutional structure (e.g., smaller school districts than would otherwise be the case), or by failure of the market to exist at all, not by directly measuring the supposed opportunistic behavior.

To summarize: Characterizing the relationship between Congress and the bureaucracy as a principal-agent problem yields a more optimistic view of bureaucratic behavior than characterizing the relationship as a game where the rules are exogenously determined by nature. Even in principal-agent models, problems may arise—commitments might not be credible, or performance bonds might not be possible. I have argued that these problems have been exaggerated. They are not unique to bureaucracy, and political institutions have been designed to correct for them. Finally, I have shown that others have derived incorrect conclusions from any agency costs that remain.

32. The fact that the voters have not consistently voted for the candidate promising (or demonstrating a commitment to) lower government expenditures suggests that government expenditures are not too large.

A COMPARATIVE STATIC ANALYSIS OF THE OVERSIGHT FUNCTION

So far the emphasis has been on why we might expect optimizing bureaucratic behavior. We now turn our attention to the design of the government bureaucracy and present a series of comparative statics results.[33]

Prior Regulation versus Post Liability

Insight into the control of government bureaucracies can be gained by considering control in other areas. Automobile accidents are controlled both by regulation of the inputs (drivers are licensed, speeders are fined) and by liability for the output (reckless drivers pay for the damage). The choice between prior and post depends upon the relative costs of monitoring and the relative capacity of the incentive structure to internalize costs. Some drivers may be judgment-proof because they have limited wealth. Imprisonment as a substitute for a fine imposes costs not only on the individual punished but also on society (guards cost money). Once again, the full costs do not fall onto the individual driver. Because of this possibility of limited liability for accidents, the system fines people for inappropriate inputs (for example, speeding) even when there is no accident.

Bureaucrats can be punished for poor performance by forfeiting raises or by receiving reduced allocations to their departments. Both methods impose only limited liability on the bureaucrat. When Congress desires high bureaucratic output, cutting budgets is very costly, and the method of control will shift to input monitoring and directives detailing both the scope of the bureaucratic activity and the procedures used in the bureau (see McCubbins and Page 1987; Calvert, McCubbins, and Weingast 1989).

For similar reasons, the more difficult it is to fire a person, the more oversight there will be. Conversely, the more Congress controls the choice of personnel through the confirmation process, the less it need control actual implementation of policy.

---

33. Note that the rationale for these results differs substantially from the explanations provided by McCubbins and Page (1987) and Fiorina (1985). Their models assume that legislators delegate more power to the bureaucracy in order to shift the blame for the costs of regulation onto the bureau. Fiorina views administrators as mechanisms that add political daylight between the legislators and those who feel the incidence of legislative actions, while McCubbins and Page argue that delegation allows the "legislator [to] claim credit for addressing an important policy problem and at the same time shirk any blame for making hard policy choices" (417). Elsewhere in this book I have argued that voters and the clients of the bureaucracy are not fooled by such tricks.

Previous History

Previous problems with bureaucratic deviations from congressional intent will result in greater control by Congress. Instituting a special oversight committee, limiting appropriations, and reducing the scope of bureaucratic discretion are some of the possible methods of altering a wayward bureaucracy's behavior (see Scher 1963; Sharkansky 1968).

On the other side of the coin, the greater the historical congruence between the cabinet head and the congressional committee, the less oversight will be instituted. Congress may also choose to delegate legislative power to bureaucracies when serious differences between the two are unlikely.

The Role of the Constituents

McCubbins and Schwartz (1984) discuss two methods of control: "police patrols" and "fire alarms." The former method relies on constant oversight by Congress; the latter relies on the constituents to inform Congress of any deviation from congressional intent.

When bureaucracies can be monitored by their constituents and where the constituents' interest is in agreement with Congress, bureaucracies will need less direct oversight. In fact, Congress can decide which constituents will pull the fire alarms by determining which constituents have standing. Furthermore, Congress may reduce the cost of oversight to a particular constituency by allocating the costs elsewhere. For example, in the private sector, the Environmental Protection Agency requires the firm, and not the potential victims, to pay for environmental impact reports. Where services are provided at different prices to groups with different incomes, quality may be measured by monitoring the demand by fee-paying servers rather than directly (Rose-Ackerman 1990).

Congress can influence policy outcomes just by its choice of methods for delegating power. For example, the Office of Safety and Health Administration allowed each state to choose whether to let OSHA enforce OSHA regulations or to do so itself. This allowed each state to determine its level of enforcement, although states were required to adopt consensus standards (Moe 1989a).

Political Importance of the Bureau

The larger the budget of the bureaucracy or the more important the decision, the more oversight there will be. For example, Executive Order

12291 (46 *Federal Register* 131937) requires that executive branch agencies submit proposed major rules (defined as those having a projected economic impact in excess of $100 million per year) to OMB's Office of Information and Regulatory Affairs sixty days before the publication of notice in the *Federal Register;* while nonmajor rules require only ten days notice (see Cooper and West 1988). Although some proposals are not reviewed and those cases reviewed are typically accepted, the threat of review is often enough to make agencies comply. Similarly, the more politically salient the issues are, the more oversight there will be.[34]

Degree of Competitiveness

Breton and Wintrobe (1982) and Tirole (1986) model collusion within the bureaucracy. Collusion would most likely arise in a bureaucracy with little turnover. The greater the potential for collusion, the greater the likelihood of implementing a system of competition between the bureaucracies.

The more external competition for bureaucratic supply, the less oversight required. Each of the competitive bureaus will argue its best case against the other. Competition between the armed services is an obvious example of the use of competitive bureaus. Another important example is the competition between state and federal bureaucracies; a less obvious example is the competition between Commerce and the Treasury (see Bendor 1985).

External Effects

Bureaus are typically designed to deal with special missions (for example, the Federal Power Commission, the Civil Aeronautics Board, the Highway Transportation Department). But it is impossible to completely compartmentalize their effects. When there is a potential for large external effects, the agencies' control over the decision will be more limited. For example, Stewart (1977) noted that courts were less likely to defer to the above-mentioned agencies when their decisions might have a serious environmental impact because these agencies were not set up to protect the environment.

---

34. This runs counter to the arguments by McCubbins and Page (1987) and Fiorina (1985). See the previous note.

THE PRESIDENT, CONGRESS, AND THE BUREAUCRACY

So far the analysis has not taken into account the fact that the bureaucracy has at least two principals: Congress (which is composed of various coalitions) and the president. In this section I will consider some of the issues that arise when an agent has two or more masters.

Hill (1985), Hammond, Hill, and Miller (1986), and McCubbins, Noll, and Weingast (1990) have all considered the possibility that the bureaucracy can take advantage of disagreements between the legislature and the executive or among the legislators themselves.

McCubbins, Noll, and Weingast (1989) consider the following model: Congress passes legislation requiring the bureaucracy to behave in a particular way. The bureaucracy chooses to behave in a different way that is somewhat preferred by the president and greatly preferred by the members of the bureaucracy. Hence, Congress will be unable to create a new coalition with the presidency to override the bureaucracy and restore its original intent. Once again, rational expectations come to the rescue. In a sequential game (which most of these papers model), Congress should be able to determine by backward induction the final outcome for each policy decision and then choose the best alternative. When Congress is the first mover, which is the case when it creates an agency and/or policy, it sets the agenda. In general, this should give Congress a considerable influence over the outcome (with and without the existence of intransitivity).[35] But suppose the sequence somehow works to Congress's disadvantage. Congress can always alter the sequence. Congress can budget and appropriate, delegate fully, or have a review.

When Congress and the president jointly decide on policy, they should be able to anticipate the bureaucracy's attempts to distort policy. Congress and the president will create an agreement between them insuring that the intended outcome is the actual outcome. An important method is to choose an agency head acceptable to both Congress and the president. The confirmation process is designed to achieve this

---

35. Congress itself may not have a stable majority preference; that is, there may not be a median senator or a unique winning coalition. In such circumstances, it really does not make much sense to say that the bureaucracy goes against the wishes of Congress if a majority of its members will not overrule the bureaucracy. Because then a majority of Congress agrees with the behavior of the bureau, even though its behavior deviates from the original legislation. If when designing the original legislation Congress anticipates all this, then the actual outcome would be the original intent of Congress.

end.[36] And if this process is imperfect and the agent's preferences are not completely known, then other methods might be instituted. These include more detailed directives for the bureaucracy and the threat of reduced appropriations.[37] Even if bureaucrats undertake discretionary action contrary to the wishes of their principals, they are on average unbiased from the expected preference determined by the confirmation hearings and the bargain between the president and the Congress. In particular, bureaucrats would not, on average, be more interested in bureaucratic growth than Congress and the presidency.

Ferejohn and Shipan (1990) consider a sequential model with five actors: Congress; a congressional committee, possibly composed of preference outliers; the president; a judiciary; and an agency.[38] In their model there is perfect foresight, and the bureau moves first, then the courts, the congressional committee, Congress, the president, and, if there is a veto, Congress again. Not surprisingly, there are first-mover advantages accruing to the bureaucracy. The agency can distort policy toward its own interest, especially so if Congress and its committee are in disagreement. But the following questions naturally arise. Why did Congress delegate its statutory decision making to the bureaucracy in the first place, knowing that the agency would distort its goals? That is, why isn't Congress the first mover? And why would Congress create committees composed of preference outliers? I have argued that Congress would delegate and give first-mover advantage to the bureaucracy only if it knew that the bureau would not take advantage of such a move, perhaps because the bureaucrats have preferences close to that of the median member of Congress. As McCubbins, Noll, and Weingast (1990) note, elected officials do not like uncertainty, nor do they like to give too much power to a bureaucracy they do not control.

36. Many have argued that the Senate's ability to confirm is unimportant because it is often perfunctory and virtually all nominations are approved. However, a wise president anticipates the reactions by the Senate and hence nominates people who have a high probability of succeeding. Some evidence for this can be found by comparing the nominee to the previously defeated nominee. They are rarely similar. For example, President Reagan did not nominate anyone resembling Bork after Bork was defeated, even though persons similar to Bork had been high on his earlier lists.

See Calvert, McCubbins, and Weingast (1989), who have a model of bureaucratic choice consistent with legislative intent when there is a confirmation process.

37. See Fiorina (1985), who discusses at length the concerns expressed by congressmen regarding the implementation of the Interstate Commerce Act of 1887.

38. See Spitzer (1990) for a variation on their model.

SELF-INTEREST AND SOCIAL WELFARE

Those who rail against bureaucracy argue that bureaucrats are interested in their own welfare rather than some other goal, such as the public good. But the fact that bureaucrats are interested in promoting their own welfare no more proves political-market failure than the self-interest of businessmen proves economic-market failure. Of course bureaucrats, if they are collecting any rents, will promote the continuation and survival of the bureaucracy, just as businessmen tend to do. There is nothing special about bureaucracies trying to perpetuate themselves, but they will be able to do so only if they satisfy their demanders. Thus the fact that bureaus change and grow should not be viewed as some kind of aggrandizement. Indeed, their survival and change indicates that they have been serving their customers very well.

9

THE MARKET FOR REGULATION

In this chapter, I consider regulation. I focus on zoning because it involves local politics, an area not considered in earlier chapters, but an important, if nonglamorous, topic in American politics. Zoning sometimes is used as a prime example of political-market failure, embodying all the evils of legislative and regulatory bodies. I want to prove my point by defending the hypothesis of an efficient political market where it may be weakest.

Once again the models of political failure are contradictory. Some people view (exclusionary) zoning as a method used by the majority to shift the costs of urban amenities onto the few developers and future residents who have no vote (Ellickson 1977; White 1979). Other people view zoning as a method for the minority to take advantage of the majority. Their argument proceeds along the following lines: The costs of development are spread among the whole community, while the benefits accrue to developers and the few holders of vacant land. Diffuse householders will not enter the political arena because the benefit to any individual homeowner in so doing is small. In contrast, developers have concentrated interests and lower organizational costs, so they will be more successful in twisting democratic politics to their own ends.[1]

Other arguments against zoning are based, not on the failure of the political process, but on the problems with zoning per se: a zoning board may be incompetent to handle complex issues, and zoning regulations themselves may be inferior to a system of property rights or liability rules (a court-administered price system).

---

1. I have criticized the theoretical foundations of this argument in chapter 7.

ZONING BOARDS VERSUS JUDGES

The main thrust of the literature in economic analysis of the law is that judge-made law is efficient, while legislative regulation is woefully inept and subject to rent seeking.[2] In this section, I demonstrate that zoning is likely to be as efficient as the common law.

Judges and zoning boards (or city councils when they make zoning decisions) are either elected by the median voter or appointed by a person who is elected by the median voter. Thus, median-voter models do not provide us with any theory to explain the relative inefficiency of zoning boards vis-à-vis judges. And since appellate courts can rule various zoning decisions invalid, we would need a theory that explains why appellate courts allow inefficient behavior in one area but not the other. The gradual shift from nuisance law to zoning regulation in the twentieth century may indicate that courts and legislatures recognize that zoning boards are a more appropriate venue for resolving nuisances than the courts. Courts are designed to handle conflicts between two parties, but zoning involves a much more complex interplay of actors.

Rent seekers will use the courts as much as they use other political arenas. We have no theory to explain why diffuse and disorganized interests will do better in the courtroom than in front of the city council or zoning board. Indeed, in the absence of a class action suit, the unorganized are unlikely to be represented in the courtroom. Developers, however, with their organized and concentrated interests, may employ expensive lawyers to argue in front of either a city council or a judge.[3]

Now it may not be worthwhile for unorganized voters to come down to city hall and argue their case against developers because the transaction costs are just too high. But the city council knows this too, and they can estimate the extent of the voters' dissatisfaction, which will be expressed on election day, and make their decisions with this dissatisfaction in mind. Thus, the political advantage of concentrated interests may be more apparent than real. (For further arguments against the theory of concentrated interests, see chapter 7).

While numerous articles have attempted to account for the invisible

---

2. The majority of articles in the *Journal of Legal Studies* find the common law to be efficient; while virtually all of the articles on regulation in the *Journal of Law and Economics* find the legislative law to be inefficient. Rubin (1982) is a counterexample. He argues that in the twentieth century both common law and statute law are inefficient.

3. It can be shown that particular sets of liability rules create the same rents as zoning.

hand in the court system, their arguments have been quite weak. To the extent that these arguments are valid, almost all of them apply equally well to zoning. For example, Posner (1986) argues that court decisions are efficient because judges fear being overridden; but this assumes either that they will be overridden by the legislature if inefficient (implying that the legislature promotes efficient laws) or by a higher court. In the latter case, we would then have to explain why Supreme Court justices are interested in efficiency. One possible explanation is that presidents want to promote efficiency and therefore select justices who have shown a commitment to such a goal. If such arguments are persuasive, then the analogous argument for zoning should not be too hard to swallow. To wit: zoning board members choose efficient regulations in order to be reappointed and to avoid having their decisions overridden by city councils and courts. As another example, Rubin (1977) and Priest (1977) argue that efficient laws survive because they are less prone to litigation. By definition, the cost that a wealth-maximizing law imposes is less than the benefit it brings. Therefore, other things being equal, pressure for change is the least when laws are efficient. A similar logic would suggest that efficient zoning regulations survive because they, too, are less prone to challenge.

Competition disciplines zoning boards at least as strongly as markets discipline judges.[4] Even if the zoning authority had goals besides efficient solutions to externalities, the zoning authority would be forced to be efficient (within its borders) if the community were in a competitive land market (see Tiebout 1956).[5]

Zoning boards are likely to have the wherewithal to handle the complex problems of urban spatial design. They are capable of creating implicit trading of property rights, thereby encouraging efficient outcomes. For example, zoning agencies may sell off rights to low-density zoning if a developer pays a high licensing fee or agrees to other stipula-

4. In this section, I have argued that the cases for the efficiency of the common law and the efficiency of regulatory law are likely to stand or fall together. While I have suggested that this will lead to a new approach to politics, those who are more skeptical of the efficiency argument may believe that it will lead to a new approach to the common law.

5. Romano (1987) has shown that corporation law is efficient because states compete for corporate charters. While the location of the articles of incorporation is more mobile than housing, one would still have to ask why cities would not compete by providing better zoning laws. For recent work on Tiebout models, see Scotchmer (1994).

tions when the outcome is Pareto superior (for a more detailed discussion, see chapter 11). The expertise of the board regarding issues of zoning is likely to be greater than the judge's expertise in nuisance law. Furthermore, the information requirements for zoning are no more difficult than the information requirements for liability rules and property rights. In deciding whether an activity is a nuisance (inefficient), courts must estimate the optimum; similarly, in deciding whether zoning requirements should prohibit an activity, zoning boards must determine the optimum.

ALTERNATIVES TO ZONING

A number of authors claim that there are more efficient methods of control than zoning regulations. In this section, I counter each of their arguments in turn.

Ellickson has argued in favor of restrictive covenants. "When a developer drafts covenants that will bind people who move into his subdivision, market forces prompt him to draft efficient ones" (1973, 80). To provide flexibility for changing situations, covenants can be altered by a majority (or supermajority). This is virtually a zoning board, except with direct democracy rather than representative government. Unfortunately, restrictive covenants require that ownership initially be in one large landholding. Clearly, public governments and zoning boards are substitutes for private governments when there are no large landholdings and the transaction costs of merger are prohibitive. Zoning boards are also more appropriate for handling diverse interests (residential and commercial) than are homeowner associations.

Siegan (1972) has argued that zoning is unnecessary to accomplish the goal of reducing pollution because the market itself spatially separates incompatible land uses. A system of no zoning, with no taxes on polluters and no liability rules giving rights to "pollutees," in effect confers a property right on polluters.

In the absence of zoning or any other corrective system for nuisances, the unregulated market generally keeps pollutees out of areas already dominated by polluters when separation is the socially optimal solution. However, in the opposite case—keeping polluters out of areas already dominated by pollutees—the unregulated market performs suboptimally. Unless land values are too high, polluters may move into an area already occupied by pollutees and may possibly force the pollutees

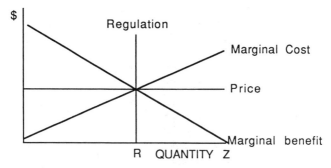

FIG. 9.1. With perfect information, regulation and pollution taxes yield identical outcomes.

to move, since polluters need not take into account the cost of pollution damage and abatement that they impose on pollutees.

In addition, spatial separation may not be optimal. Typically, there are conglomeration effects that make it efficient for both polluters and pollutees to locate near each other. Cities have residences, factories, and sewage disposal plants located in close proximity to save on transportation costs. In such cases, we want the polluter to abate pollution to the optimal level. Siegan's property-right solution will not accomplish this.

Because there are many pollutees, free-rider problems prevent them from paying the polluter not to pollute even when zero pollution is optimal. All the residents may benefit when a polluting factory moves out of the area, but each prefers that the other residents pay the bribe. In other words, the market has high transaction costs. A political organization, a zoning board, is created to reduce transaction costs because it is a better arena than the market for registering relative value.

Still another suggestion is a pollution tax. However, there is no reason this system is any better than a regulation. Consider the standard diagram (fig. 9.1) of marginal cost of pollution and marginal benefit from pollution (greater profit from higher industrial output). The vertical axis is price, the horizontal axis quantity. A pollution tax (price system) is the horizontal line; a regulation is the vertical line.[6] If neither a regulation nor a pollution tax is implemented, then the firm will produce until marginal profit (equivalently, marginal benefit) is zero, point Z. If there is perfect information, then either a regulation or a pollution tax will achieve the same output. Under a regulation, the firm will be constrained

6. If a regulation is enforced with fines, then it looks more like a price system.

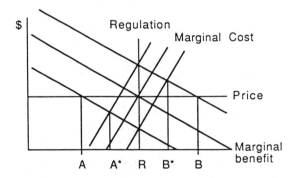

FIG. 9.2. Regulation is preferred to a pollution tax when the government has less information about the marginal benefit curve than the marginal cost curve or when the marginal benefit curve is more elastic than the marginal cost curve.

to producing no more than the optimal amount, R, where marginal pollution benefit equals marginal pollution cost. If the firm faces a pollution tax, it will continue to produce until R, where the marginal benefit from pollution equals the marginal tax from pollution.

If there is imperfect information (that is, regulatory agencies are uncertain about the intercept of one or both of the curves), then the two methods achieve different results, but, in general, there is no bias in favor of a price system over a regulatory system. The appropriate method depends on the relative elasticities of the two curves and the relative sizes of error. In figure 9.2, the expected cost and benefit curves are the middle lines. Half the time the actual benefit curve is below the expected benefit curve, and half the time above. The actual benefit curve is known by the polluter but unknown to the government agency, which knows only the expected marginal cost and benefit curves. Under a price system, the polluter equates actual marginal benefit with the price she pays for pollution. The levels of output are A and B under a price system and R under regulation, while 25 percent of the time the optimal level is A* (when marginal benefit is low and marginal cost is high), 50 percent of the time the optimal level is R (when the marginal benefit and cost curves are either both high or both low), and 25 percent of the time the optimal level is B* (when marginal benefit is high and marginal cost is low). In figure 9.2, A* is halfway between A and R, and B* is halfway between R and B. Thus 50 percent of the time regulation and pollution taxes have equivalent deadweight losses. But 50 percent of the time R is optimal. In this circumstance, regulation yields an optimal result, but pollution taxes produce deadweight losses. So in the example in figure 9.2, regulation is superior to a pollution tax.

COMPARATIVE ADVANTAGE

In this chapter, I have tried to shift the focus from the evils of regulation to the comparative advantage of various institutional arrangements. Clearly, zoning is more appropriately done at the local than the national level. More subtly, I have argued that the common law is not as effective as zoning boards in handling complex spatial interactions. Courts have devised rules, such as standing (which limits plaintiffs to those with significant interests), to facilitate the resolution of two-sided conflicts. Other institutional arrangements are needed for planning cities. Regulation by the government is a substitute for regulation within the market. Again the method chosen reflects comparative advantage. Restrictive covenants work better when the land use is relatively homogeneous and the initial landholdings are large scale. This does not describe urban areas, and thus zoning rather than restrictive covenants is most commonly employed in cities.

10

THE CONSTITUTION AS AN OPTIMAL SOCIAL CONTRACT AND THE ROLE OF TRANSACTION COSTS IN CONSTITUTIONAL DESIGN

The Federalist Papers IS THE PREMIER DOCUMENT in applied political philosophy. By arguing that the provisions of the proposed U.S. Constitution were superior to the alternatives, the authors of *The Federalist Papers* implicitly demonstrated that the Constitution was the optimal social contract for the citizens of the thirteen states. In this chapter, I provide an economic analysis of *The Federalist Papers* and of the Constitution as interpreted by the Supreme Court. I show that those who created and interpreted the Constitution tried to design a set of efficient political institutions.

The concept of transaction cost is integral to our understanding of institutional design. I demonstrate how low transaction costs obscure the separation of powers and, at times, the constitutional separation of power. I also demonstrate the converse—how high transaction costs make certain institutional differences, not merely apparent, but real.

There are both historical and substantive reasons why economic efficiency might provide an especially cogent explanation for constitutional design. The same intellectual currents that influenced political philosophy and led to the American revolution also led to Adam Smith's *Wealth of Nations* in 1776. Within economics itself, there has been a long and abiding interest in the design of efficient institutions and optimal contracts.

Economics provides a strong theoretical framework for understanding the Constitution and a methodological basis for the scientific testing of hypotheses regarding constitutional design. In contrast to the practicing lawyer who searches for exceptions, economic methodology searches for tendencies and similarities. Just as it would be wrong to argue that higher prices do not lead to reduced demand because a few consumers responded in the contrary direction, it would be inappropriate to dismiss the efficiency explanation of constitutional design because there are a few exceptions to the rule.

This chapter is composed of four major sections. First, I show how the notion of transaction costs gives new insight into the concept of separation of powers and how the Federalists made intuitive use of this notion. This section, of necessity, provides a broad sweep over a subset of issues. In the next section, I discuss federalism and show how the minimization of transaction costs explains the legal relations among the states. In the third section, I investigate the takings clause in detail. I claim that the Supreme Court's decisions regarding compensation can be explained by society's need to economize on transaction costs. Finally I contrast my economic efficiency explanation with Beard's "economic" analysis of the Constitution. His explanation for certain constitutional provisions is that they distributed wealth to particular groups. I demonstrate that many of his examples are efficiency enhancing rather than distributive.

THE FEDERALIST PAPERS AND TRANSACTION COSTS

Both the federal and state constitutions of the United States have clearly defined separation of powers. The president is to be the chief executive, the Congress is to legislate, and the Supreme Court is to judge. This separation of powers is carried out in similar, although not identical, ways in other countries, even those without written constitutions. In the following two subsections, I will demonstrate that separation of powers occasionally has no practical effect and what is promoted is separation of power, rather than separation of powers.

Separation of Powers Having No Effect

The U.S. Constitution (art. 1, sec. 7) mandates that all revenue bills be initiated by the House of Representatives; then, in order to become law, the revenue bill must also be passed by the Senate. It thus makes little difference who initiates the bill, as both houses must agree. Under the present constitutional framework, the Senate might inform the House of its preferences before any bill is formulated, or else it might reject a bill that does not meet its preference. This is a telling example of the law being transacted around when there is an ongoing contractual relationship. Madison was aware of this, as can be seen from the following excerpts from his Constitutional Convention notes: "Experience proved that it [the exclusive privilege of originating money bills] had no effect. . . . If both branches were to say yes or no, it was of little consequence which should say yes or no first, which last."[1]

The principal counterargument to Madison's reasoning is that the agenda setter often has considerable control over the outcome in a sequential game. Even if the Senate can reject a bill and compel the House to sponsor a new one, the House will have additional power whenever delaying legislation becomes costly.[2]

Political Parties and Coalitions

> Ambition must be made to counter ambition.
>
> *Madison,* The Federalist Papers *(1961, 322)*

> The different governments will control each other, at the same time that each will be controlled by itself.
>
> *Madison 51 (p. 323)*

The authors of *The Federalist Papers* wanted to prevent a monopolization of political power.[3] Their primary instrument was the separation of power, which would foster competition among the several branches of government. Madison was quite aware that if a coalition were to form, it might overcome the separation of power built into the Constitution. However, he felt that there was little possibility of such a coalition in a republic. "If a majority be united by a common interest, the rights of the minority will be insecure. There are but two methods of providing against this evil. . . . The other [second method], by comprehending in the society so many separate descriptions of citizens as will render an unjust combination of the majority of the whole very improbable" (Madison 51, p. 323).

The transaction costs involved in creating an extensive political coalition were overestimated by Madison. Indeed, the possibility of a political

---

1. Kurland and Lerner (1987, 2:376–77).

2. This alternative view does not undermine my basic argument for the efficiency of political markets. (A more in-depth analysis of sequential games can be found in chapters 6, 8, and 12).

3. Throughout this book, I have emphasized the beneficial effects of competition; so it should not be surprising that a democratic constitution should try to promote a competitive system.

party held together by implicit contracts is never explicitly considered in *The Federalist Papers*. However in the history of the United States there are several periods in which one political party has dominated more than one branch of government, enabling the party to transact around the branches-of-government concept. Is it really the Senate, the House and the Presidency, who are in competition with each other, or is it the Democratic Party in competition with the Republican Party, or is it ultimately just the liberals versus the conservatives? The Constitution creates positions of power for individual players. Individual Senators and Representatives promote their own (possibly their constituents') interests, ideological or otherwise, by entering into coalitions with other players in the Congress and the Presidency.

Separation of Powers or of Power?

> [Montesquieu] did not mean that these departments [legislative, judicial, and executive] ought to have no *partial agency* in, or no *control* over, the acts of each other.
>
> *Madison 11 (p. 482)*

I suggested at the beginning of this section that we should view the political process as a coalition acting across constitutional lines, rather than viewing the House as being in competition with the Senate and both being in competition with the presidency. Here I show that we do not have separation of powers even if we view Congress as a coalition against the presidency.

Because there are relatively few people involved, implicit trading of powers among branches is feasible. Logrolling within each branch of Congress has been well documented. Even when one branch has no visible control over a particular activity, such quid pro quo can also exist across branches. For example, if the president does not enforce a certain law that Congress wants enforced, Congress can use the threat of defeating a revenue bill that the president desires. In this way, Congress can effect the level of enforcement even though the Constitution delegates enforcement only to the president. Similarly, the executive may extract legislation in order to enforce the law.[4]

---

4. The ability to make treaties is a joint rather than a separate power: "He [the president] shall have Power, by and with the Advice and Consent of the Senate, to make Treaties, provided two-thirds of the Senators present concur" (art. 2, sec. 2, cl. 2).

The constitutional separation of powers means that each branch of government can accomplish very little on its own without the cooperation of other branches. This position is the threat point in the bargaining game. The surplus from cooperation is the difference between the cooperative value of the game and the outcome when each branch works on its own. "Separation of powers reduces the threat point of the strongest branch of government and increases the surplus from cooperation" (Cooter 1992).

How does the Supreme Court tie into this analysis? The exchanges between the other branches and the Supreme Court involve higher transaction costs than, for example, exchanges between the Senate and the House. Still, these transaction costs are not so high that implicit quid pro quo bargaining between the judiciary and the other branches is never possible.

Although there are only nine people on the Supreme Court, it is clearly difficult for the members of the Court to bargain with the president. For example, it is highly unlikely that a majority of the Court would agree to find a presidential bill constitutional in exchange for the presidential promotion of a policy that the Court desires.

On the other hand, some kinds of implicit trades between the Court and the president are possible. The Court can influence the president's enforcement behavior by finding certain areas of enforcement (or nonenforcement) unconstitutional. Influence can flow the other way, as well. The president makes new appointments to the Supreme Court. More subtly, the Court cannot find too many laws unconstitutional. This caution by the court implies that court decisions concerning constitutionality are influenced by the president's behavior. This two way influence suggests that there may be a partial transacting around the constitutional separation of powers.

The question still remains as to why exchanges between the Supreme Court and the other branches, although occurring occasionally, are not more frequent. The answer has several components. First, much more than the other branches of government, the Supreme Court is limited by precedent and the logic of its argument. Although it can bend precedent and stretch logic, the Court's capacity to bargain is severely limited. Second, the Court's control over lower courts is small in comparison to the president's control over his bureaucracy. The lower courts too are constrained by precedents. In the instance where the Supreme

Court does not decide the case at all, any attempt by the president and Congress to deal with the diffuse lower court system would involve extremely high transaction costs. It follow that the courts exchange their rights with the rights of the other branches far less often than the other branches exchange rights among themselves.

One role played by the United States Supreme Court is to allocate the initial distribution of property rights to the different branches of government. Given the relatively low level of transaction costs, it is easy for the branches to redelegate functions among themselves. Congress may delegate some of its legislative powers to the executive branch, for example, by legislating that an administrative agency is to set up rules for protecting the environment. The Constitution also explicitly states that Congress may delegate to other branches its power to appoint to lower-level offices.

It is possible for the federal and state governments to transact around the constitution, although such transactions have higher costs than exchanges among the branches of the federal government. States do have their representation in the figure of members of Congress. These congresspersons are to greater or lesser degrees in coalitions with local politicians. Local politicians may also have direct dealings with the executive branch. Presidents may provide either political or economic support for those mayors and governors who have supported them politically. The constitutional delegation of powers to states can be explicitly transacted around by bribing the states to undertake certain behavior. For example, the terms of trade for highway construction are ninety cents on the dollar.

The division of powers by the Constitution is sensible insofar as certain activities do naturally group together and might, thereby, promote a more efficient decision making process. By creating branches of powers which best exploit the benefits from the division of labor the Constitution presumably reduces transaction costs. However, if the Constitution has chosen an ineffective branch for a certain power, implicit trades between the branches may take place. When transaction costs are low, more important than the type of power delegated to individuals is the amount of power embodied in that type. To the extent that there are low transaction costs, the Constitution is more important for its separation of power among individuals than its separation of powers among branches.

Judicial Interpretation

". . . where the will of the legislature, declared in its statutes, stands in opposition to the people, declared in the constitution, the judges ought to be governed by the latter."

Hamilton contrasts this with the case where the constitution is not involved.

"In such a case [where there is a conflict between statute laws and constitutional questions are at issue], it is the providence of the court to liquidate and fix their meaning and operation." (Hamilton 78, p. 468)

This subsection will use economic theory to explain the difference between statute and constitutional interpretation.

When the majority of both houses is dissatisfied with the court's interpretation of a legislative statute, it is relatively easy for Congress to pass new legislation. For example, Congress could rewrite the Endangered Species Act so that it does not include minor fish species. In general, the court's role in interpreting statutes is to apply reasonably consistent rules of interpretation. This permits those who are affected by the legislation to predict the court's interpretation. It also permits Congress to write legislation in the future in light of the Court's previous interpretations. Thus, if the court interprets a list of prohibited behavior as "express mention, implied exclusion," so that behavior not specifically prohibited in the legislation is not implicitly prohibited, legislatures have two options if they want to broaden the interpretation of what is prohibited. One option is to assemble a list that encompasses every possible kind of prohibited behavior (this will be terribly costly if the law is to have a long life). The second option is to have the statute state specifically that similar but not identical behavior is also to be prohibited. Such a statute would encourage the court to interpret more broadly. On the other hand if the courts tend to broaden rather than limit the number of prohibited activities, legislature can make an addition which states that the law only applies to the actual list of prohibited activities.

The foregoing analysis greatly diminishes the arguments made in recent articles about the impact of *Chevron U.S.A. v. Natural Resources Defense Council, Inc.*[5] In this case, the Supreme Court stated that "considerable weight should be accorded to an executive department's construction of a statutory scheme it is entrusted to administer" (467 U.S.

---

5. 467 U.S. 837 (1984)

844). The Court held that so long as Congress had not directly addressed the issue before the agency and had not foreclosed the agency's interpretation, then the agency's construction of the statute should be upheld unless it was unreasonable or otherwise impermissible.

Scalia (1989, 512) described Chevron as the most important case in administrative law in years, while Sunstein (1990, 2075) found Chevron to be "one of the very few defining cases in the last twenty years of American Law." Eskridge and Ferejohn attacked the decision and argued that by "limiting judicial review of agency interpretations of statutes, the Court in Chevron . . . shirked its obligation to maintain the constitutional balance among the branches" (1992, 187).[6] In contrast, our analysis suggests that the Chevron decision will have little impact on the balance of power between Congress and the executive. If Congress believes that Chevron gives too much freedom to the bureaucracy, then, in the future, legislation will directly address more issues. In this way the power of the agency is reduced. The real question is not whether Chevron alters the balance of power (it does not), but whether it facilitates the making of legislation. Is it easier to write legislation when issues not specifically addressed cannot be decided by an agency or when issues not specifically addressed can be decided by an agency?

Because legislative transaction costs are relatively low compared to those incurred in amending the Constitution, one would expect the courts to make use of background material, in order to discover intent, more frequently for constitutional interpretation than for statute interpretation. After all, with regard to statute making, it is easier for the legislature to expressly indicate its intent than for the courts to sift through background material. If the courts do not sift through background material, then in the future Congress will be more likely to expressly put in the intent when writing a statute. They know their intent better than the courts.[7] The same cannot be argued for constitutional interpretation.

The degree of detail and specificity in legislative statute is determined by the tradeoff between flexibility and clarity and the comparative advantage of courts and legislatures in working out specifics (see Ehrlich and Posner 1974). In areas undergoing rapid technological change, spe-

---

6. See also Macey (1992); Pierce (1990); Farina (1989); and Breyer (1986).

7. This may be the underlying explanation for Justice Scalia's antagonism toward the use of background material in determining legislative intent.

cific rules would rapidly become obsolete; therefore, general standards would be used instead. In areas where the policy might reasonably be inferred from the standard, standards are more likely to be invoked, with the details being left to the courts.

FEDERALISM AND EFFICIENT INTERSTATE RELATIONS

In the previous section, the focus was on the separation of power between the executive, legislative, and judicial branches. In this section, I consider federalism and show that the Constitution creates efficient interstate relations.

Commerce Clause

> The interfering and unneighborly regulations of some States, contrary to the true spirit of the Union, have, in different instances, given just cause of umbrage and complaint to others, and it is to be feared that examples of this nature, if not restrained by national control, would be multiplied and extended till they became not less serious sources of animosity and discord than injurious impediments to the intercourse between the different parts of the Confederacy.
>
> *Hamilton 22 (p. 144).*

Article 1, section 10 of the Constitution disallows states from imposing export or import duties without the consent of Congress unless absolutely necessary for executing inspection laws, and the Supreme Court has maintained that there are constitutional limitations upon state interference with interstate commerce. States and other jurisdictions may enact legislation that affects interstate commerce when these regulations serve valid goals, such as safety. However, the courts are not likely to find constitutional "state efforts to protect local economic interests by limiting access to local markets by out of state suppliers" (*Dean Milk Company v. City of Madison, Wisconsin et al.*).[8] Thus the Supreme Court struck down a municipal ordinance forbidding the local sale of milk that had not been pasteurized and bottled at an approved plant within five miles of the center of the city. This ordinance was clearly economically inefficient. For the system as a whole, such an ordinance is a net loss.

While the court does not always swing with the economic argument,

---

8. 340 U.S. 349 (1951).

as sometimes local interests reduce competition from other states under the guise of safety, the rulings are predominantly toward economic efficiency. Courts have consistently struck down those state taxes that they conclude unjustifiably benefit local commerce at the expense of out-of-state commerce. For example, in *Hale v. Bimico Trading, Inc.*[9] the Supreme Court held unconstitutional a Florida statute that imposed an inspection fee sixty times the actual cost of inspection upon cement imported into the state, because that statute excluded locally produced cement from all inspection and inspection fee requirements. This Florida statute was to reduce competition from out-of-state suppliers.

One might ask why the Court does not allow the states to decide, since presumably the states would be interested in promulgating optimal contracts. In the absence of such a proscription by the Court, there would be some tendency for states to engage in efficient contracting with each other. Unfortunately, there are relatively high transaction costs between the states and among the citizens. There might be numerous attempts to gain a bargaining advantage by threatening to pass tariffs and other restraints of trade to increase the rents accruing to the citizens. Hence, it is more efficient to just outlaw inefficient transactions in the first place.

Supreme Court decisions have also prevented states from imposing clearly extraterritorial taxes and tariffs on imported goods from other states. If such taxes were allowed, free trade would be restrained, and the beneficial effects of comparative advantage would be diminished. Recently, both Posner (1992) and Epstein (1993) have argued that the severance tax and the compensating use tax allow states to impose inefficient taxes under names that conceal the true economic effect.[10] In the following paragraphs, I will argue to the contrary and show that these taxes are efficient.

Any system of taxes inevitably creates distortions. The only taxes that would not distort incentives would be taxes on a fixed asset such as land. But land by itself cannot provide a sufficient tax base, and a land tax may have other undesirable properties. Thus the search is for the best possible tax, not a perfect tax without problems. The difficulties are compounded by a federal system. On the one hand, a uniform tax system

---

9. 300 U.S. 375 (1939)

10. Tribe (1988) is also part of the chorus against the Court's decision regarding severance taxes in *Commonwealth Edison Co. v. Montana*, 453 U.S. 609 (1981).

across the states would reduce the distortions created when there are different prices for the same thing. On the other hand, a uniform system would undermine the benefits of federalism, most especially the tailoring of the government apparatus (including taxes and expenditures) to the wants of the people in each state.

States can collect compensating use taxes in lieu of sales taxes from out-of-state mail order firms. To understand why it makes sense to collect such taxes, consider the economic distortions that would arise if compensating use taxes were not allowed. Suppose that there were two identical firms with identical constant marginal costs of production in two identical states that charged 5 percent sales tax. Assume also that delivering the item to the other state costs an additional 3 percent. Without the compensating use tax, residents of each state would only buy the item from out of state, thereby saving 2 percent. But the social cost of shipping is 3 percent.[11] The residents of both states would be better off if there were no sales tax and residents bought only from the mail order firm within the state. Excessive shipping costs would be eliminated. This is the key to the rationale behind compensating use taxes. In a symmetric situation, they are necessary to maintain efficiency. In their absence, consumer choice would be distorted by differential taxation depending on point of origin.[12]

Posner provides an asymmetric example: In one state, property taxes raise average cost by 5 percent, while in the other state sales taxes raise average cost by 5 percent. In this asymmetric situation, it would be inefficient to have a compensating use tax, since the producer in the property tax state would be paying 10 percent in taxes when selling in the sales tax state and could not compete even if his nontax costs including shipping were 4 percent lower than the producer in the sales tax state. Of course, there is still a tax advantage for the mail order firm in the sales tax state shipping to the property tax state, since it avoids all taxes. In theory, one could then charge a special tax on this firm, but accounting would become a nightmare.

More generally, once there are asymmetric tax structures, the ac-

---

11. In this very simple example, no taxes are collected. The argument does not depend on this result.

12. The Court has used the tax symmetry test in a number of cases. For example, in *Armco, Inc. v. Hardesty*, 467 U.S. 644 (1984), the majority ruled that "the tax must be such that, if applied in every jurisdiction, there would be no impermissible interference with free trade."

counting of taxes and tax incidence becomes impossible. So the courts use a first-order approximation—the outcome when the situation is symmetric. Hence compensating sales taxes have been instituted not only in the United States but are now being implemented for the European Common Market.

The case for (or against) severance taxes is more muddled. It depends to a large extent on whether severance taxes are viewed as royalties or taxes. But even the tax view is not an unalloyed negative. When the ultimate consumers are mainly nonresidents and the demand is inelastic, severance taxes shift the cost of government onto residents of other states. From the viewpoint of wealth maximization, the issue is not who pays, but whether the tax is inefficient. Optimal taxation suggests that taxes be placed on commodities with inelastic demand curves. The more inelastic the demand, the less the tax is likely to distort. But as already noted, the more inelastic the demand, the more the tax will be displaced onto nonresidents. So efficient commodity taxation and tax shifting go hand in hand.[13] Posner argues that externalizing the tax base leads to socially excessive government expenditures since the voters of the state gain the benefits but do not pay the taxes. However, the voters can always choose to convert taxes into refunds for the state's citizens. For example, Montana repealed its income tax at the same time the state instituted a 30 percent severance tax on coal. Hence, the state's budget is optimal in that the marginal benefit from expenditures equals the marginal cost to the taxpayers.

Writers, inventors, and musicians are often paid royalties or some combination of up-front payments and royalties. A common explanation for such arrangements is to shift risk. But individual writers are likely to be relatively risk averse. So this explanation is not compelling. A more likely reason for this arrangement is that schedules require less information than a fixed payment because a fixed payment requires not only knowledge of the schedule relating profit to quantity sold, but also an estimate of the quantity sold. Obtaining such costly information would be imperative if rights were sold outright. Thus a royalty system saves on information costs. Royalties in the form of severance taxes may make economic sense in the same way that royalties in the private sector create optimal arrangements.

13. This is not a perfect fit because some commodities may have inelastic demands, but not from the viewpoint of any one state's suppliers.

In the absence of agreements to the contrary, *sovereign* states are likely to undertake policies that shift costs onto other states. It is easy to demonstrate that when all the states undertake such strategies, the equilibrium outcome is inefficient. But a federal system is composed of *semisovereign* states. The constitutional rules regarding interstate relations are designed to limit such predatory behavior and to provide efficient outcomes. The interesting question is not how states behave in a noncooperative game, but rather how the courts can create rules that turn the noncooperative game into a more cooperative one while maintaining the states' semisovereignty.

Choice of Law

Which state's laws should take precedent when the laws of different states are in conflict?[14] Again, a transaction cost analysis provides the answer.

Federalism is based on territory. And in many cases, making territory the basis for rule-of-law choice minimizes information costs. Suppose, for example, that a driver from Alabama runs into a pedestrian from Florida while both are in California. Which state's rule should be operative? California is the obvious choice. If not, drivers and pedestrians would constantly be looking at license plates to determine which state law applied. Since pedestrians do not identify themselves by state, the most reasonable expectation is that the pedestrian is from California (even if the stereotype is that Californians don't walk). Not surprisingly, the courts have upheld the view that the place of an automobile accident determines the prevailing law.

For similar reasons, there is a general rule that estates are administered under the law of the decedent's domicile, not the heir's. Suppose that the opposite were true. Wills would have to be rewritten every time one of the potential heirs moved, and if there were more than one potential heir, it would be unclear which state law would prevail.

The laws that regulate a married couple's relationship (say community property) are those of the state of domicile, not the state where they happen to invest (*Veazey v. Doremus*).[15] And if one spouse moves to a new state, that unilateral act cannot change the legal relationship—the

14. See Baxter (1963); Brilmayer (1991); and especially Laycock (1992), whose ideas form the basis of this section.
15. 510 A. 2d 1187 (1986).

law of the original common-home state continues until both spouses move elsewhere. Again this makes sense. In the absence of such a rule, neither spouse would know the marriage contract.

Not all such choice-of-law cases are so transparent. Phone orders may simultaneously involve two states. Since consumers are unlikely to know the state (if they call an 800 number), let alone state law, it makes sense that the location of the consumer tends to be the operative factor. This reasoning is especially persuasive if the seller specializes in phone orders, so that the cost of learning state law is amortized over many customers and the price can vary to reflect the differential in product liability law among the different states.

Another solution to choice of law would have the federal government choose the better law. But this would undermine the whole structure of federalism since there would no longer be different laws for different states (see *Erie R.R. v. Tompkins*).[16]

Treatment of Nonresidents

> The Citizens of each State shall be entitled to all Privileges
> and Immunities of Citizens in the several states.
>
> *U.S. Constitution, art. 4, sec. 2, cl. 1*

Efficiency dictates limits to this doctrine. Unless there are compelling reasons to act otherwise, nonresidents may have to pay more than residents for state-subsidized activities, such as a college education.[17] Since resident taxpayers on average pay more state taxes than nonresidents, subsidizing nonresidents as well would encourage free riding by other states. In defense, the subsidizing state would reduce its subsidy and underprovide the public good. The only solution to the free riding among states would then be to have the federal government provide the good, but this would undermine the whole concept of federalism.

This rule, too, has a limit. People from out of state cannot be charged more for driving on a state's roads. Typically, gasoline taxes pay for the roads, and out-of-staters are likely to pay for their share. Furthermore, nonresidents are unlikely to use a state's highway system because their own state underprovides. Finally, higher charges for people engaged in

16. 304 U.S. 64 (1938).

17. See *Sturgis v. Washington*, 368 F. Supp. 38 (1973), which upheld differential tuition for out-of-state students attending a state university, and *Martinez v. Bynum*, 461 U.S. 321 (1983), which upheld a residence requirement for tuition-free public education.

interstate commerce reduce trade and comparative advantage (see the section on the commerce clause).[18]

Judicial Federalism

The federal courts have argued that they have a "virtual unflagging obligation . . . to exercise the jurisdiction given them."[19] Yet the Supreme Court has developed, without congressional encouragement, three distinct arguments for abstaining from meddling into state judicial decisions. Not surprisingly, the motivating explanation is efficiency. In *Pullman* the Court argued that "federal courts should abstain from decision when difficult and unsettled questions of state law must be resolved before a substantial federal constitutional question can be decided."[20] Such abstention avoids "both unnecessary adjudication of federal questions and 'needless friction with state policies' from possibly erroneous state law interpretation."[21] A second and related rationale, known as the *Burford* abstention, argues that federal courts abstain in cases where decision of state law issues would intrude greatly on especially important state interests believed to be particularly well suited to state court consideration.[22] Both of these decisions argue that the state judiciary has a comparative advantage in deciding the issue. *Pullman* also emphasizes the unnecessary cost of deciding a case before the facts are in. The strongest abstention doctrine is found in *Younger v. Harris*.[23] It is designed to promote institutional autonomy of state judicial processes by limiting the ability of litigants to obtain federal declaratory or injunctive relief on constitutional grounds when such relief may interfere with ongoing state proceedings. To allow relief would interfere with the

18. The straightforward cases explain the principle, but as always there are hard cases where the appropriate answer is not so clear. An important example is welfare. Welfare subsidies encourage export of people to high-welfare states, suggesting that welfare should not be available to nonresidents. On the other hand, welfare enables smoother transition from one job to another, suggesting that it should be available to everyone who needs it. The courts have been persuaded by the latter argument. See *Shapiro v. Thompson*, 394 U.S. 618 (1969).

19. *Colorado River Water Conservation Dist. v. United States*, 424 U.S. 817 (1976)

20. The decision is efficient but not the grammar.

21. *Railroad Comm'n of Texas v. Pullman C.*, 312 U.S. 496 (1941) and *Hawaii Housing Auth. v. Midkiff*, 467 U.S. 236 (1984), quoting Pullman at 500.

22. *Burford v. Sun Oil Co.*, 319 U.S. 315 (1943). See also *Colorado River Water Conservation Dist. v. United States*, 424 U.S. 814 (1976).

23. *Younger v. Harris*, 401 U.S. 37 (1971). See Tribe (1988) for a discussion of this and the other rules.

smooth running of state judicial systems. Furthermore, such injunctions would imply that the states were incapable of handling constitutional issues, thereby undermining the federal system. Only if the state's judicial process were so infirm that it cannot handle constitutional issues appropriately would such a usurpation be justified.

TRANSACTION COSTS AND THE TAKINGS CLAUSE

. . . nor shall private property be taken for public use, without just compensation.

U.S. Constitution, Amendment 5

Why is there a "takings" clause? Should it be applied to regulation? If coastal land is rezoned so that development can no longer take place, should the owner of the land be compensated for diminished value? Should a polluter be compensated for undertaking pollution control? In this section I use economic theory to *systematically* answer these and related entitlement questions and show that court decisions on the takings issue are consistent with efficiency goals. Once again, transaction costs play a central role in explaining institutional design.

Previous Literature

Traditionally, the harm-benefit distinction and the notion of causation have been used to supply answers to the above questions.[24] However, in a zero-transaction-cost world there can be no such distinctions. Consider *Miller v. Schoene.*[25] In this case, the Supreme Court upheld a Virginia statute requiring uncompensated destruction of cedar trees infested with a pest deadly to nearby apple orchards but harmless to the host cedars themselves. Both cedar trees and apple trees are input into the production of damaged apples. As a consequence, causality cannot offer an acceptable explanation for whether the owners of cedars should be compensated, because both the cedars and the apple trees caused the damage. Nor can the harm-benefit distinction be a guide. Growing cedars harms apple growers and benefits owners of cedar trees; cutting cedars harms owners of cedar trees and benefits apple growers.

---

24. For causality explanations see Epstein (1979a,b, 1985). I will ignore the tradition that relies on textural analysis of the Constitution to explain Supreme Court decisions on the takings issue. I am asking a deeper question—why a takings clause. In addition, I claim that the best textural analysis is the one that promotes economic efficiency.

25. 276 U.S. 272 (1958)

This apparent symmetry led other researchers to create a variety of ad hoc theories. For example, Michaelman (1967) claimed that compensation exists in order to avoid demoralization costs (people may be upset if they are not compensated and this may cause social unrest) or to promote some just notion of distribution. Ellickson (1973) argued that even if we cannot scientifically distinguish between harm and benefit, most people have a concept of "normalcy" and that one should be compensated for being forced below the norm of normalcy.[26] Costonis (1975) has a somewhat similar view of takings. He argued that people should be compensated for the benefits that they would ordinarily derive from their property. Hagman and Misczynski (1978) took the argument one step further. They argued that landowners should be compensated for government regulations that decrease the value of their land and pay the government for regulations that increase the value of their land.

As will be shown in the following pages, some of these arguments are myopic, in that they see only half the problem, some are fallacious, and all the ad hoc arguments are unnecessary. Once we consider compensation in the context of administrative costs, the answers to all the questions posed at the beginning of the section are provided almost effortlessly.

Administrative-Cost Efficiency and the Allocation of Property Rights

There can be a taking only when a property right is taken, but how are property rights determined in the first place? Do factories have a right to pollute, or do the neighbors have the right to pollution-free air? If transactions were costless, it would make no difference; but when there are transaction costs, efficiency dictates that these costs be taken into account. Suppose that the efficient outcome is for each factory to emit no more than x pounds of sulfur into the air. If the neighbors were entitled to sulfur-free air, then the neighbors would have to be compensated for the sulfur still being emitted. If the factories were entitled to put sulfur into the air, then they would have to be compensated for the partial loss of this right. Either way would involve very large transaction costs in determining the individual losses incurred when

26. See also Dunham (1958) and Freund (1976), who make use of the harm-benefit distinction. To quote from Freund, who was also quoted by the court (*Just v. Marinette*, 201 N.W. 2d 767 (1972): "the state takes property by eminent domain because it is useful to the public, and under the police power because it is harmful" (546).

rights were curtailed. The least-cost method is to give each of the n factories the right to emit x pounds of sulfur into the air and to give the neighbors the right to have air with no more than nx pounds of sulfur. This is the basic reason why takings are not applied to regulation even when regulation has a greater impact on a particular owner's wealth than a physical expropriation of part of her land. When regulation is involved, efficiency determines property rights; no one is compensated for a taking of their rights since no rights are taken.

It is useful to contrast the efficiency explanation with the approach used by Epstein (1985). In his book, Epstein argues for the *ad coelum* rule and a physical invasion test for whether there should be compensation. He is especially distressed with the Supreme Court decision in *Miller v. Schoene,* where the Court held that the owners of the cedar trees did not have to be compensated when the state ordered cedars to be destroyed. The logic of his argument is as follows. The owner of the land has the property right to grow anything on it as long as it does not physically invade others. The cedar trees did not invade others' property (as smoke does), and therefore the owners should be compensated for the trees' destruction. But what difference does it make whether the trees release spores that harm neighboring apple trees (where Epstein would approve of no compensation) or are a primary vector for pests that harm apple trees (where Epstein desires compensation)?[27]

Now consider the economic analysis of the same case. Apples are an important agricultural crop in the area, while cedars are used mainly as windbreaks or for ornamental purposes. It is quite clear where the balance lies between the cost and benefit of cutting down cedar trees. But determining the actual cost to the particular owners of cedar trees is quite costly. The efficiency explanation for entitlements argues that the landowners do not have the right to grow cedars. Therefore, they should not be compensated when the trees are cut down. The court implicitly accepted this argument.

Miller v. Schoene is important in illustrating another difference between the efficiency approach to property rights and the libertarian view of property rights (as exemplified by Epstein). Over time, technology, income, knowledge, and tastes may change, with a resulting change in

---

27. The *ad coelum* rule does not work either. Airplanes are allowed to pass at twenty thousand feet overhead without paying for the right to trespass. Again, economic efficiency provides the explanation for the allocation of the property right.

the efficient allocation of resources. At one time it was not understood that cedar trees had harmful effects on apple trees, and everyone had the right to grow cedars. After discovering their harmful effects, Virginia passed a statute requiring the destruction of cedars. The fact that owners at one time had the right to grow cedars or theoretically had the right in a state of nature is irrelevant.[28] Hence the courts do not compensate for the change in the property right.

In general, the Supreme Court does not compensate landowners when changes in land use regulations reduce the value of some parcels. Epstein is upset with these decisions because he treats the historical value as the property right. But as I have shown, the present efficient allocation should be the baseline. Any other baseline would typically involve very high transaction costs.

The Underlying Economic Rationale for Compensation

The requirement of just compensation encourages governments to take into account the economic cost of inputs. If, for example, governments did not have to pay for land, they might appropriate more than is optimal and build short, sprawling buildings instead of highrises, even when a full cost accounting would mandate the latter.

The takings clause also insures citizens against certain kinds of government behavior. But why government insurance instead of a private insurance industry? Without the takings clause, the insurance industry itself could be faced with an uncompensated takings. Even if this were not a serious threat, it would be very hard to insure against government action because of adverse selection. Suppose that the takings clause did not exist and that citizens could buy insurance for government appropriation of land. A race would be on between the insurance company and citizens to find out which parcels the local, state, and national governments were planning to take. Ordinary citizens might very well have a comparative advantage over the insurance companies in finding out this information, especially at the local level. So citizens would only insure property with a higher risk of takeover than was indicated by the price of the insurance. This state of affairs could not last. The insurance prices would rise further, with citizens responding by no longer insuring those

28. This argument also holds against Nozick (1974) and other historically based property right theories.

parcels whose risks were now insufficient to justify paying the higher price for insurance. There would be a complete unraveling and a failure in the insurance market.

Insurance is not costless. It involves administrative costs and encourages "moral hazard" (inappropriate incentives when the costs fall on another party—for example, not bothering to lock your car because you know that it is insured). These transaction costs must be balanced against the benefits of insurance—reduced risk.

In making public policy, the government first decides which policy is most efficient and then determines whether insurance is cost effective. Insurance is most likely to be provided under the following circumstances: (1) There is a possibility of incurring a substantial loss. The risk from small losses is likely to be outweighed by the administrative costs of an insurance scheme. The government does not have a comparative advantage in insuring small losses since the individual can self-insure against uncorrelated small risks. (2) The probability of a loss is low. When the type of loss is commonplace, there are a great number of payments, making the administrative costs higher than otherwise. In the extreme case, when the timing and the outcome are certain, there is no risk and hence no need for insurance. (3) The insurance does not discourage the insured from undertaking the optimal amount of self-protection.

I will now consider the problem of moral hazard in more detail. If zoning rules force a factory to move but the government compensates factories for moving costs, then factories will be less cautious about where they locate in the first place. Such a system would not punish factory owners for bad predictions about future policy. At the same time, one has to be concerned about the moral hazard of government. If governments do not pay the costs of relocation, they *may* not take these costs into account when making decisions. The word "may" is emphasized, since other forces are present to encourage efficient behavior by the government.

Governments regulate land use, automobile safety, and a variety of other areas. With regard to compensation, there are three possibilities: (1) the government can compensate those who are hurt by regulation (e.g., a factory is compensated for being forced to reduce smoke); (2) the government can compensate those who are hurt by nonregulation (e.g., the factory's neighbors are compensated for smoke damage when the factory can produce as much smoke as it wants to); (3) no one is compensated in either event.[29] We now consider particular issues and show why one of these three possibilities is most appropriate.

Compensation When the Government Is Inefficient: *Averne Bay Construction v. Thatcher*

In general, the courts do not question the wisdom of the government (if a constitutional question is not involved). The courts presume that the government is acting efficiently. However, on occasion, the government does act inefficiently and creates negative externalities. In such cases, the victim of the externality should be compensated. Not compensating the person hurt by the inefficient regulation (i.e., doing nothing when the government acts inefficiently) would result in people undertaking self-protection from possible future inefficient regulation. This behavior itself would be inefficient.

When the courts find the regulation to be clearly inefficient, they either find it to be invalid or rule that a taking has occurred (when the damage cannot be reversed by just finding the regulation to be invalid). A classic case is *Averne Bay Construction Co. v. Thatcher*.[30] The plaintiff wanted to build a gas station, but the city zoned the property residential. The trial judge had established that there were no residences within a mile of the proposed gas station, and for good reason. In the vicinity, the city operated an incinerator that "gave off offensive fumes which permeated the plaintiff's premises." Near the premises, "sanitary sewage emptied into an open creek resulting in nauseating odors which permeated the . . . property."[31] The zoning regulation was clearly inefficient, and the court found the regulation unsuitable given the conditions of the surrounding area. The court held that "an ordinance which permanently so restricts the use of property that it cannot be used for any reasonable purpose goes, it is plain, beyond regulation, and must be recognized as a taking of the property."[32]

29. For surveys of the case law on compensating for government regulation see Berger (1976) and Ackerman (1977).

30. 278 N.Y. 222, 15 N.E. 2d 587 (1938)

31. Id. at 591.

32. Id. at 591. Another example in this genre is *San Diego Gas and Electric v. City of San Diego*, 146 Cal. Rptr. 103 (1978). In this case, land suited for industrial purposes was downzoned to open-space use. A witness testified that the land could not be used for agriculture because of its high salt content, could not be used for residences because it was in a flood plain, could not be used economically for grazing, could not be used for

In *Foster v. City of Detroit* the city froze the use of the plaintiff's land in 1950 for use in a redevelopment program and began a condemnation suit.[33] After ten years of delay, the city dropped the suit. By then the property had deteriorated in value substantially. The court found the conduct of the city so unconscionable (that is, inefficient) as to reach the level of a taking.

For the remainder of this section, I will only consider cases where the government has acted efficiently.

There Should Be No Compensation for Minor or Common Harms

There should be no compensation for minor or common harms when the efficient choice is made.[34] The courts have specifically addressed this issue. For example, Justice Holmes in *Pennsylvania Coal Co. v. Mahon* said: "[D]ifference of degree is one of the distinctions by which the right of the legislature to exercise police power is determined. Some small limitations of previously existing rights incident to property may be imposed for the sake of preventing manifest evil; larger ones could not be except by the exercise of the right of eminent domain."[35]

The explanation for this policy has already been provided. When there are minor harms, it is foolish to have compensation in order to provide insurance because the victims are risk neutral to the sum total effect of a large number of minor risks (and the administrative costs would overshadow any benefit from reduced risk).

Once again we consider *Miller v. Schoene*. Even ignoring our previous analysis, the owners of cedar trees should not be compensated. The harm is likely to be minor, and therefore insurance is less appropriate. When people are risk averse, compensation is like an insurance policy because it reduces risk to the party receiving compensation. If the benefits of reduced risk are large enough, they may outweigh the costs of courts' decision making and possible misallocation. However, in this

---

a golf course because of poor drainage, and that the land's only use was for industrial purposes.

33. 254 F. Supp. 655 (E.C. Mich., 1966). A similar case is *Klopping v. City of Whittier*, 8 Cal. 3d 89, 104 Cal. Rptr. 1 (1972) where the city so mishandled the precondemnation proceedings that the court held that they were tantamount to a taking and granted the landowner's request for payment on a theory of inverse condemnation. Also see *Richmond Elks Hall Assn. v. Richmond Redevelopment Agency*, 561 F. 2d 1327 (1977).

34. This rule does not hold in nonexternality cases.

35. 148 Mass. 372 (1889).

case, the reduced risk to the cedar owners was not so great that it was efficient to have an insurance policy.

Anticipated Outcomes: *Consolidated Rock Products Co. v. City of Los Angeles*

The prohibition against surface mining of rock and gravel has frequently been upheld in urban areas, but in rural areas attempts to prohibit mining have often been found unconstitutional.[36] This makes economic sense. In cities, the benefit of having a gravel quarry nearby (reduced transportation costs) is clearly outweighed by the harm (increased pollution). The cost of shutting down the quarry is less than the cost of having the city grow in a wide circle around the quarry. In contrast, in the countryside the costs of pollution are not so large, and it is relatively easy for homeowners to avoid the pollution (quarries have less choice of where to do their quarrying). Thus, prohibition of quarrying is less likely in a rural setting.

In an urban setting, regulation or possible prohibition of quarrying without compensation reduces courts' administrative costs (in comparison to a system of compensation) and is efficient if people are risk neutral. If people are risk averse, compensation may be desirable in order to reduce risk. However, in these urban-quarrying cases, compensation is not needed to reduce risk of a large loss, for there is no risk. Indeed, it is a certainty that quarrying in a city will be highly regulated, if allowed at all. When outcomes are fully anticipated, insurance does not reduce risk (it only changes the timing of the payment from later to earlier). If the quarry owner is compensated for shutting down, then she will pay more for the quarry in the first place (in a competitive market, people will bid more because they know that they will be compensated). Thus, compensation would be a totally useless act. The courts seem to agree with this economic intuition, as compensation is not allowed in these cases. For example, in *Consolidated Rock Products v. City of Los Angeles*,[37] the Supreme Court stated that the zoning regulation was not

---

36. Cases upholding prohibition of mining in urban areas include *Goldblatt v. Hampstead*, 369 U.S. 590 (1962), and *Town of Waterford v. Grabner*, 155 Conn. 431, 232 A. 2d 481 (1967). Cases not upholding prohibition of mining in rural areas include *Lyon Sand and Gravel v. Township of Oakland*, 33 Mich. App. 614, 190 N.W. 2d 354 (1971), and *Midland Electric Co. v. Knox County*, 1 Ill. 2d 200, 115 N.E. 2d 275 (1953).

37. 371 U.S. 36 (1962)

a taking even though there was no dispute that the restriction left the complainant's land utterly unusable for any productive purposes.

Quarrying cases are not the only example of not compensating for reasonably anticipated changes in property rights. As cities expand into surrounding areas, noxious industries that previously operated outside the city limits will inevitably be restricted. In *Hadacheck v. Sebastian*,[38] the Supreme Court upheld a city ordinance outlawing the operation of a preexisting brickyard within recently expanded city limits as a proper exercise of police power and denied any compensation.[39]

More generally, most land use regulations (including zoning) should be anticipated, and therefore any compensation by the government cannot be justified on insurance grounds. In addition, insurance would create inappropriate incentives, as poor predictors would be rewarded for making inappropriate investments (including paying too high a price for the land). This, added to our earlier argument regarding the high administrative costs that would typically arise if people could be compensated for the negative effects of regulation, suggests that compensation for land use regulation should arise only in the most unusual circumstances.

Epstein (1985), using the physical-invasion rule, sides with the court on *Consolidated Rock* and *Hadacheck* and chides Michaelman (1967), who comes to the opposite conclusion, using a "fairness" explanation. However, Epstein's physical-invasion rule leads him astray in other cases. Consider *Usdin v. Environmental Protection Department of New Jersey*.[40] In this case, the court held that in order to promote flood control the state could designate certain uplands as unfit for construction and that this was not a taking.[41] Epstein argues that this is a partial taking because construction is not an invasive conduct, and "the prevention of misfortune of nature is not the same as the prevention of wrongs by the property owner" (1985, 124). But he does not deny that efficiency dictates

38. 239 U.S. 394 (1915)

39. According to our analysis, the same logic holds for nuisance law. Preexisting nuisances must go without compensation as the city expands. *Campbell v. Seaman,* 63 N.Y. 568 (1876) is the analogous liability rule to *Hadacheck*. In this case, the court held that operation of a brick manufacturing plant could be enjoined and damages for past injuries recovered, and that it did not matter that the brickyard was used before the plaintiffs bought their land or built their houses.

40. 173 N.J. Super. 311 (1980)

41. There are analogous cases regarding restrictions on building in flood plains.

no building in this area. From the prospective of efficiency and of the court, landowners do not have the property right to build in inappropriate areas. Therefore, the landowners should not be compensated for a taking since a right has not been taken from them. Furthermore, we do not want to reward people for bad judgment (in this case, not anticipating that flood control will prohibit building on watershed). Finally, if people fully anticipate the regulation, there is no uncertainty, and the insurance function of the takings clause is undermined.

Regulation versus Physical Expropriation of a Property Right

As a general rule of thumb, compensation for regulation is less likely than compensation for physical expropriation of the property right. This is because, as a general rule, expropriation is less likely to (1) involve an externality, (2) require significant transaction costs in implementing a system of compensation, and (3) be anticipated.

Often the government enters the ordinary economic market as a participant (for example, to purchase a computer or rent a building). In such cases, no externalities are involved. In ordinary economic markets, compensation produces an efficient outcome with low transaction costs. Any other method either creates inappropriate incentives or is infeasible. For example, if the government does not compensate for its purchases of computers, people will be deterred from supplying computers. Methods to minimize these long-run incentive effects are totally impractical. It would take an inordinate amount of information for the government to identify potential computer suppliers who might be discouraged from producing any computers at all by a policy of noncompensation by the government and then force these nonproducers to pay a fine for not supplying computers to the government.

When the government engages in an ordinary economic market, the additional transaction cost of paying for the purchase is trivial. If the government orders computer A from company B, then the cost of writing a check and sending it along with the order form is minimal. This should be compared to the transaction cost involved in compensation for noise regulation. First of all, when the person is acting efficiently and not making too much noise, the government is not dealing with the person. A special transaction would have to be set up just for the compensation payment. In the second place, there is no ongoing economic market for the reduction of noise (an externality does not have a market), and, therefore, it is relatively more costly to determine the appropriate amount of compensation.

Generally, regulations of land use are much easier to anticipate than purchases of land by the government. When outcomes are anticipated, compensation by the government is a needless and ineffectual transaction. Therefore, compensation for regulation of land use would be less likely than for physical expropriation of the land. Such regulation is typically easier to anticipate because it is usually formulated in general terms (even if it only affects one or two participants). For example, it is very common to have a zoning regulation against smoking factories in a residential area. Factories should be able to anticipate such a rule. Even if the area is vacant, a factory should reasonably be able to anticipate what areas are most likely to be residential. In contrast, it is often hard to anticipate just where a particular highway will be located.[42]

Streets versus Highways

In the previous section it was suggested that physical expropriation of land is more likely to be compensated than regulation of land. However, some kinds of expropriations are more likely to be compensated than others. Again, the relative ability to anticipate plays an important role in determining whether the expropriation will be compensated. Another important factor is the benefit accruing to the owner of the land. If owners accrue most of the benefits of expropriation, they clearly should not be compensated for their own benefit.

If a highway is placed across a farmer's land, he is compensated for the loss of his land. If the farmer builds a large housing tract on his land, he usually has to deed the streets to a government jurisdiction.[43] This is consistent with our theory. The benefits of the streets clearly

---

42. The positive correlation between a regulation ruling and anticipation should be seen as a continuum: The archetypal regulation case being anticipated; the archetypal property expropriation case being unanticipated. There are exceptions. For example, the topography of the land may make one location uniquely suitable for an airport. The cost of unnecessary compensation in such cases may be outweighed by the ease of administering a rule of compensating for all cases of physical expropriation. According to our analysis, this rule will, in general, give the right economic answer. Some regulations are easier to anticipate than others. Regulation of factory smoke in urban areas is easier to predict than ordinances that restrict growth. Accordingly, compensation is more likely for the latter than for the former.

43. See *Ayres v. City Council,* 34 Cal. 2d 31, 207 P. 2d 1 (1949).

accrue to the farmer because his land is worth more as a housing tract with streets than as plain farmland. A new highway across the farmer's land may or may not improve its value, but, in any event, the bulk of the benefits accrue to those who use the highway and do not pay the farmer directly or indirectly for its use.

In addition, it is generally easier to anticipate that the housing development will need streets than to anticipate that a highway will need to cross through the farmer's land. Unless the land is uniquely suited for a highway, the farmer is unlikely to fully anticipate that a highway will run through his, as opposed to someone else's, land. In contrast, a housing development always needs streets. Since highways are less anticipated than streets, it is more reasonable for the government to insure property owners against the risk of highways than to insure large-scale developers against the risk of streets.

THE DISTRIBUTION OF POLITICAL WEALTH

It is useful to contrast my economic interpretation of the Constitution with Beard's *An Economic Interpretation of the Constitution of the United States* (1948). For Beard, the constitutional provisions were fundamentally redistributive (from farmers and debtors to commercial interests, creditors, and slave owners). In this section, I will argue that many of Beard's examples are efficiency enhancing rather than distributive, and that the most important redistributive effects were of a different level and kind from the ones considered by Beard.

Beard argued that the following rules increased the wealth of creditors at the expense of debtors or the general taxpayer: (1) All debts contracted and engagements entered into before the adoption of the Constitution were to remain valid; (2) states were forbidden to impair the obligation of contract; and (3) the emission of paper money was prohibited.[44] It is true that in the short run, after a contract is made, one side may gain by changing the rules of the game (the contract is no longer valid, debts are discharged by worthless money). But in the long run, undermining contractual obligations makes both sides worse off: If contracts cannot be enforced, then fewer contracts will be made. If money is unstable, then lenders will not lend in the first place or lend

44. I concentrate on chapter 6, "The Constitution as an Economic Document."

at a much higher nominal rate. Constitutions structure long-run relations, and in the long run, the three rules mentioned by Beard cannot redistribute income, but they can increase efficiency.[45]

Beard considered the imposition of free trade among the states a victory for manufactures, who "paid for their victory by large concessions to the slave-owning planters of the South" (1948, 175). Even without the economists' strong belief in the Pareto superiority of free trade, it is hard to come up with a convincing story demonstrating that the South was hurt by such a policy. Southern farmers and consumers would both benefit from lower prices for their purchases and greater demand for their cotton. So once again, Beard has provided a questionable redistributive explanation for a constitutional provision that is clearly efficiency enhancing.

Beard viewed the takings clause as a redistributive policy. While the takings clause does help to protect the original distribution of wealth, it also promotes economic efficiency by reducing the risk to all citizens from government policy (as shown in the previous section).

Many of the substantive sections in the Constitution are efficiency enhancing rather than distributive. However, certain sections, especially those concerned with voting procedure and the Bill of Rights, do have an effect on the distribution of political power among the citizenry. The Constitution allocates political wealth by distributing votes. Each state has two senators, regardless of population. This obviously increases the power of small states in comparison to a legislature based solely on population.[46] Since small states have more power in the Senate than in the executive branch, allocation of power between the branches of government also affects the relative power of small states.

Slaves were not given equal weight to freemen when seats were being allocated in the House or when electoral votes were being counted in the presidential election. This reduced the power of the South in comparison to a situation where slaves would be counted whole (al-

45. If contracts were not upheld by the state, then there would be redistribution from those who used the state to enforce contracts to those who were willing to use other means to enforce contracts.

46. Only owners of immobile wealth (landowners and slave owners wanting to move north) are affected by granting more power to small states. With no restrictions on internal migration, immigration will equalize wealth. Hence once again the redistributive argument is partially undermined.

though this also reduced their potential tax burden) but increased Southern power in comparison to a situation were slaves did not count at all.

If one were interested in redistributing power with minimal losses of efficiency, it would be wise to operate at the level of allocating votes and rights rather than substantive rules. In the economic sector, the basic unit of account is money. Economists prefer redistribution of wealth and property rights over special subsidies or rules to redistribute income because the former have fewer costs. In the political sector, the basic unit of accounting is the number of votes, and the maximum efficiency is achieved by allocating votes and political rights rather than creating inefficient rules. The U.S. Constitution follows these precepts.

Beard argued that the designers and ratifiers of the Constitution were motivated by self-interest. I do not disagree with the view that self-interest existed (although perhaps in a different way than he characterized); rather, I disagree about the implications.[47] Self-interest does not imply inefficient institutions, but the opposite: efficiency-enhancing institutions increase the rewards to those affected by the Constitution. The intuition behind my argument is best developed by considering a contract between a monopolist and a consumer. In such a situation, both sides have self-interest, but one side has greater economic power. Suppose the contract involves dispute resolution with the following possibilities: (1) a judge is chosen by the monopolist, or (2) a judge is chosen by both parties, and if there is no consensus, a coin is flipped to determine which judge is chosen. Even a greedy and powerful monopolist is likely to agree to the second proposal. Any additional cost to the monopolist from unbiased judgments is more than made up for by the higher price that the consumer is willing to pay for a contract specifying fair judgments. That is, the monopolist has less to gain by biased judgments than the consumer has to lose. Therefore, both prefer unbiased judgments as long as the consumer pays.

---

47. Beard's empirical work demonstrated that votes on ratification were consistent with his theory. There is a long list of critics (Brown 1956 and McDonald 1958 have been the most influential), but his detractors, as well as his supporters, have generally failed to make use of the basic techniques of statistical analysis and instead have relied on ocular tests. Recent work by McGuire and Ohsfeldt (1989a,b), using more powerful statistical techniques, yield some results contrary to those of Beard. For example, they hypothesized and their data confirmed that slave owners were less inclined toward ratification than other groups.

The same logic holds in designing the Constitution. Inefficient rules create greater losses for the loser than gains for the gainer. Both sides are made better off by designing efficient judicial (and other political) institutions and paying off the more powerful with more votes and more political rights.

CONCLUDING REMARKS

In this chapter, I have argued that efficiency considerations determine constitutional arrangements and court interpretations. Even those sections of the Constitution that Beard and others claim to be distributive I have shown to be efficiency enhancing. Except for the takings clause, I have not covered the Bill of Rights. While these and the other amendments to the Constitution have often been viewed as promoting justice, there is an underlying efficiency explanation. Farber (1991) has shown that the optimal level of knowledge requires freedom of speech to be constitutionally protected; while Posner (1992) shows that the limits on freedom of speech can be understood in terms of a simple cost-benefit rule. For example, a person advocating an immediate lynching can be prosecuted, even though a person advocating the eventual overthrow of the United States cannot. Although overthrow of the government is the more serious outcome, the likelihood is small and the opportunity for hearing opposing views is high. Hence the expected damage is slight. Due process can also be justified on grounds of economic efficiency. Needless error involves unnecessary economic costs. The greater the cost of error, the more economically justified it is to expend resources on avoiding error, and the more due process is guaranteed. Hence, putting someone in jail requires more due-process safeguards than denying the person food stamps. Admittedly, critical constitutional questions remain unanswered until further research is completed. For example, under what circumstances is bicameralism more (or less) efficient than unicameralism? Or when is a confederation more (or less) efficient than a more centralized federation? Dealing with these questions is beyond the scope of this chapter and of necessity requires research efforts by a great number of people.

11

MAJORITY RULE AND PREFERENCE AGGREGATION

SOME PESSIMISTIC VIEWS OF DEMOCRACY are not based on the irrationality of voters, shirking by politicians, or rent seeking by special interests; rather, they are based on the perceived failure inherent in the aggregation mechanism of majority rule. Three separate problems have been isolated: (1) Majority rule is concerned with numbers of votes, not intensity, (2) majority rule trajectories may lead anyplace in the feasible set, and (3) majority rule maximizes benefits to this generation at the expense of future generations. In this chapter, I show that the potential for these three problems has been greatly exaggerated.

THE MEDIAN VOTER MAY CHOOSE AN INEFFICIENT OUTCOME

Consider the provision of a public good. For a given tax structure, voter i's optimal point is where his marginal valuation (V_i) is equal to his marginal tax (T_i). If two candidates are competing to win the election, then the equilibrium strategies will be at the median voter's most preferred position. Thus the amount of public good provided will be where the median voter's marginal valuation equals his marginal tax. More formally, majority rule equilibrium results in the following:

(11.1) $V_m = T_m$ (m being the median voter).

In contrast, the conditions for economic efficiency are that the sum of marginal valuations of the good equal the sum of marginal taxations (marginal costs), or more formally,

(11.2)
$$\sum_{i=1}^{n} V_i = \sum_{i=1}^{n} T_i.$$

In general, the conditions for 11.1 need not coincide with the conditions for 11.2. Hence the median-voter outcome may be inefficient.[1]

This result is not very devastating. If the median voter's marginal valuation and marginal tax bracket are equivalent to the mean voter's marginal preference and tax bracket, as would be the case with symmetric distributions, then the median-voter outcome is efficient.[2] Even if there were not exact equivalence, under many conditions there is not a great deal of difference between the median and the mean of a distribution.[3]

This median-voter model does not provide the efficient answer primarily because only one instrument controls two policies: (1) the amount of the public good, and (2) the distribution of the tax burden. That is, in the model there is a fixed relationship between the provision of the public good and the tax incidence. There is no end to the number of failures one can create by forcing multidimensional policies into a one-dimensional method of control. This is only one example, but why should politicians restrict their platforms in the way posed in this model?[4]

If the median-voter result were truly inefficient, then there would exist a different tax policy (possibly multidimensional) coupled with an efficient amount of the public good that would dominate the inefficient

1. This result can be found in Bergstrom (1973); Shepsle and Weingast (1984); Holcombe (1985); and others.

2. Bergstrom and Cornes (1983) show that when utility functions are of the following form, $A(Y)X_i + B_i(Y)$ where X is the amount of the private good and Y is the vector of public goods, and B_i is symmetrically distributed around the mean, then the median is Pareto optimal, incentive compatible, and a Lindahl equilibrium (that is, the taxes are adjusted in such a way that there is unanimity).

3. Probabilistic voting may also move the outcome from the median toward the optimal. If voter i's probability of voting for candidate X is a linear function of the utility differential between the two candidates $(A + B[U(W_i^x) - U(W_i^y)])$ where W_i^j is the wealth that voter i receives if candidate j wins, and candidates maximize expected plurality, then both candidates will maximize the total utility from wealth. If the utility of wealth is also linear, then both candidates will choose that platform which maximizes total wealth.

4. Barzel and Deacon (1975) and Eysenbach (1974) have still another variant on the failure of the median voter. Voters may choose an inefficient level of public provision over a set of private alternatives with different levels of expenditure for different groups. But the public provision need not be unitary and monolithic and hence need not be inefficient.

median-voter result. A candidate might come upon this by trial and error, or perhaps there exists a demand revelation mechanism that yields the efficient outcome. Either way, the political market would achieve an efficient result. We would have a "median"-voter outcome, but it would be in a multidimensional space.[5]

To more fully understand why the median of the unidimensional-issue space may not be the majority outcome, it is useful to reconsider local land use decisions (chap. 9). Suppose a developer wants to build two hundred housing units on vacant land. Because of increased congestion costs and the loss of green space, the median voter (that is, the majority) may oppose such a development. However, after meeting with the city council and hearing all sides, a bargain is struck—the developer agrees to donate some of the land for open space and to build a primary school. The median voter may favor this plan, which includes an implicit tax on the developer. Note that if the majority votes for the expanded plan, this is not because the developer is rich or has concentrated interests in comparison to the diffuse interests of the voters. Rather, a trade has been made making both the median voter and the developer better off. A city council that is successful in exploiting all potential gains from trade will be reelected. That is what good politicians do: create coalitions and find acceptable compromises. They are not constrained to unidimensional solutions only.

Maybe no such demand revelation mechanism exists because no method can force voters to reveal their true desire for the public good. Nevertheless, there will be an impetus to choose that feasible mechanism which is likely to generate more efficient outcomes.[6]

INTRANSITIVITY AND UNBOUNDED TRAJECTORIES

McKelvey (1976, 1979) devised the following model demonstrating inefficiency in multidimensional spaces. Assume that there are two candi-

---

5. Income redistribution arising out of different taxation policies has a great potential for intransitivity; so there may be many possible efficient outcomes (see chap. 12). For a discussion of why the outcomes are likely to remain in the Pareto-optimal set, see the next section.

6. The aggregation of preferences may be imperfect in comparison to a situation of zero transaction costs and perfect (or costless) information about others' utility functions, but this is an unfair standard by which to judge the efficiency of either economic or political markets.

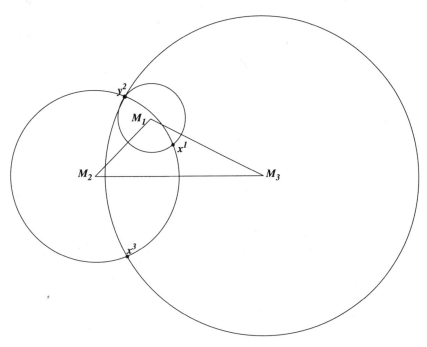

FIG. 11.1. The Pareto-optimal set is the triangle formed by the set of most preferred positions M_1, M_2, and M_3. x^1 is the incumbent's position in period 1. Assume that indifferent voters will vote for the opposition (this assumption makes the graphing simpler). Then y^2 is the winning position in the second election (voter 1 and voter 2 will vote for y^2 over x^1); and x^3 is the winning position in the third election (voter 2 and voter 3 will vote for x^3 over y^2). x^3 is further away from the Pareto-optimal set than y^2.

dates (X and Y) with two-dimensional policy vectors, x and y, respectively, and three voters (1, 2, and 3). Each voter has a most-preferred point M_i in the policy space with circular indifference curves (utility being a monotonic function of the distance from the most preferred point). Further, assume that the winning candidate must stick with her policy in the next election and that the opposition candidate is concerned only with winning the present election. Then the trajectory of possible winning platforms can go anywhere in the space, and in particular it can go outside the Pareto-optimal set. An example is drawn in figure 11.1, in which x^1, the winning position in period 1 and the incumbent position in period 2, loses to y^2 in period 2, which in turn loses to x^3 in period 3.

The arguments in previous chapters suggest many possible solutions to this problem. Politicians are likely to be more sensitive to the interests of the voters than the automatons in McKelvey's model. If the opposition candidate were at all interested in the voters' welfare, then she would, at a minimum, have the following lexicographical ordering: looking only at winning platforms, choose only Pareto-optimal policies. If the opposition candidate were interested only in her own welfare, then she would, at a minimum, have the following lexicographical ordering: looking only at winning platforms, choose that set of policies which maximizes her own utility. This too, would restrict the set of possible outcomes (Wittman 1977). I will now consider a slightly different set of assumptions, which I believe are more realistic than McKelvey's. These will be shown to yield a stable outcome within the Pareto-optimal set.

Assume that a voter is more likely to vote for a candidate the closer the candidate's position is to the voter's most preferred position. More formally, assume that

(11.3) the probability that voter i votes for candidate X is $P_i (\|M_i, x\|, \|M_i, y\|)$ and the probability that i votes for Y is $1 - P_i$

where $\| \ \|$ is the distance operator and P_i is strictly concave in x and convex in y. The probabilities may arise because the voters are imperfectly informed or because they value other attributes, such as competence and honesty, which are only imperfectly known. Alternatively, we can interpret (11.3) as follows. The voters vote with certainty, but the candidates' knowledge of how voter i votes is characterized via equation (11.3).

We further assume that candidates X and Y want to maximize their expected vote.

It is now clear that all trajectories will be in the Pareto set defined by the triangle. For given any choice by X (the incumbent), any point y' outside the Pareto set will yield a lower probability of Y winning than some point y within the set. Indeed, we can throw out the awkward assumption that the candidates take turns presenting platforms. Assume that the candidates present their positions simultaneously (and the set of strategies takes place within a closed and convex subset of R^n). Then there exists a unique equilibrium outcome within the Pareto set. The proof follows immediately from our assumptions. Maximizing expected vote is equivalent to maximizing the sum of the individual probabilities. Since these are strictly concave in x and strictly convex in y, their sums are strictly concave and convex. We therefore can appeal to a theorem by Nash (1951) on existence and uniqueness. So, at least in this case, we have not only rid ourselves of inefficiency but intransitivity as well.[7]

Furthermore, if voters register their preferences sincerely (that is, they do not vote strategically), then even if both candidates have initially chosen inefficient (disequilibrium) positions and the candidates lack global knowledge of the expected vote functions, trial and error will lead to the efficient outcome. The winning candidate will have a higher probability of being closer to the efficient outcome. So if the candidate on the right is behind in the polls, she knows that a move to the left will enhance her position; if the candidates are tied in the polls and the efficient outcome is still further to the left, a small move to the left by either candidate will increase her probability of winning. In this way myopic behavior will eventually lead to an efficient equilibrium.

Another way to overcome the possibility of a wandering trajectory is to assume that the candidate's objective is more than just winning. For example, Grofman et al. (1987) assume that a candidate will choose a position that defeats or ties the greatest number of alternatives. This will result in a position being chosen within a subset of the Pareto-optimal set.[8]

Income distribution cannot be characterized in terms of the same issue space that McKelvey considered, but a similar analysis can be applied. Ward (1961) demonstrated that any income distribution (including Pareto-inferior distributions) that provides an amount of pie strictly greater than zero to a majority of players can be on the intransitivity set (a more detailed description is found in chapter 12). That is, the trajectory can go anywhere. Thus Ward and McKelvey have similar results, and the solutions to their puzzles are analogs also. Assume that the election is devoted to dividing an income pie in which crumbs may be left on the table. Assume also that the probability that voter i votes for candidate X is an increasing function of the amount of pie that candidate X offers

7. See Coughlin and Nitzan (1981) for related results. Probabilities introduce a kind of friction into the vote mechanism. Friction can be introduced in other ways. For example, Tovey (1991) assumes a bias for the status quo. His model yields an equilibrium at the median of an n-dimensional symmetric distribution.

8. Intransitivity within legislatures has been solved by Baron (1989). See chapter 12.

to voter i (if X wins) and a decreasing function of the amount of pie that candidate Y offers to voter i (if Y wins). Assume further that this probability is a strictly concave function of X's offer and a strictly convex function of Y's offer. Again assume that each candidate maximizes her expected vote. Then we will have a unique equilibrium, and it will be efficient. The existence proof is similar to the one above.[9] Efficiency follows immediately (even in the absence of the assumptions required for transitivity) since any crumb needlessly left on the table reduces the expected vote of the candidate.

If we combine the approach used here with that provided in the previous section, we can demonstrate that policy is wealth maximizing. Restricting our attention to the case where voters have circular indifference curves for policy, assume that the price that a voter is willing to pay for a policy is independent of wealth (this implicitly assumes that the voter always has some wealth) and that demand curves are strictly downward sloping (that is, the closer a position is to a voter's most preferred policy position, the less the voter is willing to pay for an additional movement closer). Assume also that the voters vote probabilistically: the greater the utility that a voter derives from implementation of X's policy and income distribution plan, the greater the probability that the voter will vote for X. Finally, assume that each candidate maximizes expected vote. Then there exists a unique point, P^*, in policy space that will be chosen by majority rule. Given any other policy point, P', and an income distribution, I', all voters will prefer P^* and income distribution, I'', which occurs after the voters have paid for the policy move from P' to P^*. Hence the candidates will always choose P^*, the wealth-maximizing policy.[10]

SHIFTING THE BURDEN OF THE DEBT ONTO FUTURE GENERATIONS

Voters may well maximize their own utility, but won't it come at the expense of future generations, who do not even have a vote? For example, the present generation may force the next generations to pay for

9. Coughlin (1986) has an existence proof when voters' choices can be characterized by a logistic function. See also Coughlin (1991).
10. In this third model, the political determination of income distribution is left unspecified.

debts incurred by this generation.[11] While this argument may seem to have some plausibility, it ignores the other half of the equation. To illustrate, suppose that in the next generation, land will be taxed an additional billion dollars to pay off the debts from this generation. People in this generation who own the land will want to sell it and consume the proceeds before they die. But they will receive one billion dollars less from the sales, so this generation ultimately pays for the debt. The burden of the debt falls on the present generation, and they will there-fore choose the optimal discount rate, just as they choose the optimal policy in other areas.

OVERVIEW

In this chapter I have undertaken an abstract characterization of democratic systems. Pessimistic results found in the work of McKelvey (1976), Holcombe (1985), and others were shown to rely on two inap-propriate assumptions—the no-trade rule and lack of strict monotonicity in the outcome functions.

If policy choices are restricted so that implicit trades cannot be made, then majority rule outcomes, not surprisingly, could be inefficient. Of course, a similar no-trade rule would also destroy the efficiency of economic markets, as the following example illustrates: Suppose I have pears and you have apples and each prefers what the other has, but we are allowed to decide only one issue at a time. You want my pears, but I won't give them to you, because I can't get apples or money in return, since that is a different issue, decided on independently. For the same reason, you will not give me your apples. So we will have a Pareto-inferior outcome. Assuming a no-trade rule, the unanimity requirement for consensual trade leads to inefficiency in the economic sphere; assum-ing a no-trade rule, majority voting leads to inefficiency in the political sphere. But as I argued earlier, the art of politics is making good trades.

Inefficiency is also likely if there are no costs to being inefficient—lack of strict monotonicity. Thus in Ward's classic example of inefficient

11. A number of authors have considered this possibility. See, for example, Tabellini (1991) and Cukierman and Meltzer (1989), both of whom consider the possibility of debt repudiation by later generations. See also Kotlikoff and Rosenthal (1993). If voters are concerned with the welfare of their children, they may not be so callous toward future generations. See Barro (1974) for the classic argument in favor of "Ricardian equivalence."

majority rule, if the status quo allocation of apples is 30, 30, and 30, the challenger can beat the incumbent with an allocation of 35, 35, 0 or 45, 45, 0. Given Ward's characterization, the challenger is indifferent between the latter two choices, so that the inefficient allocation, 35, 35, 0, is possible. But if voters respond to better platforms by increasing their probability of voting for, or politicians skim off the surplus for themselves, inefficiency disappears.

If voters have concave probability-of-voting functions, there is an efficient equilibrium that is dynamically stable. That is, even if both candidates have initially chosen inefficient platforms, myopic behavior by the candidates will lead to both choosing an efficient outcome.

The stronger result of wealth maximization can also be derived. We start with the Coase theorem. If there are zero transaction costs, and aggregate preferences are independent of the distribution of income, then production will be the same whatever the initial allocation of property rights. Using Coase's example, whether farmers have the right to nondamage of their crops or ranchers have the right to damage farmers' crops, the outcome will be the same. If ranchers have the right to damage, farmers will pay ranchers to reduce the damage until marginal cost equals marginal benefit; if farmers have the right to nondamage, ranchers will purchase the right to damage until marginal cost equals marginal benefit. This theorem has been used to justify private exchange, but it applies equally well to democratic politics, *even in the presence of high transaction costs* between the farmer and the rancher. In the second section, we used a version of this theorem to show that vote maximization leads to wealth maximization in democratic markets, in the same way that profit maximization leads to wealth maximization in economic markets. The logic is especially transparent when the election is to decide the amount of damage to the farmer. If either candidate does not choose the optimal amount of damage, the other candidate can always win with the following policy: choose the optimal amount of damage and redistribute income from the party who benefits from the policy to the party who is hurt by the policy, so that both are better off. This is possible since the wealth-maximizing policy is worth more in total than the suboptimal policy. So the candidate with the wealth-maximizing policy can gain both votes; and even if the first candidate changes her position, a wealth-maximizing choice by the second candidate can never get less than one vote (unless both platforms are identical and the second candidate loses both times in a coin toss). Hence, the same conditions that lead to wealth maximization in private markets will also lead to wealth maximization in democratic markets, even if the private market has high transaction costs. Winning platforms provide the implicit trades and efficient outcome that would exist if market transactions were costless.

A more fully specified model would include the transaction costs of democratic decision making. When these costs are too high, issues may be left to the private sector. However, the same underlying logic still remains. Winning platforms will be those in which the benefits outweigh the costs, including transaction costs.

12

THE DISTRIBUTION OF ECONOMIC
WEALTH AND POLITICAL POWER

IN PREVIOUS CHAPTERS, I have emphasized issues of efficiency and, for the most part, have downplayed the distribution of political rewards. There is a reason for saving distributional questions to this, the last substantive chapter. As I will demonstrate in the first section, intransitivity of income distribution undermines almost all distributional analysis. So one must discount most of the extensive political science literature on the distribution of political power and remain agnostic.

Indeed, skepticism about distributional explanations of political outcomes pervades the whole chapter. In the second section, I show that despite appearances to the contrary, many laws are incapable of affecting the distribution of income. If income cannot be redistributed, then rent-seeking and power explanations cannot be used to explain legal choice. Next I briefly show that many of the arguments in favor of efficiency also undermine theoretical constructs based on the unequal distribution of political power.

INTRANSITIVITY AND THE DISTRIBUTION OF INCOME

The first and overarching problem in discussing the distribution of income within the context of majority rule is the issue of intransitivity. If people are selfish and sensitive to even small differences in income, then no distribution of income will command a majority over every other distribution of income, and every distribution of income save those that give absolutely nothing to the majority is on the cycle of intransitivity. This is illustrated in table 12.1, where A, B, and C are the three voters,

Table 12.1. Distribution of the Income Pie

Platform	Voter		
	A	B	C
1	33.3	33.3	33.3
2	50.0	50.0	0.0
3	70.0	0.0	30.0
4	0.0	4.0	31.0
5	0.0	5.0	95.0
6	1.0	0.0	99.0
7	33.3	33.3	33.3

and 1, 2, 3, . . . are the sequence of income distribution policies offered to them. The amounts are percentages of the income pie.

In an election between platforms 1 and 2, platform 2 will win since a majority of voters (A and B) prefer platform 1 over platform 2. Similarly, platform 3 is preferred over platform 2 by A and C; and platform 4 is preferred over platform 3 by B and C. Note that in platform 4, not all of the pie is consumed (perhaps the policy creates inefficiencies). Platform 5 is preferred over platform 4 by B and C, and so forth. But then both platforms 7 and 1 are preferred to platform 6. Now throughout the book, I have presented reasons why the inefficient platform 4 will not be presented (see especially the discussion in chapter 11). But all of the remaining platforms are efficient and none dominates all of the others. The example need not be limited to voting or to the division of income. For example, A, B, and C may be three coalitions, and the allocations may represent the geographic area controlled by each coalition.

Every theory of income distribution must deal with the problem of income intransitivity. Do the defense industry and the dairy farmers have their hands in the taxpayers' pockets? Why don't the dairy farmers join with the taxpayers against the defense industry? Why doesn't the defense industry join in a coalition against the dairy farmers? Or why doesn't the auto industry, organized labor, or another group form some other coalition to bring down the present winners? Why doesn't the majority vote to confiscate the wealth of the wealthiest 10 percent of the population? Why don't the wealthiest 60 percent of the population take away (more) wealth from the bottom 40 percent? Every theory of distribution must confront these issues, but much of the literature on the distribution of political rewards shows no sign that the authors are even aware of the problem.[1]

One answer to the intransitivity problem is that people are not so selfish as the numerical example assumes. Instead, there are shared values that overcome the presence of intransitivity. I am not averse to such an answer. Perhaps the majority of the population believes that the economic market should remain unfettered except for certain safety nets such as Social Security. That is, there may be a consensus about the way income should be distributed in a liberal society.[2] But most who talk about the distribution of income do not have such a benign view of this consensus. To authors in the Marxist tradition, it is based on false consciousness among the workers who are ideologically dominated by the bourgeoisie and manipulated by privately owned mass media. For example, Edelman (1964) and Gaventa (1980) argue that the powerless are kept quiescent by elites who manipulate their tastes and values. Similarly, Miliband (1969) claims that the ownership of the means of production extends to the means of intellectual production and that these are used to persuade people to hold beliefs contrary to their interests. I am not ready to let such a view come in through the back door of taste generation. False consciousness would have to assume that the disadvantaged are manipulated but not the ruling elite, that the disadvantaged do not realize it (even though Edelman, Gaventa, and Miliband do), and that there is no competition among the rulers to create different preferences (the intransitivity problem at the deeper level of preference creation). Arguments against such assumptions have been provided in the previous chapters.[3] Furthermore, we have been able to observe the effects of extreme indoctrination in nondemocratic Communist societies. Seventy-five years of Communist rule in the Soviet Union did not create a consensus that the party leaders deserved more than

1. A class-based analysis does not resolve the problem because capitalists are interested in maximizing their own profits even at the expense of other capitalists.

2. This consensus may be motivated by fear of revolution by the working class if they receive too little of the income pie (see Przeworski and Wallerstein 1982).

3. Even Marxists have argued against a cohesive class consciousness of the bourgeoisie. "The interest of 'capitalism' and of 'capitalist' is not the same: the survival of capitalism is not in the interests of individual capitalists" (Przeworski 1990, 92). "We cannot take a coherent and consistent class consciousness of the ruling class as a starting point for a reconstruction of the class character of the state activity" (Offe 1975, 34)

the populace, nor even agreement that there should be Communism in the first place.

Another approach to the intransitivity problem is to assume that voters are less sensitive to income differentials. If probability of voting is based on utility differentials and utility for income is concave (that is, there is diminishing marginal utility of income), then expected vote-maximizing candidates will choose policies promising equality of income. This has been worked out formally by Wittman (1988) and alluded to in chapter 11. The intuition is that an extra dollar transferred to a poor person increases the probability that he will vote for the candidate more than the dollar transferred from a rich person decreases the probability that she will vote for the candidate. When candidates maximize their expected plurality, marginal effects are equalized, and all voters will be promised the same share of the pie. This model is a divide-the-dollar game. In the real world, incentives would have to be taken into account—equal after-tax incomes would reduce the incentive to work, reducing the amount of dollars available. A system that takes into account the effect of taxes and subsidies on the size of the income pie would result in a less equal distribution of after-tax income.

Baron (1991) places the income distribution game within the legislature. Representatives want to maximize wealth for their districts. Legislators are chosen randomly to propose income allocations. Not passing a proposed allocation causes delay, and in his model, delays are costly. If the allocation gives too little to too many other districts, then a majority will vote against. Therefore, the first legislator chosen promises just enough so that a majority does not expect to do any better by delay. Baron's model predicts more income to the district represented by the chosen legislator. While it attempts to explain the size of coalitions, it does not explain income distribution ex ante (since each legislator has an equal chance of proposing) or over time (since each year the process is repeated). A number of interesting variations of the basic model are possible. Ferejohn and Baron (1991) show that an open rule tends to make the allocation of income more universal. Another variant would assign higher probabilities of being chosen as the agenda setter to those who had provided good allocations in the past.[4] If this probability were

---

4. The model allows each session to be infinitely long. So each session decides only the income distribution for that year (even if it is theoretically possible that the decision is made after the year is over).

a positive monotonic function of the sum of utilities received in the last division and utilities were a concave function of income, then there would be a tendency for a more uniform distribution of income. This addition to Baron's model accords roughly with how majority leaders are chosen—they are rewarded for past good behavior.

WHEN DO LAWS REDISTRIBUTE WEALTH?

Commentators often explain government policy as probusiness and anticonsumer (or the reverse). If such policies do indeed redistribute wealth from the demanders to the suppliers (or vice versa), then distributional politics may explain policy outcomes.[5] However, in this section, I show that government policy is virtually incapable of shifting wealth between demanders and suppliers and that such explanations are therefore suspect. Most of the examples come from the common law, an area I have slighted so far; however, the logic holds equally well for statutory law and executive policy.

Although numerous authors have argued that the common law is efficient (see, for example, Posner 1977), a substantial number have argued that distributive issues determine the nature of the law. For example, Gilmore (1970) argues that biases in contract law in the nineteenth century increased the profitability of new industry, thereby promoting economic progress. As another example, Horowitz (1974) argues that the courts are tools of the ruling class and therefore breach-of-labor contracts are biased in favor of employers. As a third example, Whitford (1968) and Slawson (1974) argue that limited consumer warranties can be explained by the weak market power of consumers in comparison to the market power of large manufacturers.

In this chapter I argue that in many instances government policy is incapable of affecting the distribution of wealth.[6] The argument fits in with my earlier claim that efficiency, not distribution of power, determines policy. Although the essence of a judicial decision appears to be a distributive one (the immediate outcome is a zero-sum game for the participants), in many areas—such as contracts; torts between contracting parties; corporate, family, and even some aspects of nuisance law—there can be no redistribution between the *class* of defendants

---

5. Even here the redistribution should be efficient.
6. Arguments along these lines have been made by Posner (1986).

and plaintiffs. This holds true whether one or both of the litigants is a perfect competitor or a monopolist. Thus, in many areas of law and politics, distributive theories are inappropriate because no redistribution goes on (at least in the ways presented by the distributive theorists).

In the following subsections, I develop this idea in increasing stages of complexity.

Exculpatory Clauses Allowed

To make the analysis concrete, I will focus on product liability. As my first example, I consider liability for exploding pop bottles.

If exculpatory clauses are allowed, the only difference between liability for the bottler and no liability is the writing of the exculpatory clause, if needed.[7] If the law says that Coke is liable, but Coke's profits are higher if it is not liable, then Coke will print a label on the bottle saying that it is not liable. If Coke is more profitable when liable, it will have no need to print anything on the Coke bottle. Thus the law's only effect, when exculpatory clauses are allowed, is on the amount of printing and other (transaction) costs associated with writing the exculpatory clause.

Why might it be profitable for Coke to assume liability? It is possible that Coke can produce two kinds of bottles: a fat Coke bottle that never explodes and a slim one that explodes one out of a million times causing twenty thousand dollars damage, for an average of two cents a bottle. If buyers are risk neutral, they would prefer to pay one and a half cents extra for the fat bottle. If Coke can produce the fat bottle for one cent more, then it can make more profit by producing the fat bottle. Even if Coke can only produce the slim bottle, it may be profitable for Coke to assume liability if Coke is risk neutral and some of its customers are risk averse. By assuming liability, Coke can sell its slim bottle for more than two cents extra to risk-averse buyers even though it costs Coke only two cents for liability, on average. Both sides are better off. Of course, if some customers are risk neutral or risk preferring, Coke can offer two

---

7. An exculpatory clause allows the law to not apply if there is some kind of express consent by the parties to the contrary. For example, in the absence of an agreement to the contrary, laundries might be liable for clothes left over thirty days. Thus they post a sign that they will not be responsible for clothes left over thirty days. On the other side, a manufacturer is not liable by law for an automobile engine lasting fifty thousand miles unless there is a warranty (exculpatory clause) assuming liability for fifty thousand miles.

The analysis is a variant on Coase (1960).

kinds of bottles: one with liability by Coke and one without. Just as there is sugar-free Coke, there may be liability-free (for the consumer) Coke and liability Coke, the latter selling for less. This is similar to the option for an extended warranty on new cars and appliances for an added price. By assuming liability, Coke is providing an insurance policy to the consumer. It is a tied product. The consumer buys both Coke and a specialized insurance policy.

Even if Coke is a monopolist trying to exploit the last penny from the consumer, Coke will offer additional amenities, including insurance, if this increases its profitability.

The Effect of Liability When Exculpatory Clauses Are Not Allowed

It is quite obvious that the law will have little effect when exculpatory clauses are allowed. However, the analysis sets the stage for the more complex case where the participants cannot rewrite the contract. Here I investigate the differing outcomes when one side or the other is made liable and exculpatory clauses are not allowed either way.[8]

Making the consumer liable instead of the producer means that the consumer will self-insure, buy insurance elsewhere, or buy a safer, nonexploding bottle. If the consumer can obtain insurance for the same price as Coke obtains insurance, nothing is changed, except that the consumer no longer buys an insurance policy with his Coke. In turn, this means that the consumer will pay less for Coke (if the bottle has a positive probability of exploding). Consider the possibility that only one bottle is available and that either Coke or the consumer can purchase insurance at an actuarially fair price.[9] If the bottle on average causes one cent's harm, then the consumer will pay an extra cent when Coke is liable; when Coke is not liable, the person will pay Coke one cent less but put the money in the kitty. If the nonexploding Coke bottle costs only half a cent more to produce, then the bottle will be produced whether

---

8. It is extremely rare that the producer of a product is prevented by law from assuming liability (blood donors may be a counterexample). I assume it here in order to demonstrate the differences in the symmetrically opposite situation. For analyzing the case where exculpatory clauses are allowed one way but not the other, just combine the analysis from the last section and this section.

9. Other possibilities involve a more complicated logic, but do not change the essential result that the consumer pays for liability insurance.

the consumer or Coke is liable (since it is cheaper than the insurance).

The same sort of logic applies to other areas, such as malpractice, breach of contract, and laws requiring artists to receive royalties: the insured pays for the insurance. I will briefly consider malpractice, ignoring the issues that arise because of the pervasive existence of health insurance (e.g., people may be insensitive to price when their health insurer pays all). Assume, first, that legal fees are minor so that the transaction cost of doctors' insuring patients is low. Under this assumption, the existence of malpractice liability does not affect the *total* price of medical care to any significant degree.[10] When doctors are liable for malpractice, patients are willing to pay higher fees to substitute for the patient's self-insuring, purchasing insurance, or facing risk, most likely the latter. The main effect of malpractice liability is therefore a shifting of the burden of being victimized by malpractice from the few patients subject to poor medical care to all patients, who now pay an implicit insurance premium when they visit the doctor. The average doctor is only mildly affected by the imposition of malpractice. In particular, she will not practice excessive defensive medicine (e.g., unnecessary tests) in order to prevent malpractice.

When legal costs are high (which need not mean excessive), the outcome may be quite different. High transaction costs of litigation and possibly mistaken attribution of malpractice encourage excessive caution by doctors (from the viewpoint of efficiency, not profit) in order to reduce the likelihood of mistaken attribution of malpractice.[11] But these costs of defensive medicine, expected legal fees, and expected malpractice awards are turned into higher fees by doctors.

The bottom line in all of these cases is that the consumer always pays. Making the producer liable does not shift wealth from producers to consumers. It may shift wealth from one set of consumers (those who are never harmed) to another set (those who are harmed) or from one set of producers to another, and it will definitely shift income to lawyers, but it does not shift wealth between the litigant classes.

10. If information about doctors is poor, so that patients cannot identify the quality of the doctor, then malpractice reduces adverse selection, benefiting high-quality doctors and hurting low-quality doctors.

11. Such defensive medicine is not in the interest of the patient since patients are not interested in purchasing such care otherwise.

Liability When the Individual Is an Input into the Accident Rate

Heretofore the analysis has concerned cases where the consumer has little effect on the probability of an accident or the degree of damage. In this section, I consider such a possibility.

A lawnmower accident may occur because the mower was poorly designed or because the person operating it was careless. The lawnmower company cannot ex ante discriminate among buyers.[12] For example, it cannot refuse to sell to careless buyers or charge careless buyers a higher price (as is the case with insurance companies, who can either refuse to insure high risks or charge them a higher price). The lawnmower case is thus different from the Coke bottle case. Here both sides are important variables in the production of the potential damage, but only one side can choose with whom it does business.

Once again, this is a case with low transaction costs. Consequently, when exculpatory clauses are allowed, the initial assignment of liability in the absence of a clause will have no effect on the actual final assignment of liability. If the court assigns liability to the manufacturer and the manufacturer's profits are higher when it does not have a tie-in insurance sale, then the manufacturer will just put a tag on the mower stating that the manufacturer is not liable.

What would happen if the manufacturer were forced to be liable for all the damage, which I will assume is property damage and not personal injury.[13] If manufacturers were forced to insure against all damage, then lawnmowers would be built for idiots. The careful users would be subsidizing the careless. Once again, the outcome is less a redistribution between producers and consumers than a redistribution between consumers.

In a nutshell: The law cannot redistribute income between workers

---

12. The seller might be able to distinguish after the accident whether the person was careless or not.

13. The company might offer an insurance policy for damage arising from certain types of failure of the lawnmower. If it were relatively cheap (read efficient) for the company to prevent a blade from flying through the air and causing damage, then the company would produce the safe blade and insure customers against damage from flying blades. The cost of the insurance policy would be quite low because flying blades would be quite rare. The insurance policy would be an especially good selling point if customers were not able to ascertain the likelihood of flying blades from simple (costless) inspection. Thus we see that there is likely to be some insurance but not complete coverage (the extent of insurance depending on the relevant technology).

and capitalists or between consumers and producers. Workers receive lower wages when occupational safety laws are made more stringent, and consumers pay higher interest rates when laws make repossession more difficult.[14] Of course, *unanticipated* changes in the law can affect wealth distribution if a contract is long-run. For example, if the government imposes more stringent safety standards and if this imposition was not anticipated at the time a wage contract was negotiated, then the more stringent standards will not have an effect on wages until the contract is up for renegotiation. In the meantime, workers will be capturing the benefit of more safety at no cost to them.

Nuisance Law and Other Cases Not Involving Contracting Parties

The previous subsections were devoted to situations in which people have some kind of exchange relationship. In this subsection, I consider relationships between noncontracting parties (for example, laws regarding pollution). Although the results are not nearly as strong as those when there are exchange relationships, I am able to demonstrate that in some cases the law is incapable of affecting the distribution of wealth between the classes of litigants (for example, polluters and pollutees) and that in other cases the distributive effects are minor.

I first consider a situation in which some land is uniquely suited for a particular use (say a limestone quarry). In the section on the takings clause (chap. 10), I showed that compensation for regulation of urban quarries would have no effect on the profits from quarrying. Compensation for regulation would only induce the quarry owner to pay more for the land in the first place. The same logic holds here in the absence of compensation. In the long run, limestone producers are not affected by laws regulating pollution; only the original owners of the land are.

If polluters are liable for damage caused by pollution, then limestone producers will bid that much less for land. Liability (and compensation) are internalized in the bid price. At the time of bidding, there may be uncertainty regarding potential liability for pollution damage. Limestone producers will take this uncertainty into account when they bid. If certain liability reduces the price paid for the land by ten thousand

---

14. Some studies argue that unionized workers benefit when occupational safety laws are imposed on nonunionized firms. If this is true (I am not sure that it is), the redistribution is again not from capitalists to workers, but from one set of capitalists and workers to another.

dollars an acre, then a 50 percent chance of liability will reduce bidding by five thousand dollars an acre. Those lucky polluters who are never liable for the pollution gain a windfall of five thousand dollars an acre; while the unlucky polluters who become liable for pollution damage suffer a loss of five thousand dollars. Thus, liability for damage from pollution costs producers nothing on average ex post and nothing for each producer ex ante.[15]

If the land adjacent to the quarry is uniquely suited for residents, then residents do not gain if the law requires that they receive compensation for pollution damage, for the price of the land will go up by an equivalent amount. Once again, it is the original landowner that benefits from such a rule. If the original landowner also owned the land for the quarry, then the owner would be interested only in the efficient solution that maximized the sum total value of all of her land.

In general, land use may not be unique. Making polluters liable to pollutees may result in more land being used by pollutees. The analysis is more complicated in such cases. To the extent that landowners can act as discriminating monopolists, the surplus value is captured by the original landowners, and, hence, the distribution of wealth between polluters and pollutees will not be affected by the choice of liability rule.[16] When the landowners cannot discriminate, the rule can affect the distribution of wealth. However, wins and losses do not cancel out, and efficiency gains coincide with the largest net gain or loss in the distribution of wealth. For example, consider the situation where the demand for land by polluters is highly elastic and the demand by pollutees is highly inelastic. This means that polluters are able to find substitutes for the land and experience no great cost if less land is devoted to activities that pollute. Making the polluter liable will result in a significant decrease in the value of the land because the increase in demand by the pollutees will not match the decrease in the demand by the polluters. The pollutees will now have less pollution and lower prices for land. Their wealth will increase. The loss of wealth by the polluters will be small. So the wealth effect and the efficiency choice will coincide.

When laws are unanticipated, there are short-run distributional consequences. Consider California Proposition 13, which effectively lowered

15. Of course, there are great rewards to the polluting firm from *unanticipatedly* changing the law in favor of polluters.

16. A choice of liability rule means choosing whether the polluter is liable for the damage to the pollutee or the polluter is not liable for the damage to the pollutee.

property taxes. To the degree that this law was unanticipated, it was a windfall for those who owned property. After passage of the proposition, the price that people were willing to pay for property increased by approximately the amount that they saved in property taxes. New owners of property have not benefited from Proposition 13 because it was already in effect and therefore anticipated before their purchase. Renters have not benefited either (except possibly in some minor second-order effects on the supply of housing).

Even when there are no land markets, competition creates zero excess profits for an industry.[17] Allowing trucking companies to pay lower road taxes will, in the short run, yield higher profits. But in the long run, new competitors will either eat away at the higher profits or, if there are barriers to entry, raise the price of purchasing established trucking companies, so that the rate of return on the investment is equal across industries.

Though I have argued that the scope of redistributive politics is narrower than sometimes believed, there are still many arenas of redistribution. Aid to Families with Dependent Children (AFDC), the progressivity of income taxes, public schooling—all have an important effect on the distribution of disposable income. But as will be shown in the following section, there are economic constraints on the extent of this redistribution. This section thus serves as a cautionary tale. One must be careful in applying redistributive theories, for sometimes, but not always, the wins and losses are more apparent than real.

COMPETITION, INFORMATION, AND THE DISTRIBUTION OF INCOME

At the opening of this chapter, I remarked that there is an extensive body of research in political science devoted to distributional questions.[18] The task of directly confronting this literature is so daunting that I will not do it at all. Instead, I will provide an outline of the kinds of arguments that can be made. But in many ways the groundwork has been laid. In the first two sections of this chapter, I argued that income distribution is intransitive and that many laws and policies cannot redistribute income. This argument undermines a large body of research. In

17. See Polinsky (1980). Economic rents might be gained if there were factors unique to a particular industry.
18. See Alford and Friedland (1985) and Przeworski (1990) for useful surveys.

this section, I will undertake a different tack: competition and information undermine Marxist theories, pressure group theories, elite theories, and most other theories of political distribution. Since most of the arguments for the efficiency of democratic markets hold equally well against theories of concentrated political power, much of my case has already been made in earlier chapters.

Theories of Politically Powerful Elites

Schmitter (1974, 1977, 1986) provides a neocorporatist model of politics. He argues that business organizations, labor unions, and a handful of other associations enjoy a virtual monopoly of representing functionally defined interests. This monopoly endows these associations with coercive powers over their members and allows their leaders to collude with the government bureaucracy.[19] It is a pretty good trick to label voluntary organizations as coercive and to call a multitude of overlapping and competing organizations a monopoly. The communications industry, for example, has literally hundreds of organizations representing it, and new ones are created all the time. If one organization does not do the bidding of its members, they will go elsewhere. And when so many organizations and bureaucracies are involved, collusion is extraordinarily difficult. Clearly, competition is a more appropriate characterization.

The old corporatist model emphasized the role of corporations in influencing government agencies. (See, for example, Lindblom 1977 and McConnell 1970.) This model also required the ignorance of the voters, absence of competition within the political system, and no congressional oversight.

Elite theories provide a different variant on class politics. Dahrendorf argues that relations of authority within the state are highly skewed: There is a clear division between ordinary citizens, who possess only the right to vote, and the elites, who "are in the position to exercise regularly control over the life chances of others by issuing authoritative decisions" (1959, 293). In his view, the function of democratic institutions, such as voting, is to maintain stable control by the elites, rather than to provide representation and benefits. Domhoff (1970) concen-

---

19. My two-sentence characterization of his work of necessity conflates three different arguments.

trates on the staffing of the elite in positions of power and argues that Congress is reduced to legitimizing policies made elsewhere. Both Domhoff and Dahrendorf assume barriers to entry, little competition between elites, and the inability of democratically elected representatives to control the bureaucracy in any meaningful way.[20] As in much of this literature, elections are peripheral to the theory.

Finally, Wilson (1973) and Olson (1982) employ pressure group theories of politics: concentrated interests will win out over more diffuse and unorganized interests. I have already taken this approach to task in chapter 7.

Structural-Dependence Theory

Most of the Marxist and elite theories of democratic politics leave out the democratic part entirely. The best justification for ignoring elections is found in structural-dependence theory: "Structural-dependence theory asserts that the private ownership of productive assets imposes constraints which are so binding that no government, regardless what its objectives might be, can pursue policies adverse to the interests of capitalists" (Przeworski 1992, 92). Because the government allows the capitalists autonomy in the productive sector, the capitalist class decides on the nature of the exchange relations. The entire society depends on the allocation of resources chosen by the owners of capital. "The political power of the capitalist class does not reside in what its members do politically . . . but rather in what its members can refuse to do economically . . . , i.e. invest" (Offe 1975, 9). The state is structurally dependent because no government can simultaneously reduce profits and increase investment. "[C]apitalists, in their collective roles as investors, have a veto over state policies in that their failure to invest at adequate levels can create major problems for state managers" (Block 1977, 15). "Because public functions in the market system rest in the hands of businessmen, it follows that jobs, prices, production, growth, the standard of living and the economic security of everyone all rest in their hands"

---

20. Their analysis requires that elites share similar values. In an ironic twist, a recent paper by Sniderman et al. (1991) undermines classic work on elites by McClosky, Hoffman, and O'Hara (1960) and McClosky (1964) by using McClosky's own data. McClosky had claimed a greater consensus among elites in favor of civil liberties than among their followers; Sniderman et al. reanalyzed his data and showed that elites had a bimodal distribution of attitudes, making the elites farther apart than their "followers."

(Lindblom 1977, 172). Politicians seeking reelection must anticipate the impact of their policies on the decisions of capitalists because these decisions affect employment, inflation, and the personal income of voters. If capital is internationally mobile, the ability of governments to manipulate the economic structure is even more constrained.

Now the Marxists have it about 98 percent right, but the remaining 2 percent makes all the difference in the analysis. It is true that democratic governments are severely constrained in their policy choices by economic forces.[21] But the Marxists are wrong in attributing these forces to capitalist control or to capitalism itself. Capitalists don't control, markets do. The capitalists, like the workers, face supply and demand curves. These curves, in turn, are determined by marginal costs and benefits. Goods are allocated to their highest use, and investment takes place until the forgone consumption equals the present value from increased consumption in the future. That is, efficient economic markets constrain the behavior of democratic markets. If vote-maximizing politicians try to monkey with the economy, it backfires—the economy becomes less efficient, and workers and capitalists vote them out of office. So politicians are restrained from such maneuvers in the first place. The Coase theorem again applies; this result does not depend on who owns the means of production. Suppose, for example, that a socialist economy could perfectly emulate a capitalist one. The trade-off between investment and present consumption would be the same, and, more generally, the marginal benefits and costs would be the same. Vote-maximizing politicians would again be constrained in their choices by requirements of an efficient economy. Making different choices would ultimately yield fewer votes.

CONCLUDING REMARKS

In a pure voting model, each voter has equal weight in determining policy. Once we allow factors other than the vote to enter in, political power is less equal. But the question is: how unequal? Unfortunately, no general equilibrium model has been developed to answer the question. The Baron (1991) and Wittman (1988) models are too simplistic, but they may serve as the basis for more complex models in the future.

21. For an alternative view, see Przeworski and Wallerstein (1988).

For the most part, the other theories are too vague to handle the complexities of the problem. Theories of the elites' control of democratic politics tend to leave out the *democratic* part entirely: either policies are formed and conducted outside the democratic domain, or the elites lull the mass of voters to sleep. Throughout the book I have argued against the latter interpretation.

Part III

Methodology

13

THE TESTING OF THEORY

NO DOUBT THE READER HAS COME UP WITH a litany of examples to contradict my hypothesis of an efficient political market. Rent control, tariffs, and farm subsidies are some of the favorite examples thrown back at me. In this chapter, I first argue that many examples of political-market failure are mutually contradictory and methodologically unsound. I then provide some suggestions for a more useful research strategy.

INHERENT INDIVISIBILITIES AND THE DEMAND
FOR MARKET-FAILURE THEORIES

The great advantage of the (economic) market . . . is that it permits wide diversity. . . . Each man can vote, at is were, for the color of tie he wants and get it; he does not have to see what color the majority wants and then, if he is in the minority, submit.

Friedman (1962, 15)

Economic markets do provide more variety than political markets. Friedman's explanation is that political markets are inherently incapable of offering as much variety. Here I offer a different explanation. It is the nature of government policy rather than the nature of government itself that accounts for this differential. Obviously, a country cannot have two foreign policies.

Certain policies (both in governments and in firms) by their very nature must be bundled together. Policy cannot be implemented without budgetary decisions. Diplomatic and military policy are complementary activities. If unbundling is infeasible, then no problem arising from bundling can be labeled inefficient, because there is no feasible alternative.

More important, the fact that government policy is indivisible and a public good (or bad, as the case may be) means that many people will be dissatisfied with the chosen policy. If the dissatisfied believe that the policy is mistaken, then the natural retort to their argument is, If you are correct, why didn't the government choose the correct policy? And the dissatisfied can only answer—a market failure. Thus, at the same time, we have theories of political-market failure to explain why we spend too much on foreign aid and too little, why we give too much support to right-wing dictators and too little, and so on.[1] So, while just about everyone has her own theory of government failure, at least half must be wrong.

QUESTIONABLE SAMPLING, AD HOC EXPLANATIONS, AND IMPROPER TESTING

Other methodolgical problems include questionable sampling, ad hoc explanations, and improper testing.

For example, it has been argued that agricultural-marketing orders have been enacted in favor of the organized growers and against the diffuse consumer. Assume that these orders benefit all growers (this may not be true). How would rent-seeking theory predict that farmers would overcome the pressure by intermediate purchasers of the good, such as processors, which may or may not be similarly concentrated; final suppliers of the good, which may be more or less concentrated; diffuse consumers; and possibly suppliers of farm inputs? Indeed, whatever the outcome, one could claim that there was rent seeking. At present, the theory of rent seeking does not give us a clear guide in operationalizing the theory. Hence, any undertaking is subject to numerous ad hoc explanations.

There is also the problem of arbitrary choice of samples. Subsidization of tobacco growing by the government, which serves as an insurer, is given as an example of successful rent seeking, but tobacco growers are unsuccessful in preventing special taxes on tobacco products, and farmers, in general, are unsuccessful in preventing quotas and other

---

1. Both the far right and the far left have their conspiratorial (read collusive) theories of government.

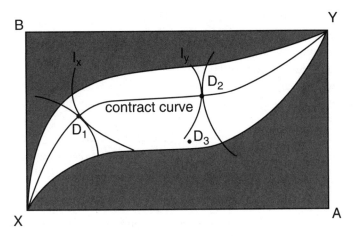

FIG. 13.1. Allocation D_3 is relatively efficient.

restrictions on the importation of cheap farm machinery. There are a large number of pressure groups engaged in political activity. The examples of successful rent seeking appear to be culled. One would prefer a test of the hypotheses where the sample was not so rigged.[2]

A more serious problem is that evidence of inefficiency may in fact support the hypothesis of an efficient political market. The logic can be illustrated via the Edgeworth-Bowley box (see fig. 13.1).[3] The box represents a distribution of two goods, apples and bananas, to two people, Xavier and Yvonne. The contract curve is the set of efficient points (the tangencies of X's and Y's indifference curves). Thus D_1 and D_2 are efficient points, but not D_3 since both people prefer D_2. A theory claiming efficient outcomes eliminates most of the box. If one counters with a vague theory claiming that governments produce inefficient results, then the set of possible outcomes is hardly restricted at all—everything but the contract curve is consistent with inefficiency. In order to compare a relatively precise efficiency theory with a diffuse inefficiency theory, one needs to make them equally predictive (equivalently, equally restrictive). I will provide first an intuitive exposition and then a more precise argument based on statistical theory.

One way of comparing a precise efficiency theory with an imprecise

2. This point has been made by Posner (1974). Data mining and other methodological errors are not limited to those who believe in market failure.

3. A similar analysis could be undertaken with the aid of the production possibility frontier diagram.

inefficiency theory is to make them equivalently imprecise by making the zone of rejection of equal size. In the diagram, I have made the theories comparable: efficiency is the unshaded area, and inefficiency is the equivalent-sized shaded area. We now see that allocation D_3 is a rejection of the hypothesis that the system is *inefficient*. So "inefficient" outcomes may support the efficiency hypothesis if they are not too inefficient. Some theories of inefficiency are more precise and predict inefficiency in a certain direction (consumers subsidize dairy producers rather than vice versa). In the context of the Edgeworth-Bowley box, a unidirectional inefficiency might be characterized as the area below the contract curve. In figure 13.2, I have drawn four zones. In zones ERIR, both hypotheses are rejected; in zones EAIR, the efficiency hypothesis is accepted (or more accurately, not rejected) and the inefficiency hypothesis rejected; in zones EAIA, neither are rejected; and in zones ERIA, the inefficiency hypothesis is accepted and the efficiency hypothesis rejected. Once again, the existence of mild inefficiencies does not reject the efficiency hypothesis. This is different than merely saying that the observation is not statistically different from zero inefficiency. If the hypothesis is that government budgets are too small (see Downs 1960), and we observe thirty government budgets, each expending one dollar less than the optimal, then government budgets are significantly less than the optimal (in a statistical sense). Nevertheless, as a predictive theory, one would choose efficiency over the Downsian alternative, since much smaller budgets are consistent with the latter, yet they are not observed. In figure 13.3, a precise inefficiency theory is compared with the hypothesis of an efficient political market. Again, certain inefficient outcomes (those in zone EAIR) support the efficiency theory and reject the theory of inefficient government behavior.

The argument can also be understood in terms of classical hypothesis testing. The usual testing of hypotheses is extremely asymmetric. One rejects the hypothesis of efficiency if the observation falls within the tail of the distribution. But one should also test the hypothesis of inefficiency. This is done in two stages: (1) taking each possible inefficiency and finding the likelihood of the observed value given that inefficiency; and (2) weighting the likelihood by the a priori expectations regarding the distribution of inefficiencies. To illustrate the whole procedure, suppose that there are eleven possible values 1, . . . 11, where 6 is efficient and the other values are inefficient. Suppose further that the likelihood

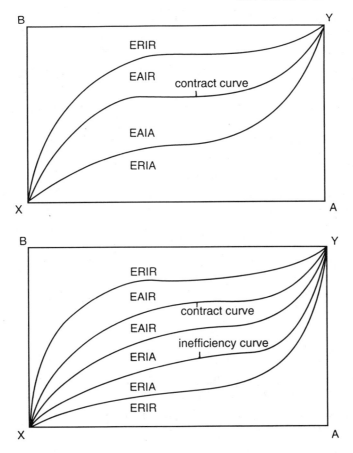

FIGS. 13.2 AND 13.3. REGIONS OF REJECTION. The Edgeworth Bowley box is divided so that the areas of rejection are equivalent for the inefficiency and efficiency theories. The inefficiency hypothesis is diffuse in (13.2). A precise inefficiency hypothesis is pitted against the precise efficiency hypothesis in (13.3).

of the observation being the true value is .75 and that the likelihood of the observation being one unit away in either direction is .125. Finally, assume that the observation was 7. The hypothesis that the outcome is efficient can be rejected at the .125 level (if conceived as a one-tailed test). Most researchers stop their hypothesis testing here, but choosing between the efficiency and inefficiency theories requires the symmetric test for inefficiency. If there is an equal ex ante probability of any inefficient point, then the hypothesis that the outcome is inefficient can also be rejected. Given equal ex ante probabilities, there is a .10 chance of the inefficient point being 7, which is multiplied by .75 (the chance of observing 7), plus a .10 chance of the inefficient point being 8, which is multiplied by .125 (the chance of observing 7), plus a .10 chance of the inefficient point being 9, which is multiplied by 0 (the chance of observing 7), and so on. The hypothesis of inefficiency can be rejected at the .0875 level. Consequently, the maximum-likelihood choice between efficiency and inefficiency is efficiency.

Thus, pointing to examples of rent control as proof that political markets are not wealth maximizing may not be proof at all. The theory of efficient political markets would predict that rent control would be uncommon, and, in fact, a very low percentage of cities enact such legislation. Likewise for tariffs. Efficient political markets would predict that tariffs would tend to be mild. So the existence of tariffs is not necessarily evidence against the efficiency of democratic markets, and, depending on the alternative formulation of the inefficient-market hypothesis, tariffs may be evidence against inefficiency.

Furthermore, pointing out political-market failures is not very helpful unless a substitute *general* theory provides a reasonable guide to the understanding of political phenomena.[4] A model of political-market failure that does better than the model of efficient markets in explaining tariffs is not of much consequence if the former is not as successful as the latter in explaining the many other areas covered by the efficient market hypothesis.

MEASURING THE UNOBSERVED

Many models of political-market failure rely on the inability of the principal (voters) to monitor the agent (politician). If the principal cannot observe the agent, then the researcher cannot either. Thus if government agents tend to be empire builders, researchers cannot observe this fact. If they could, then the principal could also. And since we are looking at long-term relationships, the principal could correct for such problems. Hence, measuring such opportunism involves an internal contradiction. When recontracting is possible, the potential for shirking is best mea-

---

4. This argument and other issues regarding anomalies have already been discussed in chapter 5.

sured, not directly, but indirectly by observing changes in the institutional structure (e.g., piece rate instead of an hourly wage, referenda instead of representation) or by failure of the market to exist at all.[5]

METHODOLOGICAL SCHIZOPHRENIA

Researchers of inefficient democratic markets often demonstrate methodological schizophrenia—they employ techniques that they eschew when studying economic markets. In this section, I draw attention to this inconsistent methodology; in the following section, I outline a different research strategy for the study of political behavior.

A number of studies have compared the technological efficiency of private and public firms. Most, but by no means all, have shown private firms to be technologically more efficient than public firms.[6] Economists rarely compare different firms within the private market, and if an economist did find one firm more efficient than another, few would believe the results.[7] Moreover, studies comparing the efficiency of public and private enterprise are poor methodologically—maybe the enterprise is public *because* it is less technologically efficient rather than it is technologically inefficient because it is public. Evidence from Eastern Europe suggests that the most efficient enterprises are privatized first. A more interesting approach would be to confront this endogeneity and predict which enterprises would be public.

Other researchers have pointed out inefficient government regulations. However, this is, in general, not the methodology used in establishing whether economic markets are efficient. For example, economists do not typically study individual businesses and consumers and observe whether they implicitly use certain decision rules, such as price ceilings,

5. This point has been discussed in greater detail in chapter 8. We are assuming that commitments are credible.

6. Since technological efficiency is not necessarily equivalent to economic efficiency (public firms may choose to satisfy other concerns that are important to voters), efficient political markets could have technologically inefficient public enterprises. Atkinson and Halvorsen's survey (1986) of empirical studies of the relative efficiency of public and private utilities found that there was no significant difference in four studies, that private firms were significantly more efficient in two studies, and that public firms were significantly more efficient in four studies. Borcherding, Pommerehne, and Schneider's survey (1982) of research from five countries showed the private sector in a much more favorable light: thirty-four studies found the private sector to be more efficient, only four studies found the private sector to have higher costs, and four studies were inconclusive.

7. Of course, output per man-hour might differ if the capital equipment differed.

that are inefficient.[8] Nor do economists tend to perform cost-benefit studies on private decisions to see whether these decisions are cost effective. For example, they do not study consumer purchases on energy conservation devices to see whether the consumer was "rational."[9]

Economists typically test their theories of consumer and firm behavior using comparative statics. Thus if the price goes up for one good, the demand for it will go down (holding real income constant). One ought to go about testing government behavior in the same way.

ORGANIZATIONAL DESIGN AND THE FUTURE FOCUS OF RESEARCH

Studies of government inefficiency may not be the most fruitful area of research. Once again, we take our clue from studies of the private sector. We do not have studies seeking to determine whether firms are generally superior (or inferior) to markets. Rather, economists try to predict under which circumstances a firm is a form of organization superior to the market (Coase 1937; Williamson 1975). Looking at the sphere of government influence, one can view purchases, taxes, and subsidies as a market solution, regulation as a long-term contract between firms (government and the private sector), and the government bureaucracy as the firm (hierarchy). The research agenda should then be: from an efficiency perspective, under what circumstances is one of these three modes of government intervention most likely?[10] The answer, of course,

8. Although economists rarely dwell on mistakes by private enterprise, one can always come up with numerous examples of stupidity in the private sector. For example, *Business Week* (August 11, 1986) alleged that the head of Allegheny International engaged in extremely opportunistic behavior and that its board of directors was not exercising any control. One of the directors was Richard Cyert. As an academic, he has argued strongly against optimization models. Perhaps he was trying to prove that firms satisfice rather than optimize. As another example, Downs and Larkey (1986) report that General Motors did not use any of its purchasing power to obtain discounts from steel companies for sheet metal. As a final example, Iacocca (1984) presents a litany of problems with Ford, but, for good reasons, this book has not undermined the economist's view that corporations maximize profits.

9. Looking at the studies that have been done, a large proportion are experimental studies, and a significant proportion of these have been devoted to decision making under uncertainty. Some of these find nonoptimal behavior (see chap. 5). For example, individuals tend to treat compound lotteries as being different from simple lotteries with equivalent outcomes. As another example, consumer purchases of safety equipment do not result in equal marginal-damage reduction per dollar.

10. Power relations might determine the amount of control but not the degree of vertical integration, just as wealth does not determine the organization of exchange.

depends on transaction costs and the comparative advantage of each organizational form in reducing opportunism. Different policies will yield different institutional responses and different degrees of vertical integration by the government. Consider, for example, the different institutional arrangements for developing advanced weapon systems and purchasing standard typing paper. There are many suppliers and demanders of standard typing paper. The potential for opportunism by either the government or the suppliers of paper is relatively slight. Neither side can easily "hold up" the other side by taking advantage of the monopoly power established by a contract to deliver, and it is relatively easy to determine the quality of the item without observing the production process. Not many firms produce their own typing paper, and we would not expect the government to. In contrast, there are no off-the-shelf purchases of advanced weapon systems. At a minimum, we would expect very involved contracting. Determining the efficient choice between government and private development would require an involved study, parallel to an analysis in the private sector determining whether it is the suppliers or the demanders of a product who should be responsible for product design.

Another avenue of research is to provide efficiency explanations for the structure of political institutions. Optimal institutional design has been a major theme of this book (see, for example, the sections devoted to interstate relations, congressional structure, and the nature of bureaucratic control). I will now show how this focus can illuminate our understanding of comparative politics.

Under systems of proportional representation, parties may have to compromise their positions to form a majority government. This compromise takes place after the representatives have been elected. The party and its ideology are very important under such a system because it is relatively difficult for a voter to judge the role of a candidate in any compromise. Thus the voter will tend to rely on the party's reputation and ideology as an indication of how the candidate will behave. In contrast, under systems of plurality rule, such as the U.S. presidential election, the winner need not compromise with the loser; rather, the compromise takes place with the voters (the well-known convergence to the median). Hence, the role and influence of the party is lessened. As a consequence, systems of plurality rule have significantly less centralized political parties.

Viewing the issue from a different perspective, one might ask why some countries have plurality and others have majority rule. It is quite possible that majority rule systems are much better at resolving conflict when there are more than two clear divisions in society. I believe this to be a more fruitful approach than saying that one form was chosen over the other by historical happenstance or that one form is always superior.

A related approach is to understand the importance of organizational substitutes. I have argued that political parties are coalitions that create positive-sum gains for their members. But suppose that parties are weak; then one should look for other institutions that perform such a function. For example, the president can create a cohesive policy minimizing the possibility that the legislature will focus too narrowly. The president can also reward or punish particular members of Congress for supporting or undermining presidential policy. For example, the president can give public credit for individual assistance on major legislation, provide campaign appearances, or focus the attention of the media on selected representatives.[11] In a still different context, committees in congressional systems can be viewed as substitutes for party caucuses in parliamentary systems (see Breton 1991).

A fourth avenue for future research is to demonstrate that what were previously believed to be examples of political-market failure are in fact examples of market success. I illustrate this approach with the following.

"What is really striking about these political leaders and political office-holders . . . is not their many differences but the extent of their agreement on truly fundamental differences" (Miliband 1973, 64). Miliband's explanation for this similarity is that the capitalist elite colludes to offer no alternatives to the proletariat voter.[12] However, there is an efficiency explanation for this observed behavior. In systems of plurality rule, as opposed to systems employing proportional representation, there tend to be only two candidates running for one political office (see Riker 1982). The optimal strategy is for both candidates to converge to the majority position when the majority feels strongly about an issue.

---

11. See Sullivan (1987) and Fitts and Inman (1992) for discussion of presidential leadership.

12. In the United States, changing the property rights system (capitalism) is never a political issue. Bachrach and Baratz (1962) claim that this nonissue indicates control of the political system by the capitalists. However, a system of property rights protects owners of human capital also. Furthermore, many nonissues benefit noncapitalists. For example, regressive income taxes in the lower tax brackets, slavery, and ending government support of education are also nonissues.

My final suggestion for a research strategy is to use models of political-market failure as an intellectual arrow. Each model makes a critical assumption that creates the failure. This assumption may be lack of credible commitments, asymmetric information, or the like. But if the failure is a serious one, political entrepreneurs will try to devise solutions to mitigate it. By putting herself in the role of the political entrepreneur, the researcher may rediscover and understand the nature of these institutional solutions.

14

EPILOGUE:
THE BURDEN OF PROOF

BEHIND EVERY MODEL OF GOVERNMENT FAILURE is an assumption that voters are
poorly informed, serious competition is lacking, and/or transaction costs
are excessively high. Economists are very suspicious of similar assumptions regarding economic markets. This skepticism should be carried
over to models of political-market failure.

The arguments used in demonstrating efficiency can also be used
in demonstrating the relative equality in the distribution of political
power in democratic systems. Democracies provide equal votes, but if
the voters are poorly informed or there is little competition, then some
actors may be extremely powerful. But here I have argued that voters
make informed judgments and that democratic markets are competitive.
I have thereby undermined the intellectual foundations of theories that
claim political power is concentrated in the hands of corporations or a
small class of individuals.

This book cannot explain all aspects of democratic politics, but it
does provide a research strategy for understanding democratic institutions. The presumption is that individuals are rational and that democratic structures promote wealth-maximizing outcomes. If some health
care is provided by the private sector and some provided by the public
sector, one's initial stance should be, not that one form of delivery is
inferior to the other, but rather that each has a comparative advantage
in delivering a particular service. Similarly, if democratic arrangements
differ across countries, the presupposition should not be that one arrangement is better than the other, but rather that each structure is
appropriate for the circumstances. Or if some women favor the Equal
Rights Amendment and others oppose it, the initial response should not

192

be that one side is misguided, but rather that there are good reasons for a woman to take her particular position on the issue. Democratic decisions should be treated as innocent until proven guilty, and they deserve a lawyer arguing their side of the case.

To say that democratic political markets tend toward efficiency does not imply that political markets are superior to economic markets; rather it implies that democratic governments will allocate to economic markets those tasks in which the economic market is most efficient. Nor does it say that democratic markets are just, for they merely aggregate (equally or unequally) the preferences of the participants in the political process. Nor does it imply that people are uninterested in power or that they desire efficiency for its own sake, only that self-interest will lead to efficient results. Nor does it imply that mistakes are never made, just as efficient economic markets do not imply that consumers and business executives never err.[1]

The weakness of the view of democratic societies as imperfect markets can be illustrated by applying the same view to another society—an anthill, the prototypical example of an efficient society. One could argue that the military is too large in an anthill, that there is a coalition between the military and the queen to inefficiently shift the costs onto the workers, who are poorly informed about the defense industry, and that prisoners' dilemma problems, insufficient internal competition (there is only one queen), and high transaction costs prevent an efficient outcome. Perhaps such a view is inappropriate for ant societies and yet appropriate for political units. The competition between human societies may not be so fierce that only the fittest survive. There may not have been sufficient time to weed out inefficient democracies. And members of democracies are not closely related genetically. But I find it strange that our models of group (and at times individual) irrationality are only applied to the one animal capable of rational thinking.

1. Economists do not dwell on business error or pathological consumer behavior (e.g., compulsive drinking); instead economists analyze the normal and look for efficiency explanations for abnormal market behavior. Similarly, political scientists should not dwell on the mistakes made by political markets.

REFERENCES

Ackerman, Bruce. 1977. *Private Property and the Constitution*. New Haven: Yale University Press.

Aldrich, John H., and Richard D. McKelvey. 1977. "A Method of Scaling with Application to the 1968 and 1972 Presidential Elections." *American Political Science Review* 71:111–30.

Alesina, Alberto. 1987. "Macroeconomic Policy in a Two-Party System as a Repeated Game." *Quarterly Journal of Economics* 102:651–78.

———. 1988a. "Credibility and Policy Covergence in a Two-Party System with Rational Voters." *American Economic Review* 78:796–806.

———. 1988b. "Macroeconomics and Politics." *NBER Macroeconomic Annual,* pp. 11–55. Cambridge: MIT Press.

Alesina, Alberto, John Londregan, and Howard Rosenthal. 1993. "A Model of the Political Economy of the United States." *American Political Science Review* 87:12–33.

Alesina, Alberto, and Jeffrey Sachs. 1988. "Political Parties and the Business Cycle in the United States, 1948–1984." *Journal of Money, Credit, and Banking* 20:63–82.

Alessi, Louis De. 1969. "Implications of Property Rights for Government Investment Choices." *American Economic Review* 69:13–24.

Alford, Robert R., and Roger Friedland. 1985. *Powers of Theory*. Cambridge: Cambridge University Press.

Arnold, R. Douglas. 1990. *The Logic of Congressional Action*. New Haven: Yale University Press.

Arrow, Kenneth J. 1982. "Risk Perception in Psychology and Economics." *Economic Inquiry* 20:1–9.

Atkinson, Scott, and Robert Halvorsen. 1986. "The Relative Efficiency of Public and Private Firms in a Regulated Environment: The Case of U.S. Electric Utilities." *Journal of Public Economics* 29:281–94.

Austen-Smith, David. 1990a. "Credible Debate Equilibria." *Social Choice and Welfare* 7:75–93.

———. 1990b. "Information Transmission in Debate." *American Journal of Political Science* 34:124–52.

———. 1991. "Rational Consumers and Irrational Voters: A Review Essay on Black Hole Tariffs and Endogenous Policy Theory." *Economics and Politics* 3:73–92.

Auten, Gerald, Barry Bozeman, and Robert Cline. 1984. "A Sequential Model of Congressional Appropriations." *American Journal of Political Science* 28:503–23.

Bachrach, P., and M. S. Baratz. 1962. "The Two Faces of Power." *American Political Science Review* 56:947–52.

Banks, Jeffrey S. 1989. "Agency Budgets, Cost Information, and Auditing." *American Journal of Political Science* 33:670–99.

———. 1990. "Monopoly Agenda Control and Asymmetric Information." *Quarterly Journal of Economics* 105:445–64.

———. 1991. *Signaling Games in Political Science.* Chur, Switzerland: Harwood Academic Publishers.

Banks, Jeffrey S., and Barry R. Weingast. 1992. "The Political Control of Bureaucracies under Asymmetric Information." *American Journal of Political Science* 36:509–24.

Baron, David P. 1989. "A Noncooperative Theory of Legislative Coalitions." *American Journal of Political Science* 33:1048–84.

———. 1991. "Majoritarian Incentives, Pork Barrel Programs, and Procedural Control." *American Journal of Political Science* 35:57–90.

Baron, David P., and John A. Ferejohn. 1989. "Bargaining in Legislatures." *American Political Science Review* 83:1181–1206.

Barro, Robert. 1974. "Are Government Bonds Net Wealth?" *Journal of Political Economy* 81:1095–1117.

Barzel, Yoram, and R. T. Deacon. 1975. "Voting Behavior Efficiency and Equity." *Public Choice* 21:1–14.

Baxter, William F. 1963. "Choice of Law and the Federal System." *Stanford Law Review* 16:1–33.

Bazerman, Max H. 1983. "Negotiator Judgement." *American Behavioral Scientist* 27:211–28.

Beach, L. R., and T. R. Mitchell. 1978. "A Contingency Model for the Selection of Decision Strategies." *Academy of Management Review* 3:439–49.

Beard, Charles A. 1948. *An Economic Interpretation of the Constitution of the United States.* New York: Macmillan.

Becker, Gary S. 1983. "A Theory of Competition among Pressure Groups for Political Influence." *Quarterly Journal of Economics* 98:371–97.

———. 1985. "Public Policies, Pressure Groups, and Dead Weight Costs." *Journal of Public Economics* 28:329–47.

Bendor, Jonathan. 1985. *Parallel Systems.* Berkeley and Los Angeles: University of California Press.

———. 1988. "Formal Models of Bureaucracy." *British Journal of Political Science* 18:353–95.

Bendor, Jonathan, Serge Taylor, and Roland Van Gaalen. 1985. "Bureaucratic Expertise versus Legislative Authority: A Model of Deception and Monitoring in Budgeting." *American Political Science Review* 79:1041–60.

Berg, S. 1993. "Condorcet's Jury Theorem, Dependency among Jurors." *Social Choice and Welfare* 10:87–96.

Berger, Curtis. 1976. "The Accommodation Power in Land Use Controversies." *Columbia Law Review* 76:799–823.

Bergstrom, Theodore C. 1973. "A Note on Efficient Taxation." *Journal of Political Economy* 81:187–91.

Bergstrom, Theodore C., and Richard C. Cornes. 1983. "Independence of Allocative Efficiency from Distribution in the Theory of Public Goods." *Econometrica* 51:1753–65.

Bernstein, Robert A. 1989. *Elections, Representation, and Congressional Voting Behavior: The Myth of Constituency Control.* Englewood Cliffs, N.J.: Prentice-Hall.

Block, Fred. 1977. "The Ruling Class Does Not Rule: Notes on the Marxist Theory of the State." *Socialist Revolution* 33:6–28.

Borcherding, Thomas E., W. W. Pommerehne, and F. Schneider. 1982. "Comparing the Efficiency of Private and Public Production: The Evidence from Five Countries." *Zeitschrift fur Nationalokonomie, Supplement* 2:127–56.

Boyce, Rebecca R., Thomas Brown, Gary H. McClelland, George Peterson, and William D. Schulze. 1991. "An Experimental Examination of Intrinsic Values as a Source for the WTA-WTP Disparity." Working paper, University of Colorado.

Braybrooke, David, and Charles E. Lindblom. 1963. *A Strategy of Decisions: Policy Evaluation as a Social Process.* Glencoe, N.Y.: Free Press.

Brennan, Geoffrey, and James Buchanan. 1980. *The Power to Tax: Analytical Foundations of a Fiscal Constitution.* Cambridge: Cambridge University Press.

Breton, Albert. 1991. "The Organization of Competition in Congressional and Parliamentary Governments." In *The Competitive State: Villa Colombella Papers on Competitive Politics,* ed. Ronald Wintrobe. Dordrecht, Netherlands: Kluwer Academic Publishers.

Breton, Albert, and Ronald Wintrobe. 1982. *The Logic of Bureaucratic Conduct.* New York: Cambridge University Press.

Breyer, S. 1986. "Judicial Review of Questions of Law and Policy." *Administrative Law Review* 38:363–98.

Brilmayer, Lea. 1991. *Conflict of Laws: Foundations and Future Directions.* Boston: Little, Brown.

Bromiley, Philip, and John P. Crecine. 1980. "Budget Development in OMB: Aggregate Influences of the Problem and Information Environment." *Journal of Politics* 42:1031–64.

Bronars, Stephen G., and John R. Lott Jr. 1993. "Do Campaign Contributions Alter a Politician's Behavior, or Does [*sic*] a Politician's Beliefs Determine Whether He Receives the Contributions?" Working Paper, Wharton School, University of Pennsylvania.

Brown, Robert E. 1956. *Charles Beard and the Constitution: A Critical Analysis of "An Economic Interpretation of the Constitution."* Princeton: Princeton University Press.

Brueckner, Jan K., and Kevin M. O'Brien. 1989. "Modeling Government Behavior in Collective Bargaining: A Test for Self-Interested Bureaucrats." *Public Choice* 63:15–41.

Buchanan, James M., and Gordon Tullock. 1962. *The Calculus of Consent.* Ann Arbor: University of Michigan Press.

Buchanan, James M., and Richard E. Wagner. 1977. *Democracy in Deficit.* New York: Academic Press.

Cain, Bruce, John A. Ferejohn, and Morris Fiorina. 1987. *The Personal Vote.* Cambridge: Harvard University Press.

Calvert, Randall L., Mathew D. McCubbins, and Barry R. Weingast. 1989. "A Theory of Political Control and Agency Discretion." *American Journal of Political Science* 33:588–611.

Camerer, Colin F. 1989. "Does the Basketball Market Believe in the 'Hot Hand'?" *American Economic Review* 79:1257–61.

Chan, Kenneth S., and Stuart Mestelman. 1988. "Institutions, Efficiency, and the Strategic Behaviour of Sponsors and Bureaus." *Journal of Public Economics* 37:91–102.

Chappell, Henry. 1982. "Campaign Contributions and Congressional Voting: A Simultaneous Probit-Tobit Model." *Review of Economics and Statistics* 64: 77–83.

Christensen-Szalanski, J. 1980. "A Further Examination of the Selection of Problem-Solving Strategies: The Effects of Deadlines and Analytic Aptitudes." *Organizational Behavior and Human Performance* 25:107–22.

Coase, Ronald. 1937. "The Nature of the Firm." *Economica* 4:386–405.

———. 1960. "The Problem of Social Cost." *Journal of Law and Economics* 3:1–44.

Coker, David C., and W. Mark Crain. 1992. "Legislative Committees as Loyalty-Generating Institutions." Papers in Political Economy, University of Western Ontario.

Coleman, James S. 1986. *Individual Interests and Collective Action: Selected Essays.* Cambridge: Cambridge University Press.

Congleton, Roger D. 1991. "Rational Ignorance, Rational Expectations, and Fiscal Illusion." Papers in Political Economy, University of Western Ontario.

Conover, Pamela Johnston, and Stanley Feldman. 1989. "Candidate Perception in an Ambiguous World: Campaigns, Cues, and Inference Processes." *American Journal of Political Science* 33:912–40.

Cooper, Joseph, and William F. West. 1988. "Presidential Power and Republican Government: The Theory and Practice of OMB Review of Agency Rules." *Journal of Politics* 50:865–95.

Cooter, Robert D. 1992. "Constitutional Law and Economics: Powers." Working Paper no. 92-1, School of Law, University of California, Berkeley.

Copeland, Thomas, and Daniel Friedman. 1987. "The Effect of Sequential Information Arrival on Asset Prices." *Journal of Finance* 42:763–97.

Costonis, John. 1975. " 'Fair' Compensation and the Accommodation Power." *Columbia Law Review* 75:1021–82.

Coughlin, Peter J. 1986. "Elections and Income Distribution." *Public Choice* 50: 27–92.

———. 1991. "Balanced-Budget Redistribution as the Outcome of Political Competition: A Comment." *Public Choice* 70:239–43.

Coughlin, Peter J., Dennis C. Mueller, and Peter Murrell. 1990. "Electoral Politics, Interest Groups, and the Size of Government." *Economic Inquiry* 28:682–705.

Coughlin, Peter J., and Shmuel Nitzan. 1981. "Electoral Outcomes and Probabilistic Voting and Nash Social Welfare Maxima." *Journal of Public Economics* 15:115–21.

Coursey, Don L., and Russell D. Roberts. 1991. "Competition in Political and Economic Markets." *Public Choice* 70:83–88.

Cox, Gary W., and Mathew D. McCubbins. 1989. "Political Parties and the Appointment of Committees." Working paper, University of California, San Diego.

———. 1990. *Parties and Committees in the House of Representatives.* Berkeley and Los Angeles: University of California Press.

Crain, W. Mark. 1977. "On the Structure and Stability of Political Markets." *Journal of Political Economy* 85:829–42.

Cukierman, Alex, and Allan H. Meltzer. 1989. "A Political Theory of Government Debt and Deficits in a Neo-Ricardian Framework." *American Economic Review* 79:713–32.

Cummings, R. G., D. S. Brookshire, and W. D. Schulze, eds. 1986. *Valuing Environmental Goods.* Totowa, N.J.: Rowman and Allanheld.

Cyert, Richard M. 1988. *The Economic Theory of Organization and the Firm.* Hertfordshire, England: Harvester Wheatsheaf.

Dahl, Robert A. 1961. *Who Governs? Democracy and Power in an American City.* New Haven: Yale University Press.

———. 1966. *A Preface to Democratic Theory.* 3d ed. Chicago: University of Chicago Press.

———. 1985. *A Preface to Economic Democracy.* Cambridge, Mass.: Polity Press.

Dahrendorf, Ralf. 1959. *Class and Class Conflict in Industrial Society.* Stanford: Stanford University Press.

Davidson, Roger H. 1981. "Subcommittee Government: New Channels for Policy Making." In *The New Congress,* ed. Norman J. Ornstein. Washington, D.C.: American Enterprise Institute.

Davis, Otto A., M. A. H. Dempster, and Aaron Wildavsky. 1974. "Toward a Predictive Theory of the Federal Budgetary Process." *British Journal of Political Science* 4:419–52.

Dempster, M. A. H., and Aaron Wildavsky. 1979. "On Change, or There Is No Magic Size for an Increment." *Political Studies* 27:371–89.

Demsetz, Harold. 1982. *Economic, Legal, and Political Dimensions of Competition.* Amsterdam: North-Holland.

Denzau, A. T., and M. C. Munger. 1986. "Legislators and Interest Groups." *American Political Science Review* 80:89–106.

Domhoff, G. William. 1967. *Who Rules America?* Englewood Cliffs, N.J.: Prentice-Hall.

———. 1970. *The Higher Circles: The Governing Class in America.* New York: Random House.

———. 1974. *The Bohemian Grove and Other Retreats: A Study in Ruling-Class Cohesiveness.* New York: Harper and Row.

Downs, Anthony. 1957. *An Economic Theory of Democracy.* New York: Harper and Row.

———. 1960. "Why the Government Budget Is Too Small in a Democracy." *World Politics* 12:541–63.

———. 1967. *Inside Bureaucracy.* Boston: Little, Brown.

Downs, George W., and Patrick D. Larkey. 1986. *The Search for Government Efficiency: From Hubris to Helplessness.* Philadelphia: Temple University Press.

Duh, R. R., and S. Sunder. 1985. "Incentives, Learning, and Processing of Information in a Market Environment: An Examination of the Base Rate Fallacy." Working paper, University of Minnesota, Minneapolis.

Dunham, Allison. 1958. "A Legal and Economic Basis for City Planning." *Columbia Law Review* 58:650–71.

Edelman, Murray. 1964. *The Symbolic Uses of Politics.* Urbana: University of Illinois Press.

Ehrlich, Isaac, and Richard A. Posner. 1974. "An Economic Analysis of Legal Rulemaking." *Journal of Legal Studies* 3:257–86.

Ellickson, Robert C. 1973. "Alternatives to Zoning: Covenants, Nuisance Rules, and Fines as Land Use Controls." In *Foundations of Property Law,* ed. Bruce Ackerman. Boston: Little, Brown.

———. 1977. "Urban Growth Controls: Economic and Legal Analysis." *Yale Law Journal* 86:386–515.

Epstein, Richard. 1979a. "Causation and Corrective Justice: A Reply to Two Critics." *Journal of Legal Studies* 8:477.

———. 1979b. "Nuisance Law: Corrective Justice and Its Utilitarian Constraints." *Journal of Legal Studies* 8:49–102.

———. 1985. *Takings: Private Property and the Power of Eminent Domain.* Cambridge: Harvard University Press.

———. 1993. *Bargaining with the State.* Princeton: Princeton University Press.

Erikson, Robert S., and David Romero. 1990. "Candidate Equilibrium and the Behavioral Model of the Vote." *American Political Science Review* 84:1103–26.

Erikson, Robert S., and Gerald C. Wright. 1993. "Voters, Issues, and Candidates in Congressional Elections." In *Congress Reconsidered,* ed. Lawrence Dodd and Bruce Oppenheimer. 5th ed. Washington, D.C.: Congressional Quarterly Press.

Erikson, Robert S., Gerald C. Wright, and John McIver. 1989. "Political Parties, Public Opinion, and State Policy in the United States." *American Political Science Review* 83:729–50.

Eskridge, W. N., Jr., and John A. Ferejohn. 1992. "Making the Deal Stick: Enforcing the Original Constitutional Structure of Lawmaking in the Modern Regulatory State." *Journal of Law, Economics, and Organization* 8:165–89.

Eysenbach, Mary L. 1974. "Voucher Plans, Voting Models, and the Efficiency of Local School Finance." *Journal of Political Economy* 82:863–71.

Farber, D. 1991. "Free Speech without Romance." *Harvard Law Review* 105: 554–83.

Farina, C. 1989. "Statutory Interpretation and the Balance of Power in the Administrative State." *Columbia Law Review* 89:452–528.

Fenno, Richard F. 1966. *The Power of the Purse: Appropriations Politics in Congress.* Boston: Little, Brown.

———. 1973. *Congressmen in Committees.* Boston: Little, Brown.

Ferejohn, John A., and Charles Shipan. 1990. "Congressional Influence on Bureaucracy." *Journal of Law, Economics, and Organization* 6:1–20.

Fiorina, Morris. 1981. "Control of the Bureaucracy: A Mismatch of Incentives and Capabilities." In *Congress Reconsidered,* ed. Bruce I. Oppenheimer, 332–48. Washington, D.C.: Congressional Quarterly Press.

———. 1983. "Flagellating the Federal Bureaucracy." *Society* 20, no. 3:66–73.

———. 1985. "Group Concentration and the Delegation of Legislative Authority."

In *Regulatory Policy and the Social Sciences,* ed. Roger G. Noll. Berkeley and Los Angeles: University of California Press.

———. 1989. *Congress: Keystone of the Washington Establishment.* New Haven: Yale University Press.

Fiorina, Morris, and Roger G. Noll. 1978. "Voters, Bureaucrats, and Legislators: A Rational Choice Perspective on the Growth of Bureaucracy." *Journal of Public Economics* 9:239–54.

Fishburn, P. C. 1988. *Nonlinear Preference and Utility Theory.* Baltimore: Johns Hopkins University Press.

Fiske, Susan T., and S. E. Taylor. 1984. *Social Cognition.* New York: Random House.

Fitts, Michael, and Robert Inman. 1992. "Controlling Congress: Presidential Influence in Domestic Fiscal Policy." *Georgetown Law Journal* 80:1737–85.

Freund, E. 1976. *The Police Power, Public Policy, and Constitutional Rights.* 1905. Rpt. New York: Arno Press.

Frey, Bruno S., and R. Eichenberger. 1989. "Should Social Scientists Care about Choice Anomalies?" *Rationality and Society* 1:101–22.

Friedman, Daniel. 1989. "The S-Shaped Value Function as a Constrained Optimum." *American Economic Review* 79:1243–48.

Friedman, Daniel, and Donald Wittman. Forthcoming. "Why Voters Vote for Incumbents, but against Incumbency: A Rational Model Approach." *Journal of Public Economics.*

Friedman, Milton. 1962. *Capitalism and Freedom.* Chicago: University of Chicago Press.

Friedman, Milton, and Rose Friedman. 1980. *Free to Choose.* New York: Harcourt Brace Jovanovich.

Fudenberg, Drew, and Eric Maskin. 1986. "The Folk Theorem in Repeated Games with Discounting and with Incomplete Information." *Econometrica* 54:533–54.

Gaventa, John. 1980. *Power and Powerlessness.* Urbana: University of Illinois Press.

Gilligan, Thomas W., and Keith Krehbiel. 1987. "Collective Decision-Making and Standing Committees: An Informal Rationale for Restrictive Amendment Procedures." *Journal of Law, Economics, and Organization* 3:287–335.

———. 1988. "Complex Rules and Congressional Outcomes: An Event Study of Energy Tax Legislation." *Journal of Politics* 50:625–54.

———. 1989a. "Asymmetric Information and Legislative Rules with a Heterogeneous Committee." *American Journal of Political Science* 33:459–90.

———. 1989b. "Collective Choice without Procedural Commitment." In *Models of Strategic Choice in Politics,* ed. Peter C. Ordeshook. Ann Arbor: University of Michigan Press.

————. 1990. "Organization of Informative Committees by Rational Legislature." *American Journal of Political Science* 34:531–64.

Gilmore, Grant. 1970. "Products Liability: A Commentary." *University of Chicago Law Review* 38:103–16.

Gilovich, Thomas, Robert Vallone, and Amos Tversky. 1985. "The Hot Hand in Basketball: On the Misperception of Random Sequences." *Cognitive Psychology* 17:295–314

Gist, John R. 1974. *Mandatory Expenditures and the Defense of Sector: Theory of Budgetary Increments.* Beverly Hills, Calif.: Sage Publications.

————. 1977. "Increment and Base in Congressional Appropriations Process." *American Journal of Political Science* 21:341–52.

Glazer, Amihai, and Marc Robbins. 1983. "Voters and Roll Call Voting: The Effect on Congressional Elections." *Political Behavior* 5:377–89.

————. 1985. "Congressional Responsiveness to Constituency Change." *American Journal of Political Science* 29:259–73.

Goetz, Charles J. 1977. "Fiscal Illusion in State and Local Finance." In *Budgets and Bureaucrats,* ed. Thomas E. Borcherding. Durham, N.C.: Duke University Press.

Goodwin, George. 1970. In *The Little Legislatures: Committees of Congress.* Amherst: University of Massachusetts Press.

Green, Jerry, and Jean-Jacques Laffont. 1979. *Incentives in Public Decision-Making.* Amsterdam: North-Holland.

Grenzke, Janet. 1989. "PACs and the Congressional Supermarket: The Currency Is Complex." *American Journal of Political Science* 33:1–24.

Grofman, Bernard N., and S. L. Feld. 1988. "Rousseau's General Will: A Condorcetian Perspective." *American Political Science Review* 82:567–76.

Grofman, Bernard N., Guillermo Owen, Nicholas Noviello, and Amihai Glazer. 1987. "Stability and Centrality of Legislative Choice in the Spatial Context." *American Political Science Review* 81:539–53.

Hagman, Donald, and Dean Misczynski. 1978. *Windfalls for Wipeouts: Land Value Capture and Compensation,* Chicago: American Society of Planning Officials.

Hall, Richard L., and Bernard N. Grofman. 1990. "The Committee Assignment Process and the Conditional Nature of Committee Bias." *American Political Science Review* 84:1149–66.

Hamill, Ruth, Milton Lodge, and Frederick Blake. 1985. "The Breadth, Depth, and Utility of Political Belief Systems." *American Journal of Political Science* 29:850–70.

Hamilton, Alexander, John Jay, and James Madison. 1961. *The Federalist Papers.* New York: New American Library.

Hammond, Thomas, Jeffrey Hill, and Gary J. Miller. 1986. "Presidential Appointment of Bureau Chiefs and the 'Congressional Control of Administration'

Hypothesis." Paper presented at a meeting of the American Political Science Association, Washington, D.C.

Harrington, Joseph E., Jr. 1992. "The Role of Party Reputation in the Formation of Policy." *Journal of Public Economics* 49:107–21.

Harrison, Glenn W. 1989. "Expected Utility Theory and the Experimentalists." Working paper, Department of Economics, University of New Mexico, Albuquerque.

Hechter, Michael. 1987. *Principles of Group Solidarity.* Berkeley and Los Angeles: University of California Press.

Herrnson, Paul S. 1986. "Do Parties Make a Difference? The Role of Party Organizations in Congressional Elections." *Journal of Politics* 48:589–615.

Higgins, Richard S., William F. Shughart, and Robert D. Tollison. 1985. "Free Entry and Efficient Rent Seeking." *Public Choice* 46:247–58.

Hill, Jeffrey. 1985. "Why So Much Stability? The Role of Agency Determined Stability." *Public Choice* 46:275–87.

Hochman, H. M., and J. D. Rogers. 1969. "Pareto Optimal Redistribution." *American Economic Review* 59:542–57.

Hochman, H. M., and J. D. Rogers. 1969. "Pareto Optimal Redistribution: Reply." *American Economic Review* 60:977–1002.

Holcombe, Randall G. 1985. *An Economic Analysis of Democracy.* Carbondale: Southern Illinois University Press.

Holmstrom, Bengt, and Roger B. Myerson. 1983. "Efficient and Durable Decision Rules with Incomplete Information." *Econometrica* 51:1799–1819.

Horwitz, Morton J. 1974. "The Historical Foundations of Modern Contract Law." *Harvard Law Review* 87:953–56.

Iacocca, Lee. 1984. *Iacocca: An Autobiography.* New York: Bantam Books.

Jacobson, Gary C. 1987a. "The Marginals Never Vanished: Incumbency and Competition in Elections to the U.S. House of Representatives." *American Journal of Political Science* 31:126–41.

———. 1987b. *The Politics of Congressional Elections.* Boston: Little, Brown.

Jones, Charles O. 1962. "The Role of the Congressional Subcommittee." *Midwest Journal of Political Science* 6:327–44.

Kahneman, Daniel, Jack Knetsch, and Richard Thaler. 1987. "Fairness and the Assumptions of Economics." In *Rational Choice,* ed. Melvin W. Reder. Chicago: University of Chicago Press.

Kahneman, Daniel, and Amos Tversky. 1984. "Choices, Values, and Frames." *American Psychologist* 39:341–50.

Kalt, Joseph P., and Mark A. Zupan. 1984. "Capture and Ideology in the Economic Theory of Politics." *American Economic Review* 74:279–300.

———. 1990. "The Apparent Ideological Behavior of Legislators: Testing for

Principal-Agent Slack in Political Institutions." *Journal of Law and Economics* 33:103–31.

Kamlet, Mark S., and David C. Mowery. 1983. "Budgetary Side Payments and Government Growth, 1953–1968." *American Journal of Political Science* 27: 636–64.

———. 1987. "Influences on Executive and Congressional Budgetary Priorities, 1955–1981." *American Political Science Review* 81:155–78.

Kantor, Shawn Everett. 1991. "Razorbacks, Ticky Cows, and the Closing of the Georgia Open Range: The Dynamics of Institutional Change Uncovered." *Journal of Economic History* 51:861–86.

Katz, Eliakim, Shmuel Nitzan, and Jacob Rosenberg. 1990. "Rent-Seeking for Pure Public Goods." *Public Choice* 65:49–60.

Kau, James, Donald Keenan, and Paul H. Rubin. 1982. "A General Equilibrium Model of Congressional Voting." *Quarterly Journal of Economics* 97:271–93.

Kau, James, and Paul H. Rubin. 1979. "Self-Interest, Ideology, and Logrolling in Congressional Voting." *Journal of Law and Economics* 22:365–84.

———. 1993. "Ideology, Voting, and Shirking." *Public Choice* 76:151–72.

Keller, Bill. 1992. "The Veterans' Lobby as an 'Iron Triangle.' " In *Governing: Readings and Cases in American Politics,* ed. Roger Davidson and Walter Oleszek. Washington, D.C.: Congressional Quarterly Press.

Kiewiet, D. Roderick, and Mathew D. McCubbins. 1985. "Congressional Appropriations and the Electoral Connection." *Journal of Politics* 47:59–82.

———. 1988. "Presidential Influence on Congressional Appropriations Decisions." *American Journal of Political Science* 32:713–36.

———. 1991. *The Logic of Delegation.* Chicago: University of Chicago Press.

Kingdon, John. 1989. *Congressmen's Voting Decision.* Ann Arbor: University of Michigan Press.

Knetsch, Jack L. 1989. "The Endowment Effect and Evidence of Nonreversible Indifference Curves." *American Economic Review* 79:1277–84.

Kosterlitz, Julie. 1982. "PAC Inc." *Common Cause* 8, no. 4:10–16.

Kotlikoff, L., and R. Rosenthal. 1993. "Inefficiency Implications of Generational Politics." *Economics and Politics* 5:27–42.

Krehbiel, Keith. 1991. *Information and Legislative Organization.* Ann Arbor: University of Michigan Press.

Krehbiel, Keith, and Douglas Rivers. 1988. "The Analysis of Committee Power: An Application to Senate Voting on the Minimum Wage." *American Journal of Political Science* 32:1151–74.

Kroll, Yoram, Haim Levy, and Amnon Rapoport. 1988. "Experimental Tests of the Separation Theorem and the Capital Asset Pricing Model." *American Economic Review* 78:500–519.

Krueger, A. O. 1974. "The Political Economy of the Rent-Seeking Society." *American Economic Review* 64:291–303.

Kurland, Philip, and Ralph Lerner, eds. 1961. *The Federalist Papers.* 2 vols. New York: New American Library.

Laband, D., and Lentz, Bernard. 1985. "Favorite Sons: Intergenerational Wealth Transfers among Politicians." *Economic Inquiry* 23:395–414.

Ladha, K. K. 1993. "Condorcet's Jury Theorem in Light of de Finetti's Theorem: Majority-Rule Voting with Correlated Votes." *Social Choice and Welfare* 10: 69–86.

Lau, Richard R. 1986. "Political Schemata, Candidate Evaluations, and Voting Behavior." In *Political Cognition,* ed. Richard Lau and David Sears. Hillsdale, N.J.: Lawrence Erlbaum Associates.

Laycock, D. 1992. "Equal Citizens of Equal and Territorial States: The Constitutional Foundations of Choice of Law." *Columbia Law Review* 92:249–337.

Leibenstein, Harvey. 1989. *Inside the Firm.* Cambridge: Harvard University Press.

Leland, Jonathan. 1988. "A Theory of 'Approximate' Expected Utility Maximization." Working paper, Department of Social and Decision Sciences, Carnegie-Mellon University.

LeLoup, Lance T. 1975. "Agency Policy Actions: Determinants of Nonincremental Change." In *Policy-Making in the Federal Executive Branch,* ed. Grace A. Franklin. New York: Free Press.

Lindblom, Charles E. 1959. "The Science of Muddling Through." *Public Administration Review* 19 (spring):79–88.

———. 1977. *Politics and Markets.* New York: Basic Books.

———. 1988. *Democracy and the Market System.* Oslo: Norwegian University Press; distributed in U.S. by Oxford University Press.

Lindsay, C. M. 1976. "A Theory of Government Enterprise." *Journal of Political Economy* 84:1061–77.

Lodge, Milton, and D. Hamil. 1986. "A Partisan Schema for Political Information Processing." *American Political Science Review* 80:505–19.

Lodge, Milton, Kathleen M. McGraw, and Patrick Stroh. 1989. "An Impression-Driven Model of Candidate Evaluation." *American Political Science Review* 83:399–419.

Lott, John R., Jr., and Robert W. Reed. 1989. "Shirking and Sorting in a Political Market with Finite-Lived Politicians." *Public Choice* 61:75–96.

Lowi, Theodore. 1979. *The End of Liberalism.* New York: Norton.

Lupia, Arthur. 1994. "Shortcuts versus Encyclopedias: Information and Voting Behavior in California Insurance Reform Elections." *American Political Science Review* 88:63–76.

Maas, Arthur. 1983. *Congress and the Common Good.* New York: Basic Books.

Macey, Jonathan. 1992. "Organizational Design and Political Control of Administrative Agencies." *Journal of Law, Economics, and Organization* 8:93–110.

Machina, Mark. 1989. "Dynamic Consistency and Non-Expected Utility Models of Choice under Uncertainty." *Journal of Economic Literature* 27:1622–88.

Magee, Stephen P., William A. Brock, and Leslie Young. 1989. *Black Hole Tariffs and Endogenous Policy Theory: Political Economy in General Equilibrium.* New York: Cambridge University Press.

Mann, Thomas E., and Raymond E. Wolfinger. 1980. "Candidates and Parties in Congressional Elections." *American Political Science Review* 74:617–32.

March, James G., and Johan P. Olsen. 1989. *Rediscovering Institutions: The Organizational Basis of Politics.* New York: Free Press.

Massaro, D., and Daniel Friedman. 1990. "Models of Integration Given Multiple Sources of Information." *Psychological Review* 97:225–52.

Mayhew, D. R. 1974. *Congress: The Electoral Connection.* New Haven: Yale University Press.

McAdams, John C., and John R. Johannes. 1988. "Congressmen, Perquisites, and Elections." *Journal of Politics* 50:412–39.

McClosky, Herbert. 1964. "Consensus and Ideology in American Politics." *American Political Science Review* 58:361–82.

McClosky, Herbert, Paul Hoffman, and Rosemary O'Hara. 1960. "Issue Conflict and Consensus among Party Leader and Follower." *American Political Science Review* 54:406–27.

McConnell, G. 1970. *Private Power and American Democracy.* New York: Alfred Knopf.

McCubbins, Mathew D., Roger G. Noll, and Barry R. Weingast. 1989. "Structure and Process, Politics and Policy: Administrative Arrangements and the Political Control of Agencies." *Virginia Law Review* 75:431–82.

———. 1990. "Slack, Public Interest, and Structure-Induced Policy." *Journal of Law, Economics, and Organization* 6:203–12.

McCubbins, Mathew D., and Talbot Page. 1987. "A Theory of Congressional Delegation." In *Congress: Structure and Policy,* ed. Terry Sullivan. Cambridge: Cambridge University Press.

McCubbins, Mathew D., and Thomas Schwartz. 1984. "Congressional Oversight Overlooked: Police Patrols versus Fire Alarms." *American Journal of Political Science* 28:167–79.

McDonald, Forrest. 1958. *We the People: The Economic Origins of the Constitution.* Chicago: University of Chicago Press.

McGuire, Robert A., and Robert L. Ohsfeldt. 1989a. "Public Choice Analysis and the Ratification of the Constitution." In *The Federalist Papers and the New Institutionalism,* ed. Donald Wittman, 175–204. New York: Agathon Press.

———. 1989b. "Self-Interest, Agency Theory, and Political Voting Behavior: The

Ratification of the United States Constitution." *American Economic Review* 79:219–34.

McGuire, Thomas g. 1981. "Budget Maximizing Governmental Agencies: An Empirical Test." *Public Choice* 36:313–22.

McGuire, Thomas G., Michael Coiner, and Larry Spancake. 1979. "Budget-Maximizing Agencies and Efficiency in Government." *Public Choice* 34: 333–58.

McKean, Roland N. 1965. "The Unseen Hand in Government." *American Economic Review* 55:496–505.

McKelvey, Richard D. 1976. "Intransitivities in Multidimensional Voting Models and Some Implications for Agenda Control." *Journal of Economic Theory* 12:472–82.

———. 1979. "General Conditions for Global Intransitivities in Formal Voting Models." *Econometrica* 47:1085–1112.

McKelvey, Richard D., and Peter C. Ordeshook. 1985. "Elections with Limited Information: A Fulfilled Expectations Model Using Contemporaneous Poll and Endorsement Data as Information Sources." *Journal of Economic Theory* 36:55–85.

———. 1986. "Information, Electoral Equilibria, and the Democratic Ideal." *Journal of Politics* 48:908–37.

McNeil, B. J., S. G. Pauker, H. C. Sox, and Amos Tversky. 1982. "On the Elicitation of Preferences for Alternative Therapies." *New England Journal of Medicine* 306:1259–62.

McRae, D. 1977. "A Political Model of the Business Cycle." *Journal of Political Economy* 85:239–63.

Michaelman, Frank. 1967. "Justice, Utility, and Fairness." *Harvard Law Review* 80:1169–1258.

Miliband, Ralph. 1969. *The State in Capitalist Society*. New York: Basic Books.

Mill, John Stuart. 1970. *Principles of Political Economy*. Harmondsworth, England: Penguin Books.

Miller, Edward M. 1987. "Bounded Efficient Markets: A New Wrinkle to the EMH." *Journal of Portfolio Management* 13:4–13.

Miller, Gary J. 1977. "Bureaucratic Compliance as a Game on the Unit Square." *Public Choice* 29:37–61.

Miller, Gary J., and T. M. Moe. 1983. "Bureaucrats, Legislators, and the Size of Government." *American Political Science Review* 77:297–322.

Miller, Warren E., and Donald E. Stokes. 1963. "Constituency Influence in Congress." *American Political Science Review* 57:45–56.

Mitchell, William C., and Michael C. Munger. 1991. "Economic Models of Interest Groups: An Introductory Survey." *American Journal of Political Science* 35: 512–46.

Morton, Rebecca, and Charles Cameron. 1992. "Elections and the Theory of Campaign Contributions: A Survey and Critical Analysis." *Economics and Politics* 4:79–108.

Mosca, G. 1989. *The Ruling Class.* Trans. H. D. Kahn. New York: McGraw-Hill, 1939. Reprint, Cambridge, Mass.: Cambridge University Press.

Mumy, Gene E., and Stephen Turnbull. 1992. "Information and Incentive Compatible Budgetary Allocations for Public Sector Bureaucracies." Working paper, Department of Economics, Ohio State University.

Nash, J. F. 1951. "Non-Cooperative Games." *Annals of Mathematics* 54:286–95.

Navarro, Peter. 1984. *The Policy Game.* New York: John Wiley.

Neustadt, I. 1980. *Presidential Power: The Politics of Leadership from FDR to Carter.* New York: Wiley.

Newell, Allen, and Herbert A. Simon. 1972. *Human Problem Solving.* Englewood Cliffs, N.J.: Prentice-Hall.

Niou, Emerson, and Peter C. Ordeshook. 1985. "Universalism in Congress." *American Journal of Political Science* 29:247–57.

Niskanen, W. A., Jr. 1971. *Bureaucracy and Representative Government.* Chicago: Aldine-Atherton.

———. 1975. "Bureaucrats and Politicians." *Journal of Law and Economics* 18:617–43.

Nordhaus, William D. 1975. "The Political Business Cycle." *Review of Economic Studies* 42:169–90.

———. 1989. "Alternative Approaches to the Political Business Cycle." In *Brookings Papers on Economic Activity,* ed. George L. Perry. Washington, D.C.: Brookings Institution.

Oates, W. E.. 1988. "On the Nature and Measurement of Fiscal Illusion: A Survey." In *Taxation and Fiscal Federalism: Essays in Honor of Russell Matthews,* ed. G. Brennan, Bhajan Grewal, and Peter Groenewegan. Canberra: Australian National University Press.

Offe, C. 1975. "The Theory of the Capitalist State and the Problem of Policy Formation." In *Stress and Contradiction in Modern Capitalism,* ed. C. Offe. Lexington, Mass.: Lexington Books.

Olson, Mancur. 1982. *The Rise and Decline of Nations.* New Haven: Yale University Press.

Orzechowski, W. 1977. "Economic Models of Bureaucracy: Survey, Extensions, and Evidence." In *Budgets and Bureaucrats: The Sources of Government Growth,* ed. Thomas E. Borcherding. Durham, N.C.: Duke University Press.

Padgett, John. 1981. "Hierarchy and Ecological Control in Federal Budgetary Decision Making." *American Journal of Sociology* 87:75–129.

Page, Benjamin I., and Robert Shapiro. 1983. "Effects of Public Opinion on Policy." *American Political Science Review* 77:175–90.

————. 1992. *The Rational Public.* Chicago: University of Chicago Press.

Peltzman, Sam. 1976. "Toward a More General Theory of Regulation." *Journal of Law and Economics* 19:211–40.

————. 1990. "How Efficient Is the Voting Market?" *Journal of Law and Economics* 33:27–63.

Pierce, R., Jr. 1990. "Political Control versus Impermissible Bias in Agency Decisionmaking: Lessons from Chevron and Mistretta." *University of Chicago Law Review* 57:481–519.

Plott, Charles R. 1979. "The Application of Laboratory Experimental Methods to Public Choice." In *Collective Decision Making: Applications from Public Choice Theory,* ed. Clifford S. Russell. Baltimore: Johns Hopkins University Press.

Plott, Charles R., and Louis L. Wilde. 1982. "Professional Diagnosis versus Self Diagnosis: An Experimental Examination of Some Special Features of Markets with Uncertainty." In *Research in Experimental Economics,* ed. V. L. Smith. Greenwich, Conn.: JAI Press.

Polinsky, A. Mitchell. 1979. "Notes on the Symmetry of Taxes and Subsidies in Pollution Control." *Canadian Journal of Economics* 12:75–82.

Popkin, Samuel. 1991. *The Reasoning Voter.* Chicago: University of Chicago Press.

Posner, Richard A. 1974. "Theories of Economic Regulation." *Bell Journal of Economics and Management Science* 5:335–58.

————. 1977. *Economic Analysis of Law.* 2d ed. Boston: Little, Brown.

————. 1986. *Economic Analysis of Law.* 3d ed. Boston: Little, Brown.

————. 1992. *Economic Analysis of Law.* 4th ed. Boston: Little, Brown.

Powell, Lynda. 1982. "Issue Representation in Congress." *Journal of Politics* 44:658–78.

Price, David E. 1972. *Who Makes the Laws? Creativity and Power in Senate Committees.* Cambridge, Mass.: Schenkman.

Priest, George. 1977. "The Common Law Process and the Selection of Efficient Rules." *Journal of Legal Studies* 6:65–82.

Przeworski, Adam. 1985. "Marxism and Rational Choice." *Politics and Society* 14:379–409.

————. 1990. *The State and the Economy under Capitalism.* Chur, Switzerland: Harwood Academic Publishers.

Przeworski, Adam, and Michael Wallerstein. 1982. "The Structure of Class Conflict in Democratic Capitalist Societies." *American Political Science Review* 76:215–38.

————. 1988. "Structural Dependence of the State on Capital." *American Political Science Review* 82:11–29.

Quattrone, George A., and Amos Tversky. 1988. "Contrasting Rational and Psychological Analyses of Political Choice." *American Political Science Review* 82: 719–36.

Riker, William. 1982. "The Two Party System and Duverger's Law: An Essay on the History of Political Science." *American Political Science Review* 76:753–66.

Riker, William, and Steven J. Brams. 1973. "The Paradox of Vote Trading." *American Political Science Review* 67:1235–47.

Ripley, Randall B., Grace A. Franklin, William M. Holmes, and William B. Moreland. 1975. "Structure, Environment, and Policy Actions: An Empirical Exploration." In *Policy-Making in the Federal Executive Branch,* ed. Grace A. Franklin. New York: Free Press, 1975.

Roberts, Brian. 1990. "Political Institutions, Policy Expectations, and the 1980 Elections: A Financial Model Perspective." *American Journal of Political Science* 34:289–310.

Rogoff, Kenneth, and Anne Sibert. 1988. "Elections and Macroeconomic Policy Cycles." *Review of Economic Studies* 55:1–16.

Romano, Roberta. 1987. "The Political Economy of Takeover Statutes." *Virginia Law Review* 73:114–15.

Rose-Ackerman, Susan. 1990. "Comment on Ferejohn and Shipan's 'Congressional Influence on Bureaucracy.'" *Journal of Law, Economics, and Organization* 6:21–27.

Rosenberg, Shawn W. 1988. "Economic Rationality, Market Discipline, and Political Analysis." Working paper, University of California, Irvine.

———. 1991. "Rationality, Markets, and Political Analysis: A Social Psychological Critique of Neoclassical Political Economy." In *The Economic Approach to Politics: A Critical Reassessment of the Theory of Rational Action,* ed. Kristen Renwick Monroe. New York: HarperCollins.

Rosenberg, Shawn W., and P. McCafferty. 1987. "The Image and the Vote: Manipulating Voters' Preferences." *Public Opinion Quarterly* 51:31–47.

Rubin, Paul H. 1977. "Why Is the Common Law Efficient?" *Journal of Legal Studies* 6:51–64.

———. 1982. "Common Law and Statute Law." *Journal of Legal Studies* 11: 205–23.

Russell, Thomas, and Richard Thaler. 1985. "The Relevance of Quasi-Rationality in Competitive Markets." *American Economic Review* 75:1071–82.

Saunders, Peter, and Fridrich Klau. 1985. "The Role of the Public Sector: Causes and Consequences of the Growth of Government." *Organization for Economic Cooperation and Development Economic Studies* 4:11–239.

Savage, Leonard J. 1954. *The Foundation of Statistics.* New York: Wiley.

Scalia, Antonin J. 1989. "Judicial Deference to Administrative Interpretations of Law." *Duke Law Journal* 1989:511–21.

Scher, Seymour. 1963. "Conditions for Legislative Control." *Journal of Politics* 25:526–51.

Schmitter, Philippe C. 1974. "Still the Century of Corporatism?" *Review of Political Studies* 36:85–131.

———. 1977. "Modes of Interest Intermediation and Models of Societal Change in Western Europe." *Comparative Political Studies* 10:7–38.

———. 1986. "Neo-Corporatism and the State." In *The Political Economy of Corporatism,* ed. Wyn Grant. London: Macmillan.

Schumpeter, Joseph A. 1950. *Capitalism, Socialism, and Democracy.* 3d ed. New York: Harper and Row.

Scotchmer, Suzanne. 1994. "Public Goods and the Invisible Hand." In *Modern Public Finance,* ed. John Quigley and Eugene Smolensky. Cambridge: Harvard University Press.

Sharkansky, Ira. 1968. "Agency Requests, Gubernatorial Support, and Budget Success in State Legislatures." *American Political Science Review* 62:1220–31.

Shepsle, Kenneth A. 1978. *The Giant Jigsaw Puzzle.* Chicago: University of Chicago Press.

———. 1979. "Institutional Arrangements and Equilibrium in Multidimensional Voting Models." *American Journal of Political Science* 57:27–59.

Shepsle, Kenneth A., and Barry R. Weingast. 1981. "Political Preferences for the Pork Barrel: A Generalization." *American Journal of Political Science* 25: 96–112.

———. 1984. "Political Solutions to Market Problems." *American Political Science Review* 78:417–34.

———. 1987a. "The Institutional Foundations of Committee Power." *American Political Science Review* 81:85–104.

———. 1987b. "Why Are Congressional Committees Powerful?" *American Political Science Review* 81:935–45.

Siegan, Bernard H. 1972. *Land Use without Zoning.* Lexington, Mass.: Lexington Books.

Simon, Herbert. 1957. *Administrative Behavior.* New York: Macmillan.

Slawson, W. David. 1974. "Mass Contracts: Lawful Fraud in California." *Southern California Law Review* 48:1–24.

Smith, Adam. 1909. *An Inquiry into the Nature and Causes of the Wealth of Nations.* Harvard Classics. New York: P. F. Collier and Son.

Sniderman, Paul, J. Fletcher, Peter Russel, Philip Tettvik, and Brian Gaines. 1991. "The Fallacy of Democratic Elitism." *British Journal of Political Science* 21: 349–70.

Snyder, M., and W. B. Swann. 1978. "Hypothesis Testing Processes in Social Interaction." *Journal of Personality and Social Psychology* 36:1202–12.

Spencer, B. J. 1982. "Asymmetric Information and Excessive Budgets in Government Bureaucracies: A Principal-Agent Approach." *Journal of Economic Behavior and Organizations* 3:197–224.

Spitzer, Matthew L. 1990. "Extensions of Ferejohn and Shipan's Model of Administrative Agency Behavior." *Journal of Law, Economics, and Organization* 6: 29–43.

Staaf, Robert J. 1977. "The Public School System in Transition: Consolidation and Parental Choice." In *Budgets and Bureaucrats: The Sources of Government Growth*, ed. Thomas E. Borcherding. Durham, N.C.: Duke University Press.

Stewart, Charles. 1987. "Does Structure Matter? The Effects of Structural Change on Spending Decisions in the House, 1871–1922." *American Journal of Political Science* 31:584–605.

Stewart, Richard B. 1977. "The Development of Administrative and Quasi-Constitutional Law in Judicial Review of Environmental Decisionmaking: Lessons from the Clean Air Act." *Iowa Law Review* 62:712–69

Stigler, G. 1971. "The Theory of Economic Regulation." *Bell Journal of Economics and Management Science* 2:3–21.

———. 1972. "Economic Competition and Political Competition." *Public Choice* 13:91–106.

———. 1975. *The Citizen and the State: Essays on Regulation.* Chicago: University of Chicago Press.

Straussman, Jeffrey D. 1988. "Rights-Based Budgeting." In *New Directions in Budget Theory,* ed. I. S. Rubin. Albany: State University of New York Press.

Strom, Kaare. 1990. "A Behavioral Theory of Competitive Political Parties." *American Journal of Political Science* 34:565–98.

Sullivan, Terry. 1987. "Presidential Leadership in Congress: Securing Commitments." In *Congress: Structure and Policy,* ed. Terry Sullivan. New York: Cambridge University Press.

Sunstein, Cass. "Law and Administration after Chevron." *Columbia Law Review* 90:2071–120.

Tabellini, Guido. 1991. "The Politics of Intergenerational Redistribution." *Journal of Political Economy* 99:335–57.

Thaler, Richard. 1987. "The Psychology and Economics Conference Handbook: Comments on Simon, on Einhorn and Hogarth, and on Tversky and Kahneman." In *Rational Choice,* ed. Melvin W. Reder. Chicago: University of Chicago Press .

Thorngate, W. 1980. "Efficient Decision Heuristics." *Behavioral Science* 25: 219–25.

Tiebout, C. M. 1956. "A Pure Theory of Local Expenditures." *Journal of Political Economy* 64:416–24.

Tiefer, Charles. 1989. *Congressional Practice and Procedure.* New York: Greenwood Press.

Tirole, Jean. 1986. "Hierarchies and Bureaucracies: On the Role of Collusion in Organizations." *Journal of Law, Economics, and Organization* 2:181–214.

Tovey, Craig. 1991. "The Instability of Instability." Naval Postgraduate School, Monterey, Calif. Mimeograph.

Tribe, Laurence H. 1988. *American Constitutional Law*. 2d ed. Mineola, N.Y.: Foundation Press.

Tufte, Edward R. 1978. *Political Control of the Economy*. Princeton: Princeton University Press.

Tullock, Gordon. 1965. "Entry Barriers in Politics." *American Economic Review* 55:458–66.

———. 1967. "The Welfare Costs of Tariffs, Monopolies, and Theft." *Western Economic Journal* 5:224–32.

Tversky, Amos, and Daniel Kahneman. 1974. "Judgement under Uncertainty: Heuristics and Biases." *Science* 211:1124–31.

———. 1987. "Rational Choice and the Framing of Decisions." In *Rational Choice,* ed. Melvin Reder. Chicago: University of Chicago Press.

Von Neumann, John, and Oskar Morgenstern. 1947. *Theory of Games and Economic Behavior*. Princeton: Princeton University Press.

Wanat, John. 1978. *Introduction to Budgeting*. North Scituate, Mass.: Duxbury.

Ward, Benjamin. 1961. "Majority Rule and Allocation." *Journal of Conflict Resolution* 5:379–89.

Weber, Max. 1947. *The Theory of Social and Economic Organization*. Trans. A. M. Henderson. New York: Free Press.

———. 1968. *Economy and Society*. Trans. Ephraim Fischoff. 3 vols. New York: Bedminster Press.

Weber, Robert P. 1989. "Home Style and Committee Behavior: The Case of Richard Nolan." In *Home Style and Washington Work,* ed. David W. Rohde. Ann Arbor: University of Michigan Press.

Weinberger, Marvin, and David Greevy. 1982. *The PAC Directory*. Cambridge, Mass.: Ballinger.

Weingast, Barry R. 1984. "The Congressional-Bureaucratic System: A Principal-Agent Perspective." *Public Choice* 44:147–92.

Weingast, Barry R., and William Marshall. 1988. "The Industrial Organization of Congress." *Journal of Political Economy* 96:132–63.

Weingast, Barry R., and Mark J. Moran. 1983. "Bureaucratic Discretion or Congressional Control? Regulatory Policymaking by the Federal Trade Commission." *Journal of Political Economy* 91:765–800.

———. 1986. "Congress and Regulatory Agency Choice: Reply to Muris." *Journal of Political Economy* 94:890–94.

Weingast, Barry R., Kenneth A. Shepsle, and Christopher Johnsen. 1981. "The Political Economy of Benefits and Costs: A Neoclassical Approach to Distributive Politics." *Journal of Political Economy* 89:642–64.

White, Michelle J. 1979. "Suburban Growth Controls: Liability Rules and Pigovian Taxes." *Journal of Legal Studies* 8:207–30.

Whitford, William. 1968. "Law and the Consumer Transaction: A Case Study of the Automobile Warranty." *Wisconsin Law Review* 1968:1006–98.

Wildavsky, Aaron. 1979. *The Politics of the Budgetary Process*. 2d ed. Boston: Little, Brown.

Williamson, Oliver E. 1975. *Markets and Hierarchies: Analysis and Antitrust Implications*. New York: Free Press.

Wilson, James Q. 1973. *Political Organizations*. New York: Basic Books.

Wintrobe, Ronald. 1987. "The Market for Corporate Control and the Market for Political Control." *Journal of Law, Economics, and Organization* 3:435–48.

Wittman, Donald A. 1973. "Parties as Utility Maximizers." *American Political Science Review* 67:490–98.

———. 1977. "Candidates with Policy Preferences: A Dynamic Model." *Journal of Economic Theory* 14:180–89.

———. 1982. "Efficient Rules in Highway Safety and Sports Activity." *American Economic Review* 72:78–90.

———. 1989. "Pressure Group Size and the Politics of Income Redistribution." *Social Choice and Welfare* 6:275–86.

Wright, Gerald C. 1990. Review of *Elections, Representation, and Congressional Voting Behavior,* by Robert A. Bernstein. *Journal of Politics* 52:643–45.

Wright, Gerald, Jr., and Michael Berkman. 1986. "Candidates and Policy in United States Senate Elections." *American Political Science Review* 80:567–90.

Wright, Gerald Jr., Robert Erikson, and John McIver. 1987. "Public Opinion and Policy Liberalism in the American States." *American Journal of Political Science* 31:980–1001.

Wright, John. 1985. "PACs, Contributions, and Roll Calls: An Organizational Perspective." *American Political Science Review* 75:400–414.

Wyckoff, Paul Gary. 1990. "Bureaucracy, Inefficiency, and Time." *Public Choice* 67:169–79.

Zupan, Mark A. 1990. "The Last-Period Problem in Politics: Do Congressional Representatives Not Subject to a Reelection Constraint Alter Their Voting Behavior?" *Public Choice* 65:167–80.

AUTHOR INDEX

Ackerman, Bruce, 142 n. 29
Aldrich, John H., 11
Alesina, Alberto, 18, 21
Alessi, Louis De, 96
Alford, Robert R., 173 n. 18
Arnold, R. Douglas, 10, 69
Arrow, Kenneth J., 52 n. 18
Atkinson, Scott, 187 n. 6
Austen-Smith, David, 73 n. 17, 81 n. 6
Auten, Gerald, 93

Bachrach, P., 190 n. 12
Banks, Jeffrey S., 73 n. 17, 99
Baratz, M. S., 190 n. 12
Baron, David P., 68–69, 157 n. 8, 165, 176
Barro, Robert, 159 n. 11
Barzel, Yoram, 153 n. 4
Baxter, William F., 134 n. 14
Beach, L. R., 59 n. 29
Beard, Charles A., 148–51
Becker, Gary S., 1 n. 1, 9, 12 n. 4, 23 n. 5, 76–77
Bendor, Jonathan, 89, 98–99, 102 n. 25, 111
Berg, S., 16
Berger, Curtis, 142 n. 29
Bergstrom, Theodore C., 153 nn. 1, 2
Berkman, Michael, 11

Bernstein, Robert A., 11, 27, 28
Blake, Frederick, 10
Block, Fred, 175
Borcherding, Thomas E., 187 n. 6
Boyce, Rebecca R., 56 n. 24
Bozeman, Barry, 93
Brams, Steven J., 32
Braybrooke, David, 88
Brennan, Geoffrey, 23
Breton, Albert, 95 nn. 9, 12, 96 n. 14, 111
Breyer, S., 129 n. 6
Brilmayer, Lea, 134 n. 14
Brock, William A., 80–81
Bromiley, Philip, 88
Bronars, Stephen G., 84–85
Brown, Robert E., 150
Brown, Thomas, 56 n. 24
Brueckner, Jan K., 97 n. 17
Buchanan, James M., 23, 33

Cain, Bruce, 25 n. 8
Calvert, Randall L., 109, 113 n. 36
Camerer, Colin F., 54 n. 21
Cameron, Charles, 81 n. 6
Chan, Kenneth S., 97 n. 17
Chappell, Henry, 85 n. 13
Christensen-Szalanski, J., 59 n. 29
Cline, Robert, 93
Coase, Ronald, 31, 167 n. 7, 188

217

Subject Index